Java
for 3D and VRML
Worlds

Rodger Lea
Kouichi Matsuda
Ken Miyashita

New Riders

New Riders Publishing, Indianapolis, Indiana

JAVA FOR 3D AND VRML WORLDS

By Rodger Lea, Kouichi Matsuda, and Ken Miyashita

Published by:
New Riders Publishing
201 West 103rd Street
Indianapolis, IN 46290 USA

Printed in the United States of America 1 2 3 4 5 6 7 8 9 0

Library of Congress Cataloging-in-Publication Data

```
Lea, Rodger, 1962-
    Java for 3D and VRML worlds / Rodger Lea,
Kouichi Matsuda, Ken Miyashita.
        p.   cm.
    Includes index.
    ISBN 1-56205-689-1
    1. Java (Computer program language)  2. VRML
(Document markup language)   I. Matsuda, Kouichi,
1960-   . II. Miyashita, Ken, 1969-        . III.
Title.
    QA76.73.J38L43  1996
    006--dc21
    96-47534
```
                                                      CIP

WARNING AND DISCLAIMER

This book is designed to provide information about VRML 2.0 behaviors and Java. Every effort has been made to make this book as complete and as accurate as possible, but no warranty or fitness is implied.

The information is provided on an "as is" basis. The authors and New Riders Publishing shall have neither liability nor responsibility to any person or entity with respect to any loss or damages arising from the information contained in this book or from the use of the discs or programs that may accompany it.

Publisher
Don Fowley

Publishing Manager
David Dwyer

Marketing Manager
Mary Foote

Managing Editor
Carla Hall

Acquisitions Editor
Steve Weiss

Software Specialist
Steve Flatt

Development Editors
Laura Frey, Nancy Warner

Project Editor
Jennifer Eberhardt

Copy Editor
Howard Jones

Technical Reviewers
H. Sugino, S. Matsuda, T. Kamachi

Acquisitions Coordinator
Stacey Beheler

Administrative Coordinator
Karen Opal

Cover Designer
Gary Adair

Cover Production
Aren Howell

Book Designer
Anne Jones

Production Manager
Kelly D. Dobbs

Production Team Supervisor
Laurie Casey

Graphics Image Specialists
Steve Adams, Clint Lahnen,
Casey Price, Marvin van Tiem

Production Analysts
Jason Hand, Erich J. Richter

Production Team
Aleata Howard, Elizabeth San Miguel,
Rowena Rappaport, Christy Wagner

Indexer
C.J. East

ABOUT THE AUTHORS

Rodger Lea is a senior research scientist with Sony's Computer Science Lab in Tokyo. His main areas of interest are distributed systems, virtual environments, and adaptive systems. Since he received his Ph.D. from Lancaster University in the UK, he has managed to persuade several large companies to allow him to pursue these interests in France, the USA, the UK, and now Japan. In return he's published a few papers, designed a few systems, and visited some really great places. He can be reached at rodger@csl.sony.co.jp.

Kouichi Matsuda (Kou1 Ma2da) is a senior research scientist working with Sony Architecture Laboratories in Tokyo, Japan. He was the lead author of the Java binding appendix of VRML 2.0. He is interested in multiuser, interactive, shared, three-dimensional virtual environments, which enable diverse users and applications to interact with each other, thereby enhancing social participation. He is the translator of *Presenting Java* by John December, one of the translators of *VRML: Browsing & Building Cyberspace* by Mark Pesce, and the author of the X and UNIX-related books in Japan. He can be reached via the Internet at matsuda@arch.sony.co.jp.

Ken Miyashita is a researcher working with Sony's Architecture Laboratories in Tokyo, Japan. His major area of interest is graphical interfaces for computer software, especially for novice users. He is currently a member of the technical team that has developed Sony's VRML browser "Community Place." He has co-authored several articles on VRML and has recently co-translated Mark Pesce's *VRML: Browsing & Building Cyberspace* into Japanese. Ken can be reached at miyashita@soft.arch.sony.co.jp.

DEDICATIONS

To our parents.

ACKNOWLEDGMENTS

We owe our thanks to a great many people, not all of whome we can list. We'd like to thank the entire Virtual Society team at Sony for helping us build such an excellent system and to A. Takeuchi for allowing us the time to write this book. To the editing team at New Riders, especially Jennifer and Steve, we are also grateful. Our thanks to Doris for English lessons, T. Kamachi for sound advice, Y. Honda for concise explanations, and the entire team at Sony Pictures Imageworks who authored Appendix A. Last, we extend our thanks to our colleagues at the Computer Science Lab who helped launch the Virtual Society project.

TRADEMARK ACKNOWLEDGMENTS

All terms mentioned in this book that are known to be trademarks or service marks have been appropriately capitalized. New Riders Publishing cannot attest to the accuracy of this information. Use of a term in this book should not be regarded as affecting the validity of any trademark or service mark.

CONTENTS AT A GLANCE

TABLE OF CONTENTS

5 Advanced Java   161

6 Hints and Tips for Effective and Efficient VRML   231

INTRODUCTION

The dream of CyberSpace, an electronic environment where the world's data can be browsed at will, is fast becoming a reality. The Internet and its multimedia cousin, the World Wide Web, are the essential technological foundations and have been in place for several years. However, the tools to construct CyberSpace on these foundations are only now beginning to be created. Two of those tools are the network programming language Java and the 3D graphics standard for the Internet, the Virtual Reality Modeling Language (VRML).

This book is about harnessing the power of these two tools to enable you to build rich, interactive 3D scenes   scenes that people can navigate through, can interact with, and most important, can change so that each visit leaves its mark. These scenes may range from simple extensions to your Web pages, through 3D art galleries on the Internet, up to 3D shared spaces where people can visit and mingle in your part of CyberSpace. VRML provides the essential 3D building blocks to construct your worlds; Java is the glue that animates the worlds and links them to the World Wide Web.

WHO THIS BOOK IS FOR

This book has two target audiences. The first group consists of those of you who already have VRML experience. You have probably already read an introductory text on VRML 1.0 or even

VRML 2.0. You understand the potential of VRML 2.0, maybe you have built a few toy worlds, and you are probably frustrated at their simplistic nature. For you, this book opens up the true possibilities of VRML by showing, step by step, how to exploit the synergy between VRML and Java to create rich, compelling 3D worlds. The second target group is made up of those of you who are familiar with Java. You have written some interesting Java applets or programs, maybe added some simple animation to your Web pages. You are now looking for a real use of Java and the idea of 3D Web pages intrigues you. This book shows you how Java can be combined with VRML to enable you to build complex applications that have a 3D component.

Although some knowledge of VRML is assumed, we do not expect you to be experts. For those of you who feel a little nervous about your VRML knowledge, we added a primer on VRML as Appendix A, "VRML and 3D Principles."

This book isn't a primer on Java. So if you have never programmed in Java before, we suggest you take a look at the resource appendix (Appendix C, "Resources"), which lists several good Java primers. However, we have kept the Java examples as uncomplicated as possible and anybody with a basic knowledge of programming will, with the aid of a Java primer, have no problems tackling them.

A ROAD MAP

This book is structured as follows:

➤ Chapter 1, "Fulfilling the CyberSpace Dream," provides some historical perspective on VRML, where it came from, how it evolved, why we are interested in it, and where it is going.

➤ Chapter 2, "Adding Action to 3D Worlds," introduces the mechanics of animation and interactivity in VRML 2.0 and shows how to build simple animated 3D scenes without a line of Java code.

➤ Chapter 3, "Letting Java Loose," explains how Java and VRML work together and provides a gentle introduction to using Java to animate 3D scenes.

➤ Chapter 4, "Advanced VRML," explores some of the more complicated features of VRML 2.0 and shows how to enhance them with Java.

➤ Chapter 5, "Advanced Java," switches emphasis and shows how some of the powerful features of Java can be used in conjunction with VRML. Examples include a 3D directory browser and a multiuser server for shared VRML worlds.

➤ Chapter 6, "Hints and Tips for Effective and Efficient VRML," offers hints and tips for efficient, high-performance 3D worlds.

➤ Chapter 7, "The Future of VRML," concludes the book with a glimpse of the future and some discussion on the multiuser aspects of Sony's Community Place VRML system.

If you are not very familiar with VRML, the best way to get started is to read Chapter 1 and then browse through Appendix A, which is a primer on VRML 2.0. You should then return to Chapter 2 and work through it and the subsequent chapters.

If you are familiar with VRML 2.0 but not very familiar with how Java and VRML work together, you may want to quickly read through Chapter 2 to ensure you understand VRML 2.0's execution model. Then start straight into Chapter 3, which explains how Java can be used to add behaviors to VRML scene entities. If you are already knowledgeable about how VRML 2.0 works with Java, we suggest you quickly read Chapter 2 and then go straight to Chapters 4 and 5. You may want to refer back to earlier chapters to confirm your understanding of the execution model of VRML 2.0 and how it interacts with Java.

WHAT'S ON THE CD-ROM

The CD-ROM contains all you need to work with VRML and Java. It includes a fully functional VRML 2.0 browser, Sony's

Community Place, along with software manuals and sample scenes. The CD-ROM also contains the Java 1.0.2 JDK and installation instructions. Both are for Windows 95/NT. All of the examples in the book are also on the CD-ROM, laid out in the same order as in the book. In addition, there are several more complex VRML 2.0 scenes, including a multiuser VRML 2.0 scene that will connect to a public multiuser server managed by Sony.

Last, the CD-ROM contains some VRML-related utilities and a fully functional multiuser server that works with the Community Place Browser and runs on Windows 95/NT.

CONVENTIONS USED IN THIS BOOK

Most New Riders Publishing books use similar conventions to help you distinguish between the various elements used within the book. This means that after you purchase one New Riders book, you'll find it easier to use all others.

Before you continue, you should take a moment to examine the conventions used in this book:

➤ New terms appear in *italic*.

➤ All nodes appear in **bold**.

As well, this book features sidebars—special text that is set apart from the normal text by icons. These sidebars include the following:

NOTE

A Note includes extra information you should find useful, but this information complements the discussion at hand instead of being a direct part of it.

T I P

A Tip marks a shortcut or idea that helps you get your work done faster or better.

WARNING

A Warning tells you when a procedure may be dangerous. Warnings may provide, for example, information about data loss, system lockups, and damage to files or software.

NEW RIDERS PUBLISHING

The staff of New Riders Publishing is committed to bringing you the very best in computer reference material. Each New Riders book is the result of months of work by authors and staff who research and refine the information contained within its covers.

As part of this commitment to you, New Riders invites your input. Please let us know if you enjoy this book, if you have trouble with the information and examples presented, or if you have a suggestion for the next edition.

Please note, however: New Riders staff cannot serve as a technical resource for Java or VRML or for questions about software- or hardware-related problems.

If you have a question or comment about any New Riders book, there are several ways to contact New Riders Publishing. We will respond to as many readers as we can. Your name, address, or phone number will never become part of a mailing list or be used for any purpose other than to help us continue to bring you the best books possible. You can write us at the following address:

New Riders Publishing
Attn: Publisher
201 W. 103rd Street
Indianapolis, IN 46290

If you prefer, you can fax New Riders Publishing at 317-817-7448.

You can also send electronic mail to New Riders at sweiss@newriders.mcp.com.

New Riders Publishing is an imprint of Macmillan Computer Publishing. To obtain a catalog or information, or to purchase any Macmillan Computer Publishing book, call 800-428-5331 or visit our Web site at http://www.mcp.com.

Thank you for selecting *Java for 3D and VRML Worlds*!

FULFILLING THE CYBERSPACE DREAM

CyberSpace, a global electronic environment that

enables you to be anybody, do anything, and browse the

world's wisdom, is in the process of becoming reality. Its

essential components are the World Wide Web, VRML,

a few good ideas, and a handful of dreams.

A few pioneers have already started to turn these

dreams into reality by using available technology to

start building CyberSpace. This and subsequent chap-

ters will arm you with the knowledge to enable you to

join in that process.

What This Chapter Covers

This chapter offers a historical perspective on VRML, its roots, development, and current blossoming. It briefly overviews the origins of the VRML language and highlights some of the motivations and the key players who have catapulted VRML into the WWW spotlight. This chapter also discusses the development of our interest in VRML—from an advanced research project investigating online societies to our adoption of VRML 1.0, our extensions, and our co-authoring of the VRML 2.0 standard.

The role of this chapter is to set the scene, to explain the origins of VRML, and to discuss its evolution. Because VRML is such a new technology—and one that is still evolving—the goal of this chapter is to explain some of the motivations for the development of VRML. We hope this information enables you to more fully understand where VRML will go next. In particular, we hope that by the end of this chapter you will understand why we think VRML is so important, and why both we, the authors, and Sony have invested so much time and effort into its evolution. By understanding this, you will be better able to imagine what the technology can do today, how you can use it, and how it may evolve in the next few years.

The Origins of VRML 1.0

VRML can trace its origins to a fusion of science fiction, virtual reality, 3D graphics, and the phenomenon of the World Wide Web.

The Science Fiction Legacy

Science fiction authors have long been dreaming of an electronic or virtual reality through which humans can escape the drudgery of everyday life. A clutch of recent books, including cult classics such as *Snow Crash* by Neal Stephenson and *Neuromancer* by William Gibson, have built on a long tradition of electronic fantasy worlds. The details vary, but the dream is constant: some day, humans can plug into an electronic network that spans the globe—CyberSpace, where their presence has an electronic embodiment, an *avatar*, with which they can meet others, explore, play, fantasize, and with any time left over, work!

VIRTUAL REALITY

The tangible growth of virtual reality (VR) technology in the last decade, as witnessed not only by the high-tech projects at NASA but also in VR gaming theaters and home VR technology, has lent a reality to the dreams of the science fiction aficionados. Suddenly it became possible to realize a limited form of the CyberSpace dream. Given enough hardware, a compelling 3D environment could be created within a single large computer. The 3D environment and its contents could be visualized by using high-end computer graphics technology, and users could actually enter into this 3D world. In some cases, they don head-mounted display devices that give the impression of immersion in the 3D scene; in others, large-screen technology is used to surround the users with the 3D scene. As users move, the computer recalculates the correct view and redisplays it, all sufficiently fast enough to give the impression of reality. Add to this devices that enable users to interact with objects in this electronic world, and you have the basis for CyberSpace.

A GLOBAL COMPUTER NETWORK

Given that the graphics technology was available, the only part missing before work could begin on a global 3D space was a worldwide computer network. With the explosive growth of the Internet and its multimedia cousin, the World Wide Web (WWW), a number of people believed that the technology was ripe to begin to build the CyberSpace dream.

PESCE AND PARISI

Two of those people were Mark Pesce and Tony Parisi who, early in 1994, met up in San Francisco and began working on their version of the CyberSpace vision.

Inspired by normal 2D viewers of HTML pages, Pesce and Parisi put together an initial prototype of a 3D browser that could be used to view a 3D object found on the Internet. This prototype was taken to the May 1994 WWW conference in Geneva, where a "Birds of a Feather" (BOF) session brought together a group of like-minded technophiles.

The term VRML (Virtual Reality Markup Language) was coined by Dave Raggett of Hewlett Packard's European research lab who was one of the early WWW developers and had a keen interest in CyberSpace.

VRML quickly came to stand for Virtual Reality Modeling Language—the term modeling more closely reflecting its goal—and took its first major step forward with the adoption of Silicon Graphics' (SGI) Open Inventor 3D file format. Making it possible to use this, up to that point, proprietary language was the work of Rikk Carey, Paul Strauss, and Gavin Bell, all of SGI, who joined the quickly growing band of VRML enthusiasts.

VRML 1.0 HITS THE STREETS

By October 1994, VRML had progressed sufficiently far to be presented in draft form at the second WWW conference in Chicago. With enough interest generated, people and companies began working feverishly on VRML 1.0 browsers, and by the official launch date of VRML 1.0 in April 1995, several prototype browsers were available.

WHAT WAS WRONG WITH VRML 1.0

Although VRML 1.0 was a good start as an Internet-based 3D graphics format, it still had a long way to go before it could fulfill some of the goals of its original inventors. The main drawback from which VRML 1.0 suffered was the fact that it was a static scene description language. This meant that an author could build an incredibly complex scene, people could navigate through that scene and see what the author had placed there, but the users could never interact with the scene and its entities. For this reason some people speculated that the M in VRML stood for Museum—nothing ever changed in the scenes!

A goal of many in the community was to be able to build the VRML equivalent of the hands-on science museums—scenes that reacted to the user's presence. This type of reaction would enable scene authors to build scenes with doors that open, walkways that move, taxis you can really ride in, and space rockets that explore the universe. But more than these dynamic exhibits, authors wanted the ability to enable users to change the scene as they interacted with it, to let the scenes become interactive, evolving spaces, where every time the user went back, things had changed.

For those with a vision of CyberSpace—as an evolving, ever-changing electronic world where users would be embodied with avatars and would be let loose to live out electronic lives or fantasies in an electronic reality—VRML 1.0 was tantalizingly close, but not yet close enough.

SONY'S VIRTUAL SOCIETY PROJECT

We at Sony shared this CyberSpace dream, and it led us to VRML and our participation in its evolution.

The origins of Sony's involvement in the VRML community can be traced to a long-term research project initiated in Sony's Computer Science Lab (CSL) in 1994: Virtual Society. The Virtual Society (VS) project wanted to explore societal interaction in CyberSpace. Based on existing expertise in artificial intelligence, multiagent systems, and artificial life, the VS project was aimed at investigating the support infrastructure needed to build an electronic society. This society would support electronic interaction among humans represented by avatars, but also among humans and intelligent agents. A more ambitious goal was to explore the emergence of societal rules of interactions among autonomous intelligent agents who were capable of self-evolution based on the use of artificial life techniques.

The Virtual Society project and its goals led naturally to the following requirements:

➤ **Easy access.** Easy access means that the technology must work with standard home computers and that its communication model must be based on the ubiquitous Internet.

➤ **Large numbers of users.** The requirement for large numbers of users represents more of a dream than a possibility with today's technology. Our aim is to support large-crowd events, such as concerts or sports events. Obviously, given that the average user still has a 14.4 kbps modem, the amount of information that can be sent is severely restricted. However, we have our eye on the future and are assuming that in another three to five years, consumer electronic devices, such as game machines and Internet TVs, will be connected through increasingly "fat" communication pipes such as cable and cable modems. The basic premise of the project is that the infrastructure developed by Sony must be scaleable to meet the needs of increasing communications speeds.

➤ **Rich interactive worlds.** 3D environments need to be self-sustaining. This means that the people who use these environments must want to come back—again and again—to spend time in the 3D spaces and be committed to the space and its evolution. The return of users is possible only if those spaces are sufficiently dynamic to maintain interest and, perhaps more important, sufficiently open so that users can actually cause the spaces to change as users interact with them. Our goal is to build an infrastructure that enables users to build their own 3D spaces dynamically.

➤ **Multimedia delivered into worlds.** A rich set of media formats is also an important feature of a sustainable space. This implies more than just the ability to add textures to the 3D world; audio and video support are also necessary. From a long-term point of view, Sony has a strong interest in providing high-quality audio and video for 3D spaces running on consumer devices in the home. In this way, Sony can combine its extensive media content with its established consumer electronics base.

➤ **Open to experimentation by designers and users alike.** The final requirement is that the infrastructure has to be open, accessible, and usable by all. Although the initial target is to enable home PCs to run on a dial-up connection, Sony's vision for the future of consumer electronics calls for more. The goal is to provide the home user with a sophisticated home network of dedicated home devices that all work together and are linked to the outside world through a high-bandwidth communications pipe. The uses to which such an environment will be put cannot be foreseen today, so the infrastructure must be open and extensible enough to enable anyone to build any type of application by using the technology.

These features are, we believe, the absolute minimum needed to build sustainable 3D spaces. Only if users can explore rich, interesting spaces will they want to visit those spaces. Only if they are allowed to evolve the space will visitors be sufficiently engaged and so become co-owners or inhabitants of the space. Only after the threshold from visitors to inhabitants has been crossed does it become possible for an electronic, or virtual, society to evolve.

A SHARED SPACE ARCHITECTURE

Our investigations into the basic infrastructure for a shared space architecture began with the initial development of a shared virtual environment. This environment provided shared 3D spaces where users could meet and interact with each other. The initial platform for this development was Dive (Distributed Interactive Virtual Environments), an existing piece of technology from the Swedish Institute of Computer Science. This software, although an excellent starting point at that time, supported interaction only between a handful of users and required high-end workstations and high-bandwidth communication networks.

Because our goal was for a ubiquitous system that supported thousands of users in our shared spaces, we began to develop a shared space architecture that would support a large number of people and be accessible to the growing number of users in the Internet. When we began to investigate the Internet, and in particular its use of 3D graphics, we quickly came across the budding development of the VRML 1.0 language.

Already aware of VRML's existence through a previous contact with Dave Raggett, the originator of the term VRML and one of the founding architects of the Web, we quickly came up to speed with VRML and began building our own VRML 1.0 browser in early 1995.

However, in contrast to most of the VRML 1.0 browsers under development, the goal for our browser was to use VRML for our shared social worlds. We needed interactive capabilities and designed our browser from scratch to support these needs. The result was a VRML 1.0 browser that supported a set of extensions to VRML called, imaginatively, Extended VRML (E-VRML). E-VRML supported behaviors as well as shared interactive VRML worlds.

SONY'S EXTENDED-VRML 1.0 (E-VRML)

To support interactive VRML worlds, we needed a way to cause changes to entities in the VRML scene. The approach adopted was based on the notion of behavior scripts and events. Events, such as a user pressing the mouse button, were sent to event handlers. The event handlers were attached to entities in the scene and specified program scripts that reacted to the incoming events. The program scripts would then change the scene by using a set of Application Programmers Interface (API) calls that enabled them to manipulate scene entities and, if required, to generate new events. This approach separates the 3D data from the code that manipulates it and uses the event handler to bind the two.

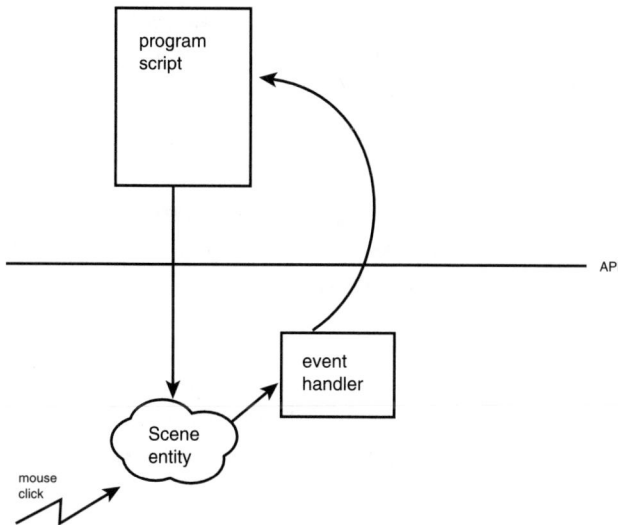

FIGURE 1.1
The E-VRML execution model.

E-VRML enabled any language to be used for the behavior script programs. However, we chose to use a language called TCL (Tool Command Language), a public domain language developed by John Ousterhout's group at Berkeley.

A set of time-related nodes were also added to enable scene authors to generate time events that could be used to animate scene entities.

Last, E-VRML added nodes to support sound and video so that multimedia data could be incorporated into the 3D scene.

This approach to extending VRML is based on the beliefs that VRML is a 3D scene description language and that animation of a scene is best left to a programming language. Our goal was to find a simple way to attach a piece of programming code, written in any language, to the VRML scene and to change the scene by using that programming code. A side effect of this approach is that VRML remains relatively unchanged; the real work—the animation—happens in the programming language scripts that are attached using the event handlers.

MULTIUSER BEHAVIORS

To this basic model, we added support for shared scenes that enabled programmers to use their scripts to send events from one machine to another. The conceptual model is simple, although the implementation issues are more complex.

Imagine a 3D scene that represents a large grocery store. Two users, Grace and Tony, are viewing the scene and are looking at the same shelf. Grace clicks on a can of beans to select the can and add it to her virtual shopping cart. The click event in Grace's browser is delivered to the can event handler. The handler calls the associated programming script that animates the can from the shelf into the grocery cart. However, because Tony is viewing the same shelf, he should see the can being removed and placed into Grace's cart. To support this, E-VRML enabled scene authors to specify that an event needed to be shared and should be sent to anyone else viewing the scene. In our case, the event that caused animation in Grace's browser is sent to Tony's browser, where it causes the same animation, thereby keeping the scene consistent. The underlying network infrastructure was responsible for making sure the details of the event were sent to everyone who needed to see them.

THE ORIGINS OF VRML 2.0: MOVING WORLDS

Our original foray into the VRML community was based on the experience we gained with E-VRML. When people began discussing the next phase of VRML's development on the VRML mailing list, we proposed (August 1995) E-VRML as a basis for VRML 2.0.

The approach used in our initial proposal was similar in approach to that being suggested by a key member of the VRML community, Mitra. Mitra, who was then with Worlds Inc. but later set up his own company, WorldMaker, had several years experience in the area of multiuser shared environments, had been involved in the work on VRML 1.0, and was a member of the VRML Architecture Group (VAG).

Our work was a natural match with Mitra's and, more important, his goals for the long-term development of VRML as a basis for CyberSpace. This match enabled us to quickly begin working together to understand whether we could merge our respective draft proposals.

Mitra not only brought his proposal to the table, but he also brought the work of the San Diego Supercomputer Center (SDSC) groups, which shared the same overall vision for VRML as we did.

During the subsequent weeks we refined our ideas, and in October 1995 we had a first draft of a joint paper that was to form the basis of future work. In early November 1995, a behaviors workshop, where several groups interested in behaviors presented their ideas, was held at the SDSC. At this meeting, Mitra, SDSC, and Sony formally agreed to work on a joint proposal for VRML 2.0. By the end of November, this joint paper had evolved into a joint proposal.

In conjunction with that work, SGI also proposed a first draft of a behavior model. This model, although having many things in common with our work, based its execution model not on the notion of events but rather on a dataflow model. In addition, the

SGI proposal didn't rely on an external scripting language that manipulated the scene through an API but used an internal language that interacted with the VRML directly. This approach had its roots in existing technology that SGI had already developed in the area of 3D graphics.

Clearly there was a certain degree of synergy between the SGI work and ours, but it was also clear to us that a dataflow model was completely unsuited for shared multiuser worlds. Because it made good sense—for both ourselves and the VRML community—to try to combine our proposals, we began discussions in November 1995. After much debate, SGI was convinced that an event-driven model was more practical, and in early December 1995 we formally agreed to combine our proposals.

Shortly afterward, at the VRML 1995 conference in San Diego, this proposal was presented as a joint offering and named Moving Worlds. At the technical session and in the demo session, we used our E-VRML multiuser system to explain the basic principles behind the Moving Worlds proposal and to demonstrate what the proposal would enable scene authors to do.

During the subsequent time-consuming and often fractious six weeks, this basic Moving Worlds proposal evolved into being acceptable to all parties. SGI devoted significant resources to the technical writing, and other companies were invited to comment and contribute to the basic final proposal.

In early February 1996, this proposal was presented to the VRML community as Moving Worlds and put forward as a possible contender for VRML 2.0.

FROM MOVING WORLDS TO VRML 2.0

The VRML community had requested, via a request for proposals (RFP), technology for the VRML 2.0 standard. This RFP was made in January 1996, with the deadline for submission being February 4. The goals of this RFP was to ensure that the best technology was evaluated, that the process was open to all members of the VRML community, and that the entire community could evaluate all technology and vote on the final choice.

OTHER CONTENDERS FOR VRML 2.0

The VRML 2.0 RFP deadline produced a clutch of proposals; all were excellent in their own right and all addressed extremely complex issues. In addition to the Moving Worlds proposal, the following five proposals were submitted:

➤ Out of This World

➤ The Power of Dynamic Worlds

➤ Reactive Virtual Environments

➤ Active VRML

➤ HoloWeb

APPLE COMPUTER—OUT OF THIS WORLD

The proposal from Apple Computer was based on its open 3D meta file format (3DMF), which is also used in its QuickDraw 3D technology. Apple's proposal basically encapsulated VRML 1.0 within a 3DMF file. This approach treats VRML 1.0 as just another data format that can be found in 3DMF files.

Behaviors are achieved by using scripts that are in complete control of the 3DMF data, including any VRML within it. The proposal also dispenses with the notion of a 3D browser; instead, it views browsers as just another script that is downloaded to the user's machine.

Last, the Apple proposal attacks the problem of multiauthored scenes by designating a master script that is responsible for talking to the browser. This script receives information, via a public interface, from other scripts that tell it what they want to do. The script then uses this information to update the view the user sees by interacting with the browser.

To achieve all this, the scripts have access to a high-level API that provides them with routines for controlling graphics data, including support for graphic data manipulation, drawing, selection, and so on.

THE GERMAN NATIONAL RESEARCH CENTER FOR INFORMATION TECHNOLOGY (GMD)—THE POWER OF DYNAMIC WORLDS

The German National Research Center for Information Technology proposal was based on its existing work in the area of Computer Supported Cooperative Work (CSCW). GMD proposed a set of extensions to the VRML 1.0 language that supported an event model, behaviors, a set of new nodes and, interestingly, multiuser worlds.

The proposed approach was to extend VRML 1.0 with enough built-in support to enable authors to build dynamic scenes without recourse to an external scripting language. The approach relied on a rich event model that was extended to work in a multiuser environment.

In the same way as E-VRML, events were sent between VRML nodes; however, these events caused the execution of behavior nodes, which manipulated the scene directly.

To support multiuser scenes, the GMD model categorized behaviors as autonomous or shared and enabled events to be propagated between browsers that supported the different categorizations.

IBM JAPAN—REACTIVE VIRTUAL ENVIRONMENTS

IBM's Japanese research lab proposed a set of extensions to VRML that used a model of reactive behaviors. Motion engines that supported reactive behaviors could be attached to entities in the scene and were used to describe how the entities changed over time.

The motion engines supported their own, built-in, simple scripting language that enabled scene authors to describe how entities change as a result of incoming events. The motion engines supported a notion of callbacks so that the system could deliver events, much in the same way as event handlers in E-VRML.

Motion engines could be linked together either serially or in parallel to enable complex interrelated animation to take place.

The IBM proposal has a number of similarities with the GMD proposal—in particular, its desire to build behaviors into the scene. However, the proposal had no specific support for multiuser scenes.

MICROSOFT—ACTIVEVRML

The proposal by Microsoft was named ActiveVRML and was part of its ActiveX strategy. ActiveVRML was an interesting proposal because the language had its roots in the functional programming world. ActiveVRML was a functional programming language, designed to support several media types as basic data types in the language.

ActiveVRML's relationship to VRML was that VRML data, like any other data, can be read in and manipulated as ActiveVRML data types. In a sense, this relationship represents the weakest binding possible between a language and VRML.

The strength of ActiveVRML comes from the power of the functional programming model. To programmers familiar with procedural or object-oriented languages such as C or Java, functional languages often seem weird and incomprehensible. However, one significant advantage of a functional language for the manipulation of rich media formats is that it abstracts from the notion of time. The passage of time is captured in the functions themselves, enabling programmers to ignore time and not have to deal with tricky issues such as synchronization.

This benefit is useful for a 3D simulation, which is what a 3D VRML world becomes when you add support for behaviors. However, the strength of a functional language, such as ActiveVRML, lies in supporting multimedia such as audio and video.

Of interest is that unlike most of the other proposals, ActiveVRML lives on. It is currently being evolved and targeted more toward multimedia presentations than 3D interactive environments. This latter change makes sense given the strength of ActiveVRML in the field of time-dependent media. The current status of this work can be found by visiting Microsoft's ActiveVRML Web page. You can find the Web address in Appendix C, "Resources."

SUN MICROSYSTEMS—HOLOWEB

The HoloWeb proposal from Sun Microsystems grew out of two internal Sun developments: its long-standing interest in 3D graphics and its recently launched WWW language, Java. HoloWeb was three things: a file format, a programming API, and a CyberSpace metaphor.

The file format of HoloWeb was a departure from VRML 1.0. HoloWeb didn't offer a selection of high-level 3D primitives; it offered a simple subset of dots, lines, triangles, and text. What's more, HoloWeb was by default a highly optimized format based on compression. This compressed format has obvious benefits for file transfer in the WWW.

The basic graphics types could be used to build more complicated 3D models and would be manipulated and managed, via the HoloWeb API, by the Java language.

The HoloWeb viewing metaphor was based on the city model. A home page would be a building in the HoloWeb universe. Viewing a page would be like entering that building; surfing the Web would be like walking down a city street. However, the city metaphor provides for more structure than possible in today's

WWW. All computer companies, for example, could be located in the same part of the virtual city, enabling surfers to easily locate information.

One interesting aspect of the proposal was that Java programs would also be spatially defined and would have their own 3D coordinates in the HoloWeb universe, enabling them to be manipulated like any other 3D entity.

THE VOTE

The vote on the proposals was taken after in-depth discussions within the VRML community via the electronic mailing list. The results of the vote are shown in figure 1.2 and represent a clear victory for Moving Worlds.

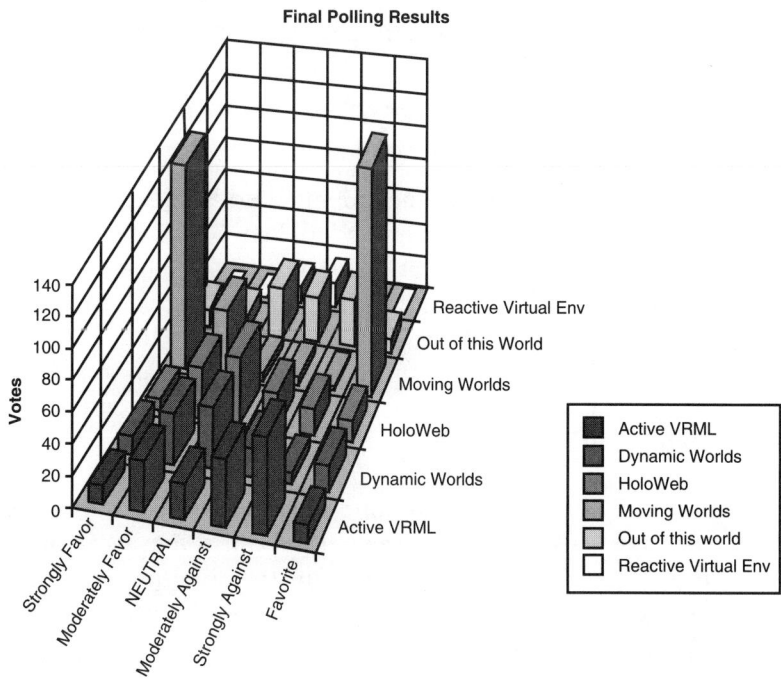

FIGURE 1.2
Results of the VRML 2.0 proposal.

There is no question that all of the proposals had something interesting to offer, and all represented significant and original work. The overwhelming choice of the Moving Worlds proposals had probably less to do with its technical merits—which, although good, were not significantly better than some of the other proposals—and more to do with the process used to develop Moving Worlds.

From the outset, the Moving Worlds proposal was born of existing expertise from Sony, SGI, and Mitra and represented a distillation of all three of the original proposals. Therefore, it was already well discussed and criticized. Further, during the drafting stage, it was well publicized within the VRML community and received a significant amount of input and comment. By the time it was proposed as a candidate for VRML 2.0, the proposal was already well honed and represented the collective wisdom of many of the key players in the VRML community.

EVOLVING A PROPOSAL INTO A STANDARD

The hard task of developing Moving Worlds into an acceptable basis for VRML 2.0 was then undertaken. Continuing the approach taken in the formation of the proposal, this process was carried out in full view and with significant participation from the VRML community. However, in contrast to the time before the vote when there were six proposals to divide attention among, now with only one proposal remaining, the entire community focused on it.

This was an immense effort and was coordinated by three SGI members: Rikk Carey, Gavin Bell, and Chris Marrin. They performed an excellent job of balancing the differing requirements and goals of the VRML community and reaching a fair consensus on contentious issues.

In parallel with this specification effort, we at Sony began the task of building a VRML 2.0 browser that would conform to the rapidly evolving specification. During the period from April 1996 to

August 1996, we publicly released five new versions of the browser, each one tracking the evolving standard and culminating in a version (demonstrated at Siggraph) that supported the final specification. Each one of these versions enabled us to perform checks on the paper specification to ensure that it was both possible to implement and useful.

At the same time, a group at Sony Pictures Imageworks developed a set of multiuser shared VRML 2.0 worlds that showed off the facilities of VRML 2.0 including movies, animation, and Java scripting.

At Siggraph (early August 1996) the VRML 2.0 specification was published and made available in its final form. The interest in VRML was now significantly higher than at previous events. A large number of companies—small and large—were all showing VRML-related technology. The majority of this was obviously VRML 1.0 related, but Sony and SGI displayed VRML 2.0 versions of their technology, proving the possibility of building the final VRML 2.0 specification and taking the first step toward the dream of CyberSpace.

VRML 2.0 CURRENT STATUS

VRML is evolving, even as you read this. The goal of VRML 2.0 is to provide an open, extensible system that supports 3D interactive scenes on the WWW. But our sights, and that of others in the community, still rest on the support for shared multiuser spaces.

VRML 2.0 is sufficiently open and extensible to enable anybody to begin experimentation into the issues of building multiuser spaces. At the time of writing, Sony, along with a handful of other companies and individuals, are experimenting to understand best how to do this. The result of this experimentation will result in new proposals in the area of multiuser standards.

As part of our own experimentation, you will find that the VRML 2.0 browser—Community Place—included on the accompanying CD is a full multiuser system. This browser will enable you not only to experiment with VRML 2.0 but also to share multiuser scenes. Because the goal of this book is to show you how to use Java to build standard VRML 2.0 scenes, we have restricted most of our discussion to standard VRML 2.0. However, in Chapter 5, "Advanced Java," we return to the issue of multiuser worlds and show you how to build a simple multiuser server of your own.

ROUNDUP

This chapter has given you an overview of the development of VRML 2.0 as seen from our perspective. That perspective is obviously biased and concentrates on events and motivations that we think are important. Clearly, VRML is many things to many people and will be used in a wide variety of ways in the coming years. For us, and for many others, a principle use of VRML will be as a building block for CyberSpace.

Building CyberSpace is a technical challenge and will not come easily. Our goal throughout the rest of this book is to equip you with enough information to be able to meld the strengths of Java and the flexibility of VRML so that you can begin building interesting, interactive 3D content. In this way, you can become part of the CyberSpace dream.

ADDING ACTION TO 3D WORLDS

The power of VRML 2.0 comes from its capability to

support dynamic, interactive 3D scenes. This

chapter is all about the underlying mechanism that

enables that interactivity.

VRML 1.0 was really only a 3D data description

language that described a static set of 3D entities

that, together, made up a scene. The program was

loaded into a display engine, or browser, and the

user could wander through the scene at will. VRML's

flexibility came from a set of built-in nodes that enabled scene authors to integrate their scene with the Web. For example, a 3D entity could be linked to an HTML page or even to another VRML 1.0 file somewhere out in the Web. Although this allowed applications such as data visualization or online museums, it was not sufficiently flexible to build the wealth of applications that would benefit from a 3D interface.

Applications such as story board animation, real-time data tracking, and shared meeting spaces all require a way to animate the VRML scene's response to external events such as user input or incoming network data.

The designers of VRML 2.0 adopted a hybrid mechanism to support this flexibility. They defined a way to send messages between entities in the scene to enable one entity to change another. The designers then added a set of predefined nodes that generated a set of useful messages so that scene authors could animate entities. Last, to support open flexibility, they added the capability to link arbitrary programming language fragments, or scripts, into the scene. These scripts could generate messages and change the scene. Because these scripts could be any language, it became possible to build complex applications that use VRML as part of their user interface but that also talk to disks, the network, and other applications.

For those of you who are familiar with graphics programming, the addition of an execution mechanism and a set of message-generating nodes into a 3D data description language may seem natural, whereas the idea of plugging programming languages fragments that also manage the scene may not. Conversely, for those of you who are more familiar with programming and using programming languages to manage state, the use of script nodes will be clear. However, the idea of a data description language that also has elements of a programming model may seem a little strange.

This chapter introduces you to the VRML 2.0 execution mechanism in such a way that by the end, no matter what your background, you will have a clear idea of how VRML 2.0 works and how to harness it to build your own type of application.

WHAT THIS CHAPTER COVERS

To be able to animate a 3D scene, you need a mechanism to change the state of the 3D entities in the scene. This mechanism must enable the scene author to specify which state must change, when state must change, and what state must change to. VRML 2.0 supports an "execution model" that is designed to do just that.

In this chapter you do the following:

➤ Work through a brief review that points out the key aspects of VRML 2.0

➤ Learn about the execution model and how it works

➤ See how sensors and interpolators are used to drive the execution model

➤ See examples of the execution model in action

A good understanding of the VRML 2.0 execution model is essential for being able to build complex animated scenes. More important, such an understanding will enable you to fully exploit the synergy between Java and VRML.

After you finish this chapter, you will have sufficient knowledge to build complex animated scenes without ever having to write a line of Java code. You will also be familiar with the basic ideas behind sensor nodes and interpolator nodes.

More important, however, you will have a sound grounding in the mechanisms that VRML 2.0 supports. This knowledge will enable you to quickly and effectively work through the subsequent chapters, which introduce Java and show you how to use it to build exciting, animated 3D worlds.

THE EXECUTION MODEL

VRML 2.0's power comes from the capability to make the worlds you develop come alive. What this means is that the 3D scenes you author are not static—there is a way to make things change. The kind of change that is interesting is change to the scene graph, such as moving an object to a new location, changing its color, or even the way it interacts with the user.

To make these types of changes, you need two essential components. The first is a way to describe what is supposed to happen, what must change, and in what way. The concept of "behavior" captures this idea. The second essential component is a way of associating that behavior with the VRML entities that need to change, a means of communicating the changes to the entities, and a method of finding out about their current state. This method of communicating changes to and from scene entities is referred to as the *execution model*.

The execution model acts to change state. *State*, in VRML terms, is the data associated with entities in the scene graph. So the coordinate position of a sphere, for example, is part of its state. Or the color of a cube is part of its state. This idea of state is no different from the state users normally manipulate in traditional programming languages. Obviously, it is the changes in the state that cause the changes in the 3D world. If a behavior causes a change to the part of the state that describes the color of a cube, the visual representation of the cube changes accordingly.

In essence, behaviors drive the changes to the scene, often in response to events such as user input or the passage of time. The execution model is the mechanism that enables behaviors to change the scene. This relationship between behavior and state can be shown with a simple diagram (see fig. 2.1).

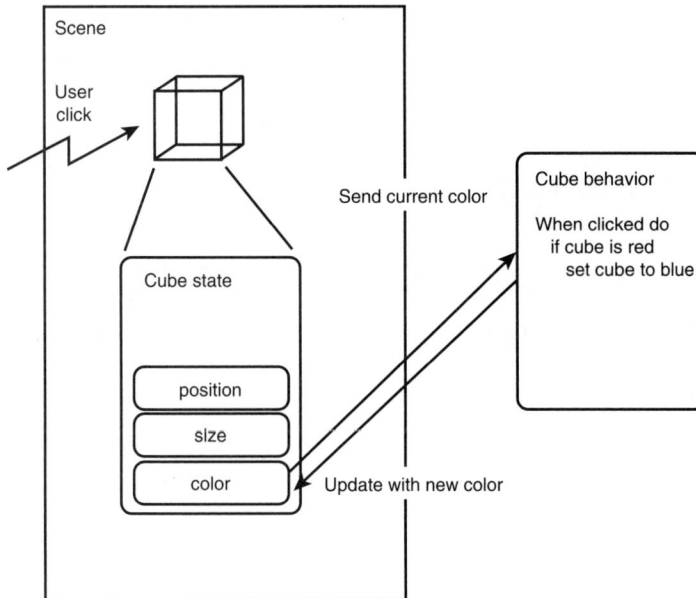

FIGURE 2.1

The relationship between scene entities, their state, and their behavior.

Assuming that user input initiates the process, the user input causes the behavior code to execute some programming logic. What happens, for example, if you want to find out the color of the cube and change it from green to red? The user input causes the color of the cube to be sent to the behavior. The behavior then uses this information to decide what to set the new color to. The result is sent back as an update to the cube's color state.

You can think of the execution model in much the same way as you think of an automobile. The engine, working with the automobile, enables you to get from point A to point B. The engine and the automobile are the execution model. The decision about where A and B are and the way you want to travel between them is yours. You are the behavior. The state of the automobile, its speed, direction, and gas level are available for reading via a set of dials in the dashboard, and you can change them through the gas pedal, gear shift, and steering wheel.

As is the case with automobiles, you can get by in life without really understanding how they work. All you need to know is how to operate them. But as is also true with automobiles, if you really want to get the best out of them, you need to understand the basic principles of their operation. This chapter introduces you to the basic workings of the execution model so that you will be able to harness the benefits of Java to build compelling interactive 3D scenes.

POSSIBLE APPROACHES TO BEHAVIOR

As discussed in the previous chapter, there are several proposals for VRML 2.0—each with its own advantages and disadvantages. The key difference between these proposals was often in the implementation of the execution model. The various proposals can be grouped into three categories: API, language, and event-based. Each proposal adopts a different approach to supporting change.

➤ **API.** The scene is manipulated through a set of procedures or method calls that are made available to the programmer.

➤ **Language.** The VRML 1.0 language evolves to be a fully fledged but specialized 3D programming language.

➤ **Event-based.** Events are used to send changes from an external language to the scene and from the scene to an external language.

THE API APPROACH

One possible approach is to base the execution model on a browser application programming interface (API) that enables application programmers to manipulate scene objects via a set of procedure calls. In this approach, the execution model is procedure-based. The behavior module makes procedure calls into the browser via the API. These calls return after the browser makes the necessary changes.

The API approach will be familiar to most programmers because the majority of existing operating systems already use this type of execution model. The key advantage of this approach is that the VRML file simply contains 3D data. There is no need to complicate the data with hooks to support the execution model.

Although this approach simplifies the VRML file, it makes it difficult for browsers to optimize the scene because the browsers do not have sufficient information of the scene author's intentions. All the browser has to work with is the scene entities. From these scene data, the browser does not receive any clues as to what the scene author intends to change in the scene.

THE LANGUAGE APPROACH

A second approach, which was also proposed, was to evolve the VRML 1.0 3D data format into a fully fledged programming language. This approach is the exact opposite of the API approach. The language approach would provide most of the basic control structures of any traditional programming language, but its base set of data types would be suitable for 3D programming. For example, the 3D cone and the 3D cube would be base types in the language.

This approach solves the optimization problem of the API approach because the browser is told everything about the scene, including the behaviors that will manipulate the scene. The browser is then capable of deciding that certain parts of the scene need not be evaluated, or even rendered, because the user will not see or interact with that part of the scene. However, the main drawback of this approach is that it requires yet another programming language, and, more important, results in a complex specification and implementation in the browser. Because one of the stated goals of the VRML 2.0 call for proposals was a desire for simplicity, this approach was not adopted.

THE EVENT-BASED APPROACH

A third approach, the one proposed in Moving Worlds and adopted in VRML 2.0, is to use an event mechanism. In this approach, VRML scene objects are self-contained entities that expose their internal state via a set of fields. These fields can be written or read by using events. Writing a field requires the generation of an event, which is sent to the field and updates the field with the value of the event. Reading a field happens when a field value changes and the change causes an event, which contains the new value, to be sent.

Events provide the basis for the VRML 2.0 execution model. An *event* is a message containing some data that is used as a trigger for action. Those of you familiar with windowing systems will have no problem understanding the notion of events. In windowing systems, input such as a keypress or mouse click causes an input event to be generated and delivered to the current application. The application will previously have registered its interests in these events and informed the windowing system where the event should be delivered. When the event arrives, the application decides what to do with the event and will then update its internal state and show these updates via the windowing system.

In VRML 2.0, events are used in a similar way—as a means to send messages that contain state between entities. However, in contrast to windowing systems, the source and target for events are fields.

As in VRML 1.0, the basic nodes in the scene graph are parameterized by a set of fields that hold the values of node's properties—their position or color, for example. In VRML 2.0, however, you can now dynamically change these field values by using events.

When a field value is updated, it is possible to generate an event message that holds the new value of the field. That event message may then be sent to another field, whose value is updated with the contents of the event message.

Figure 2.1 reveals that the communication between the behavior and the scene entity enables state to be queried and changed. The mechanism for this in VRML 2.0 is based on events. The events carry the state updates that enable you to change the color of the cube.

The advantage of the event-based approach is that it cleanly separates the essential components of the execution model. The VRML file contains a set of self-contained entities, each of which exposes an interface via a set of fields. The behaviors that drive changes to the scene are implemented externally to the VRML. The execution model provides the glue—the event mechanism— that enables events to carry state between both behaviors and VRML entities and also between individual entities in the scene.

This model has similarities to those found in most modern programming languages. The data to be manipulated is cleanly separated as a well-defined data type. The parts of the data that can be manipulated are clearly defined as a set of exposed fields via the interface.

The event-based approach resolves the essential tensions among performance, simplicity, and flexibility. Events define the relationship between the external behaviors and the VRML scene entities, and also the internal relationship among entities within the scene. This approach clearly denotes which entities will be changed and which fields will be used. The 3D data contains sufficient information to enable optimization but is not as complex as a full-blown programming language.

Before discussing events and fields in more detail, the following section provides a brief recap of the basic model that VRML 2.0 supports to describe a 3D scene.

THE VRML 2.0 SCENE

The VRML 2.0 scene consists of a set of scene entities arranged in a hierarchical fashion. This model is similar to that used in VRML 1.0.

The hierarchy is built up by using a parent-child relationship in which a parent may have any number of children, some of whom may, in turn, be parents themselves.

Listing 2.1 is a complete VRML 2.0 example that will help make this discussion more concrete. The example is simple enough to be understood without too much background knowledge but is sufficiently complex to enable you to understand the basic concepts in a VRML 2.0 scene.

Listing 2.1   A Simple VRML 2.0 Chair (chair.wrl).

```
1    #VRML V2.0 utf8
2    #
3    # chair.wrl (chair)
4    #
5    DEF CHAIR Transform {
6        translation 0 -2 10
7        children [
8            Transform {
9                translation 0.5 0.5 0.5
10               children [
11                   DEF SEAT Shape {
12                       appearance Appearance {
13                           material Material { diffuseColor 0    1 0 }
14                       }
15                       geometry  Box { size 1 0.1 1 }
16                   }
17               ]
18           }
19
20           DEF LEG Transform {
21               children [
22                   Shape {
23                       appearance Appearance {
24                           material Material { diffuseColor 0 0 1 }
25                       }
26                       geometry Cylinder { height 1 radius 0.1 }
27                   }
28               ]
29           }
```

```
30        DEF LEG2 Transform {
31            translation 0 0 1
32            children [
33                USE LEG
34            ]
35        }
36        DEF LEG3 Transform {
37            translation 1 0 0
38            children [
39                USE LEG
40            ]
41        }
42        DEF LEG4 Transform {
43            translation 1 0 1
44            children [
45                USE LEG
46            ]
47        }
48    ] # end of children for chair
49 } # end of transform
50 DEF BACK Transform {
51    translation  0.5 -1 9.7
52    rotation 1 0 0 1.2
53    children [
54        USE SEAT
55    ]
56 }
```

This example shows a simple chair, made up of a seat, a seat back, and four legs. This chair won't be the most comfortable seat in the world, but it will work for our purposes. Note that this method isn't necessarily the best way to build this model. The chair has been built in this way to highlight a number of aspects of the VRML 2.0 scene graph.

Figure 2.2 shows what the model actually looks like in a VRML 2.0 browser.

FIGURE 2.2
A simple VRML 2.0 chair.

NODES

The basic element in VRML 2.0 is the node. *Nodes* are the elements that make up the 3D scene. Each node is typed and has a set of fields that parameterize the node. In turn, each of these fields is typed. The VRML 2.0 specification defines the type, the field names and their types, and the default value for these fields.

VRML 2.0 contains just over 50 nodes, approximately 20 more than included with 1.0. This section and sections in subsequent chapters explore some of these newer nodes because the majority were added to enable scene authors to add action to their scenes.

In the previous example (listing 2.1), the geometry uses a **Box** node for the seat and seat back and a **Cylinder** node for the chair leg (lines 15 and 26). Note, however, that these geometry nodes are wrapped in **Shape** nodes, which are, in turn, wrapped in **Transform** nodes. This "wrapping" is the way we define the scene hierarchies.

NAMING NODES

Nodes are named with the **DEF** prefix, which assigns a string value to a particular example of a node. To assign the name LEG to a **Transform** node that contains the seat geometry, for example, you would use the code shown in listing 2.2.

Listing 2.2 The Transform Node.

```
1   DEF LEG Transform {
2      ...
3   }
```

DEF forms the basis of the sharing model, through which any named node can be shared at some point later in the scene graph by using the **USE** syntax. By looking closely at the example in listing 2.1, you will see that the seat is reused to create the seat back, and the chair leg is **DEF**d once and **USE**d three times for the other legs.

GROUPING NODES AND CHILDREN NODES

Nodes come in two types: grouping and leaf. *Grouping nodes*, such as **Transform**, group children. Children may be leaf nodes or other grouping nodes. The group node provides the coordinate space for the children contained within. This coordinate space is relative to the parent's coordinate space. This enables scene authors to build a hierarchy of nodes with each transformation having an accumulative effect as you move down the scene graph hierarchy.

Again referring to the chair example in listing 2.1, you can see that two hierarchies are defined. The first hierarchy—defined using a **Transform** node and named CHAIR—begins at line 5 and has five children, each of which is a **Transform** node. The first child contains the description of the seat, the second child contains the description of the leg, and the remaining three reuse the leg description to define the other three legs.

The second hierarchy (line 50) is a simple one. The hierarchy is based on a **Transform** node and contains only one child. The child that describes the seat back reuses the SEAT node to create the seat back.

The first hierarchy shows the relationships among the parents and children. The initial **Transform** node, named CHAIR, specifies a translation from the origin of –2 meters in the Y axis and 10 meters in the Z axis. Because the children of this node inherit the coordinate space from their parent, they start out with this new coordinate as their origin. Any transformations the children define are relative to their parent's coordinate space.

In addition to the **Transform** node, there are four grouping nodes: **Anchor**, **Billboard**, **Collision**, and **Group**. These nodes have a role similar to the **Transform** node and provide a hierarchical transformation space for their children. These nodes will be discussed in more detail in Chapter 4, "Advanced VRML."

LEAF NODES

Leaf nodes, such as **Shape,** place entities into a coordinate space defined by the surrounding group node. The **Shape** node is new to VRML 2.0 and contains only geometry and appearance information for visible elements in the scene. The **Shape** node was designed to support easy sharing of scene elements so that scene composition is easier than in VRML 1.0. Returning to the example, a simple shape, such as a seat, can be defined and then reused in the scene via the **DEF/USE** facility.

The geometry field is actually a node pointer and contains the node that describes the geometrical properties of the object, for example, a **Cone** or **Sphere** node. The appearance field enables the author to set visual properties, such as its color or brightness, for the geometry.

THE SCENE GRAPH

A VRML file defines a set of nodes organized into a set of hierarchies. *Scene graph* is the name used to denote the entire ordered collection of these scene hierarchies as they appear in the VRML file. Each hierarchy is a single rooted group node, with a series of one or more children.

Conceptually, a scene graph looks like figure 2.3(a). To make the scene more concrete, figure 2.3(b) shows the scene hierarchies defined by the chair example.

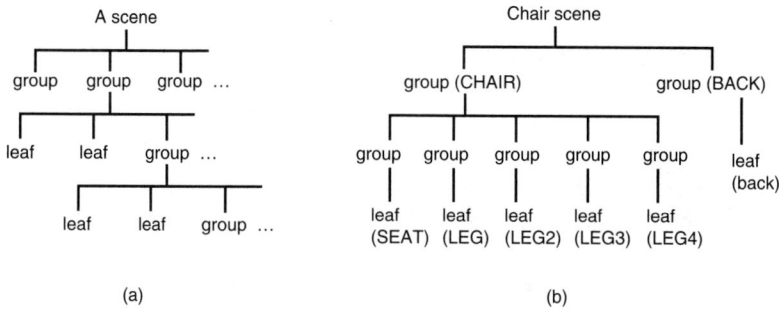

FIGURE 2.3

A conceptual and concrete scene graph.

The example, in combination with this section, gives you a good overview of the structure of a VRML 2.0 file.

In this book, we assume you already have a basic knowledge of VRML 2.0. If you are a little rusty, you may want to spend some time studying Appendix A, "VRML and 3D Principles," which is a quick primer to VRML 2.0. You will also find more information in the resources list in Appendix C, "Resources."

NOTE

THE EXECUTION MODEL: DETAILS

Having introduced the basics of VRML 2.0, let's return to the discussion of the execution model. Remember that the basic mechanism consists of a behavior that changes the state of entities in the scene via the execution model. The execution model uses events as its vehicle for change and acts on fields that hold state.

FIELDS IN VRML 2.0

As shown previously, the basic VRML 2.0 scene structure is not much different from VRML 1.0. What is new, however, is that fields are no longer simple write-once values that enable you to define the characteristics of a node. Fields are now the basis of the execution model. In VRML 2.0, fields can be one of four different classes.

The simplest class, the field class, is the same as in VRML 1.0. Fields are data values that define the characteristic of the node (for example, the radius field of the **Sphere** node).

The second class of fields is the eventIn field. An eventIn field is a field that will accept an incoming event that will change its value to the value of the event itself. In this book, we'll refer to this type of field as a *sink* for events.

The third class of fields is an eventOut field. As the name suggests, this field is one that outputs its value as an event. We'll refer to this type of field as a *source* for events.

The last class of fields is actually a combination of the eventIn and eventOut field—the exposedField. The exposedField is a field that is both willing to accept a new value via an event and to send out its new value as an event. An exposedField is a shorthand notation for the combination of the two field types and can act as both a source and a sink for events.

AN EXAMPLE: THE TRANSFORM NODE

To make all this concrete, listing 2.3—the **Transform** node—is an example from the VRML 2.0 specification.

Listing 2.3   The Full Transform Node Specification.

```
1   Transform {
2   eventIn        MFNode       addChildren
3   eventIn        MFNode       removeChildren
4   exposedField   MFNode       children         []
5   exposedField   SFRotation   rotation         0 0 1 0
6   exposedField   SFVec3f      scale            1 1 1
7   exposedField   SFRotation   scaleOrientation 0 0 1 0
8   exposedField   SFVec3f      center           0 0 0
9   exposedField   SFVec3f      translation      0 0 0
```

```
10   field         SFVec3f       bboxCenter       0 0 0
11   field         SFVec3f       bboxSize         -1 -1 -1
12   }
```

NOTE

File Syntax and the Specification

In listing 2.3, the **Transform** node is shown in its entirety, the way it is written in the VRML 2.0 specification. However, the actual version an author or authoring tool would write is a shorthand version of this. For example, the addChildren and removeChildren fields are implied and, therefore, dropped. In addition, keywords such as exposedField and the type name are also dropped. Last, the values associated with the fields are the default values used by the browser. Authors are free to specify their own values or to not specify a value or even an entire field, in which case the default is used.

In a similar vein, the full name of all eventIn fields is set_xxx and eventOut fields is xxx_changed; however, these can be left off and are inferred by the browser.

Looking back to the chair example in listing 2.1, you can see the difference between the specification version of **Transform** and the actual version you would expect to find in a VRML 2.0 file. Throughout most of this book, examples are given in the same format as you would expect to see them in a VRML 2.0 file. Where necessary, the full specification version will be used to make a particular point.

In the **Transform** node, you can see that some of the fields are of the simple field class, for example, the bboxCenter and bboxSize fields. These fields define a bounding box for an object that can be used by the browser as a hint for optimization. Because these values are typically set when the node is first authored, they cannot be changed.

Note also that the class of the field is orthogonal to the actual data type that the field holds. There is no relationship between the type of the field and whether that field can be changed.

The more interesting fields, such as translation or scale, are defined as exposedFields. This means that they are capable of both sending and receiving events (see fig. 2.4).

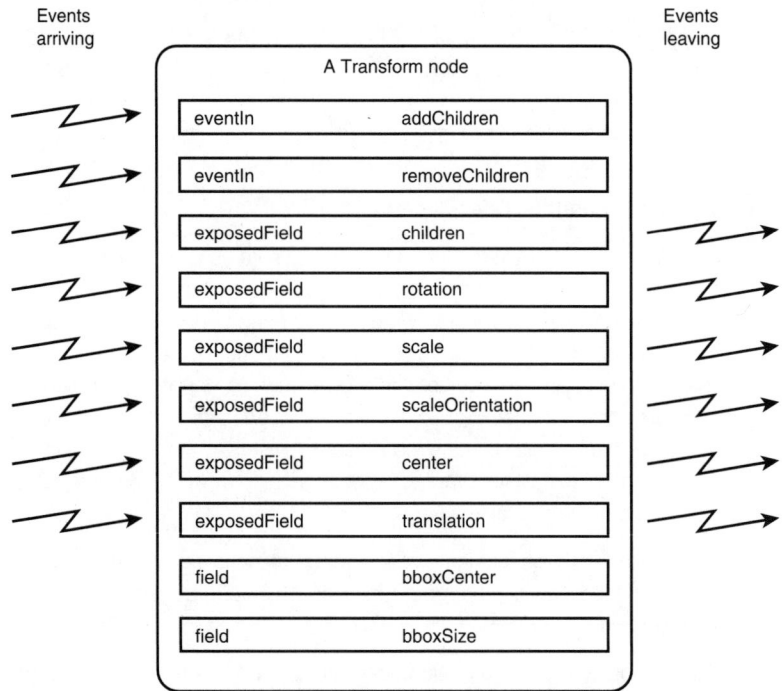

Events   Events
arriving   leaving

A Transform node

eventIn	addChildren
eventIn	removeChildren
exposedField	children
exposedField	rotation
exposedField	scale
exposedField	scaleOrientation
exposedField	center
exposedField	translation
field	bboxCenter
field	bboxSize

FIGURE 2.4

The class of the field dictates whether that field is a source, sink, or both for events.

ROUTES

So far, all that has been described is the basic building block for the execution model, the capability to denote fields of a node as either a source or sink, or both, of events. The next question is how to link those sources and sinks to enable a series of events to flow between nodes? This method of linking is based on the notion of a route.

A *route* defines the source and sink fields for an event and enables a scene author to wire nodes together. The route enables events to flow between fields, enabling you to propagate change between nodes in the scene graph.

Routes are written as follows:

```
1   ROUTE node.sourceField TO node.sinkField
```

With this mechanism, fields can be linked to enable one event in one node to cause a corresponding change in another node. This change is achieved by linking an eventOut field (via a route) to an eventIn field. Remember that routing can take place only between fields of the same type. Otherwise some form of type translation would have to be provided, an option that VRML 2.0 doesn't support.

To see how this works, imagine two related boxes, one inside the other. If the outer box is moved, the inner box should move accordingly. One way to create this relationship would be to place both boxes in separate **Transform** nodes and link the translation field of one **Transform** to the other (see fig. 2.5).

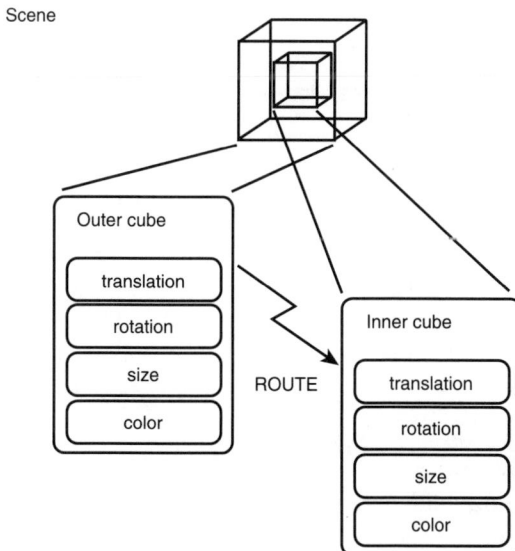

FIGURE 2.5

The inner cube moves when the outer cube moves.

CASCADING EVENTS, FAN-OUT, AND LOOPS

In the preceding example, one event from a source field is routed to a sink field and then stopped. This model can naturally be extended so that events originating in one node cause a field in another node to change, which in turn is routed to yet another node. This process is referred to as *cascading* events and implies that each event that is delivered causes another event to be generated. Obviously, for this to happen, the link field in the middle of the chain has to be both able to receive and to generate events—that is, it is an **exposedField**. In figure 2.6, a third node, "another," has been linked into the scene.

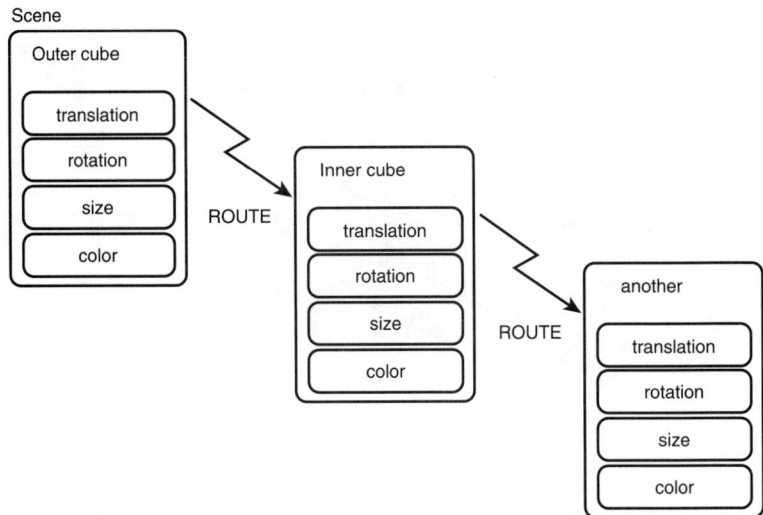

FIGURE 2.6
Cascading a translation change event.

The execution model doesn't restrict a field value that changes to generating only a single event; it is possible for a field to have several routes originating from it. When the field value changes and generates an event, the value is propagated on all routes. This model is referred to as *fan-out* (see fig. 2.7).

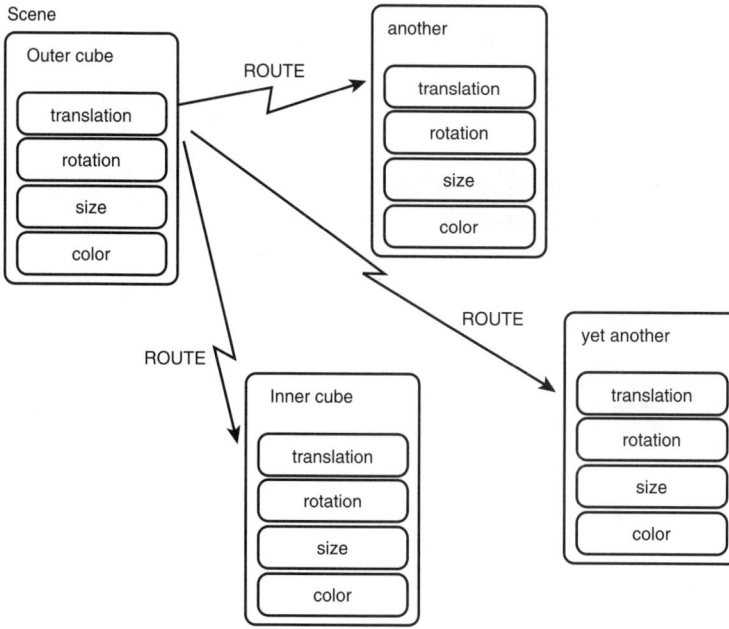

FIGURE 2.7

A single event source is sent to multiple sinks.

A final possibility is a route or series of routes that cause an event loop. In this, the start event is propagated through a series of fields, one of which points back to the start field that sourced the event. Although this is perfectly acceptable, the VRML browser ensures that during any one time period, the start of the loop will generate only one event.

RIDING A BICYCLE

To give you a better understanding of the event propagation model, here is an example that is slightly more interesting than boxes. Imagine a bicycle and its rider; these are independent entities in the scene, but they nevertheless have a relationship. As the bicycle moves, the rider should move in the same way. To achieve this, the translation field of a **Transform** will be used. Listing 2.4 shows the bicycle.

NOTE

Due to space restrictions, the following example gives only the skeleton for the VRML code. You can find the full example on the accompanying CD-ROM or at the Web page http://www.mcp.com/newriders/.

Listing 2.4   A Simple Bicycle (bike.wrl).

```
1    DEF BIKE Transform {
2        translation 0 0 0
3        children [
4        DEF FWHEEL Transform {
5            ...
6        }
7        DEF BWHEEL Transform {
8            ...
9        }
10        DEF FRAME Transform {
11            ...
12        }
13        ]
14    }
```

Note how the **Transform** for the BIKE node defines its position in the world coordinate system by using a translation field. The wheels and frame are defined relative to that position. Listing 2.5 shows the definition of the rider.

Listing 2.5   A Simple Rider.

```
1    DEF RIDER Transform {
2    translation 0 0 0
3        children [
4          Transform {
5              translation 0 3 0
6              children [
7                  ...
8              ]
9          }
10        ]
11    }
```

Again, the rider is defined by using a **Transform** that is set to the origin. To link these two independent scene hierarchies—the rider and the bicycle—use a route that links their translation fields and so ensures that when one moves, the other moves with it. This relationship is possible because the translation field of the **Transform** node is an exposedField and can both source and sink events.

```
1   ROUTE BIKE.translation TO RIDER.translation
```

This ROUTE means that when the translation field of the BIKE **Transform** node is changed, that change is routed out as an event, which is delivered to the translation field of the RIDER **Transform** node. At any point in time, the value of both fields will be the same, with the BIKE translation field dictating the value of the RIDER translation field.

EVENT SOURCES

The examples so far have explained how to link two nodes and how to route changes in the field of one node to a field in another node by using a ROUTE. However, a basic question has been ignored: Where do events originate from, and what is the initial source of change?

There are two answers to this: interpolator nodes and sensor nodes. Both of these types of nodes are designed to generate new values. As the name suggests, *sensor nodes* sense something and generate events when that something changes. *Interpolator nodes* are different in that they are designed to interpolate new values from existing values and generate events holding those new values. VRML 2.0 has six different interpolator nodes and seven different sensors nodes. The relationship between sensor nodes and interpolator nodes is extremely close; generally you will find them working together. This is because although interpolator nodes generate new events, their operation requires a start or seed value. In many cases, the sensor node provides this seed. The following section introduces the interpolator and shows how it works. Subsequently, one of the sensor nodes, the **TimeSensor**, is introduced and the relationship between interpolators and sensors is discussed in detail. A full list of the interpolator and sensor nodes can also be found in Appendix A.

INTERPOLATORS

Interpolators are designed to take the grunt work out of key-framed animation. They are nodes that take a set of values that define a range and then automatically generate the intermediate values between the range values—they interpolate the missing values. You can imagine an integer interpolator that, given a start value of 0 and an end value of 10, generates all the intermediate integer values, 1 though 9, one per second.

To generate these values, an interpolator needs to be given enough information to enable it to interpolate the missing values. This information is defined by a set of input values: the **key** and corresponding output values, the **keyValue**. You can think of these as examples given to the interpolator to help it calculate arbitrary intermediate values. VRML 2.0 defines a set of useful interpolators that help animate objects, such as the **ScalarInterpolator** that interpolates between a range of floating point values and the **PositionInterpolator** that works with sets of coordinate values.

In the bicycle example, you can use a position interpolator to generate a set of new positions for the bicycle. Listing 2.6 specifies the **PositionInterpolator**.

Listing 2.6   The PositionInterpolator.

```
1    PositionInterpolator
2    eventIn         SSFloat      set_fraction
3    exposedField    MMFloat      key           []
4    exposedField    MFVec3f      keyValue      []
5    eventOut        SFVec3f      value_changed
6    }
```

The key field is used to define the input to the interpolator function. The keyValue field defines the corresponding result values. However, as mentioned previously, these fields are really the examples that the interpolator uses to construct a function that—given any input value in the range—it can use to generate an output value. The actual input values and output values are managed via the set_fraction and value_changed field. The set_fraction field takes any arbitrary value, which causes the interpolator to calculate the interpolated value and makes this value available via the value_changed eventOut field.

For example, as in listing 2.7, using a set of three keys (0, 0.5, and 1) and an associated set of position values (0 0 0, 10 0 0, and 0 0 0), the interpolator will calculate the corresponding 3D coordinate for any value in the range 0 to 1. In this case, the calculation is simple because our three keyValues describe a straight trajectory from the origin, 10 meters in the X direction and back to the origin.

It is possible to "wire" this interpolator into the bicycle scene and use it to send a set of new positions to the bicycle, which in turn will be routed to the rider. Figure 2.8 shows this in action.

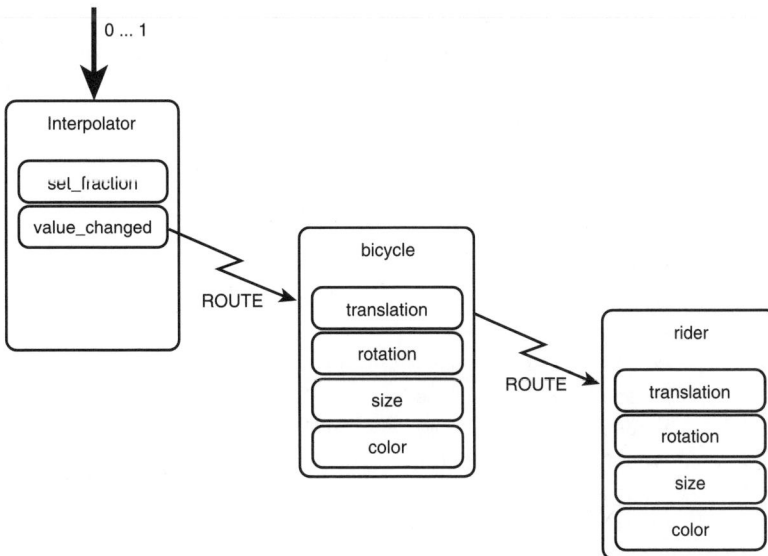

FIGURE 2.8

The interpolator drives the new position for the bicycle.

Listing 2.7   Setting Up a PositionInterpolator.

```
1   DEF P PositionInterpolator {
2       key [ 0, 0.5, 1]
3       keyValue [ 0 0 0, 10 0 0, 0 0 0]
4   }
5   ROUTE P.value_changed TO BIKE.translation
```

One final piece is necessary before you can actually animate the scene. So far, the scene objects, the bicycle, and the rider have been defined. An interpolator that can generate new positions for the bicycle has been set up, and the routing to cause the bicycle and the rider to move has been written. However, something still needs to trigger the **PositionInterpolator** to enable it to generate position coordinates.

TIME SENSORS

To be able to trigger the **PositionInterpolator** to generate position coordinates, you need a means to generate the trigger event. To do that, another type of node, the **TimeSensor** can be used. In this example, the job of the **TimeSensor** is to generate the fraction values that are the input values for the **PositionInterpolator**. The **TimeSensor** generates these values as time passes, enabling the **PositionInterpolator** to interpolate the new positions that are used to animate the bicycle. Listing 2.8 shows the **TimeSensor**.

Listing 2.8   The TimeSensor.

```
1   TimeSensor {
2       exposedField    SFTime     cycleInterval      1
3       exposedField    SFBool     enabled            TRUE
4       exposedField    SFBool     loop               TRUE
5       exposedField    SFTime     startTime          0
6       exposedField    SFTime     stopTime           0
7       eventOut        SFTime     cycleTime
8       eventOut        SFFloat    fraction_changed
9       eventOut        SFBool     isActive
10      eventOut        SFTime     time
11  }
```

The **TimeSensor** is a multipurpose node that you can use to drive continuous simulations, periodic activities, and one-off alarms. This node senses the passage of time and generates events from the startTime to the stopTime. To do this, the **TimeSensor** compares the "real time" to its start and stop times, and if the real time is after the start time and before the stop time, the sensor is active and generates events. During that period, the current time is available from the time field as an absolute value calculated as time—in seconds—since midnight GMT January 1, 1970.

The cycleInterval defines a cycle (in seconds) that repeats itself during the lifetime of the timer. At the beginning of each cycle, a time event is generated and made available in the cycleTime field. In conjunction with this, the field fraction_changed contains a value in the range 0 to 1 that indicates what proportion of the cycle has passed. If the cycleInterval is set to 10 seconds, for example, five seconds into the cycle the fraction_changed value will hold 0.5.

The code in listing 2.9 shows an example **TimeSensor** and the routing needed to wire the node into the example.

Listing 2.9   Setting Up the TimeSensor.

```
1    DEF T TimeSensor {
2        loop TRUE
3        enabled TRUE
4        cycleInterval 10
5        stopTime -1
6    }
7    ROUTE T.fraction_changed TO P.set_fraction
```

The **TimeSensor** is initialized with a loop value set to TRUE and a negative stopTime. The result of this is that the **TimeSensor** will start generating events when the scene is loaded and will continue to do so until the scene is replaced. The reasons for this are as follows. startTime, although not shown, defaults to a value of 0; therefore, startTime is larger than stopTime and so we can ignore stopTime. Because loop is TRUE, the **TimeSensor** does not stop when the current time passes the value of startTime + cycleInterval but loops back and starts the cycle again. Then, at the point of loading, the current time is greater than the startTime, so the **TimeSensor** begins generating events immediately.

The field that is most interesting for the example and which can be used to drive the interpolator is the fraction_changed field of the **TimeSensor**. This value will start from 0 at the start of the cycle and climb to 1 at the end of the cycle. This fraction_changed field is routed to the set_fraction field of the position interpolator. Note that the position interpolator is set up to accept keys in the range 0 to 1, which corresponds exactly to the fraction_changed value that the **TimeSensor** is generating.

Figure 2.9 shows all these components and their links. The **TimeSensor** is used to drive the keys needed by the **PositionInterpolator** to generate new positions. These positions are routed through to the bicycle translation field and are then, in turn, cascaded to the translation field of the rider node.

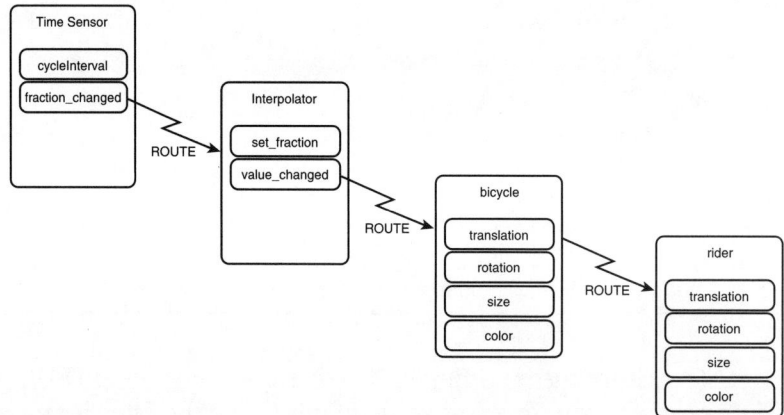

FIGURE 2.9
The TimeSensor acts as the initial event source for the animation.

Putting together the **TimeSensor**, **PositionInterpolator**, and routing information, you can see that the effect is that the bicycle and rider move continuously from the origin, 10 meters along the X axis and then back to the origin. This animation repeats indefinitely. Remember that the full source code for this example can be found on the accomanying CD-ROM and on the New Riders Web page for this book.

TIME IN THE 3D SCENE

The passage of time in a VRML scene is dependent on the VRML browser being used to view the scene. The browser causes time to pass—from the viewpoint of the scene—by causing **TimeSensor**s to generate events.

Although most browsers try to ensure that the passage of time in the scene is equivalent to the passage of time in the real world, there is no requirement for this. It is entirely possible that a specialized browser used for complex simulations may make scene time move much faster than real time to enable users to "speed up" the simulation. Alternatively, it is possible, and indeed likely, that a browser will not track real-world time accurately. This means that some nodes, such as interpolators, will generate fraction_changed events when they are able. This will not always correspond to real-world time.

SUMMARY OF THE EXECUTION MODEL

The VRML 2.0 execution model is relatively straightforward. The model is based on two key features, fields and events, and a mechanism to wire those together, the ROUTE. During each clock tick in the browser, all potential sources of events are evaluated. Sources of events are always fields that are either eventOuts or exposedFields. If any field has generated an event, the browser checks to see whether that field is routed to any other node. If so, the browser delivers the new field value to the destination, or sink, of the route.

Static Versus Dynamic Behaviors

This chapter began with a discussion of the idea of a behavior and of how the behavior used the execution model to drive changes to the scene graph. However, in all of the previous examples, there has never been a real behavior module as most people would understand it—that is, something that looks like a piece of programming code.

The reason for this is that the execution model, combined with the new nodes defined in VRML 2.0, are sufficiently rich to build animated scenes without using programming. This approach is referred to as static behaviors. The name may seem a contradiction, but it actually captures the power and limitations of the approach. A *static behavior* is one where a set of event sources and sinks are wired to enable change in the scene graph. Because there is no decision-making facility within the execution model, this mechanism is restricted in what it can do. However, it does enable you to build some interesting animated scenes.

The alternative approach—using a piece of programming logic to make decisions which then drive event generation—is referred to as *dynamic behavior*. Again, the name is chosen simply because it captures the power and flexibility of the approach.

The rest of this chapter explains further the possibilities and limitations of using static behaviors. In the next chapter, you fully explore the use of the Java programming language to build dynamic behaviors.

Going Further: User Activation

You've already looked briefly at an example of the **PositionInterpolator** used in conjunction with a **TimeSensor**. However, in that example, the entire animation starts when the browser loads the scene and runs until it loads another scene. In the following example, a **PositionInterpolator** and **TimeSensor** are used to move an object, but the movement will be executed in conjunction with another sensor, in this case a **TouchSensor**. The role of the **TouchSensor** is to enable a mouse click to start the animation.

As you might imagine, the **TouchSensor** is a sensor that tracks whether the pointing device is "over" some part of the scene. See listing 2.10.

Listing 2.10   The TouchSensor.

```
1   TouchSensor {
2   exposedField    SFBool    enabled    TRUE
3   eventOut      SFVec3f    hitNormal_changed
4   eventOut      SFVec3f    hitPoint_changed
5   eventOut      SFVec2f    hitTexCoord_changed
6   eventOut      SFBool    isActive
7   eventOut      SFBool    isOver
8   eventOut      SFTime    touchTime
```

The **TouchSensor**, when enabled, tracks the pointing device and checks to see whether the user points to any geometry contained within the **TouchSensor**'s parent group. If that is the case, the isOver field is set to TRUE.

If the **TouchSensor** is selected with the pointing device, isActive becomes TRUE and returns to false when it is deselected. If the pointing device is a mouse, for example, mouse-down indicates selected and releasing equals deselected. When the sensor is deselected, the current time is placed in the touchTime field and an event is generated. (See Chapter 3, "Letting Java Loose," for more information about the use of the **TouchSensor**.)

Here, the focus is on the fields of the **TouchSensor** that will allow a demonstration of the basic operation and, more important, how we can use this to start the animation.

The geometry that will have the **TouchSensor** attached is the bicycle. To attach it, all you need to do is make the **TouchSensor** one of the children of the BIKE node, as seen listing 2.11.

Listing 2.11   Adding a TouchSensor to the Bicycle Example.

```
1   DEF BIKE Transform {
2      translation 0 0 0
3      children [
4      DEF CLICKER TouchSensor { }
5      DEF FWHEEL Transform {
6                    ...
7                    }
8      DEF BWHEEL Transform {
9        ...
10     }
11     DEF FRAME Transform {
12       ...
13     }
14     ]
15  }
16   ROUTE CLICKER.touchTime TO T.startTime
```

You need to wire the **TouchSensor** to the **TimeSensor** to tell it to start generating time events. To do this, route the touchTime field of the **TouchSensor** to the startTime field of the **TimeSensor** and set the loop field of the **TimeSensor** to FALSE. This action is necessary to prevent the **TimeSensor** from generating events as soon as it is loaded.

Now, when the bicycle is clicked, the current time is sent to the **TimeSensor** to be used as the **startTime**. The **TimeSensor** then realizes that the **startTime** has passed and begins to generate time events. These time events cause the same animation as before, except that after one cycle, the animation stops. Clicking again on the bicycle causes the animation to repeat.

SEEING THE BICYCLE EXAMPLE IN ACTION

Now that you've become familiar with the basic features of the execution model, the best way to experiment further is to actually load the examples into a VRML 2.0 browser and experiment with them.

The following section shows how to copy from the accompanying CD-ROM or download, install, and use the Sony VRML 2.0 browser—called Community Place, or CP for short. Although this book uses the CP browser—the one we're most familiar with—the examples in this chapter are standard VRML 2.0 and will run under any browser that is VRML 2.0 compliant. If you've already installed CP or you're using another browser, feel free to skip this section and go straight to the section "Trying the First Example."

INSTALLING CP

There is a fully functional evaluation version of Community Place on the CD-ROM that accompanies this book. Appendix D, "Installing Community Place," provides full details of how to install this software.

The CP browser is also freely available from two download sites. The primary site is the Sony Virtual Society site at Sony's head-quarters in Tokyo, Japan. The CP system is also available from the Sony Pictures ImageWorks site in Los Angeles (USA). Choose whichever site is more easily accessible for you.

http://vs.sony.co.jp/   Site in Japan

http://sonypic.com/vs   Site in the USA

Follow the instructions on the download page and then double-click on the resulting executable file on your PC. The CP browser installs itself automatically.

This version of the CP VRML 2.0 browser works as a helper to Netscape. The browser can be run as a stand-alone, but you will only be able to load VRML files from your local disk.

You can use the examples in this book in one of two ways. These examples are available on the accompanying CD-ROM, laid out in the same order as the book. Alternatively, you can access the examples at the New Riders Web site at http://www.mcp.com/newriders/.

When you install the CP browser, you also install its manual. If you're not already familiar with CP, you may want to spend a few minutes browsing the manual.

You are now ready to load and experiment with the examples shown previously.

TRYING THE FIRST EXAMPLE

Load rider.wrl into CP (or your favorite browser) and you should see a figure similar to figure 2.10. You can load the example by clicking on the link on the examples HTML page or by using the File, Load pull-down menu of CP if the file is local.

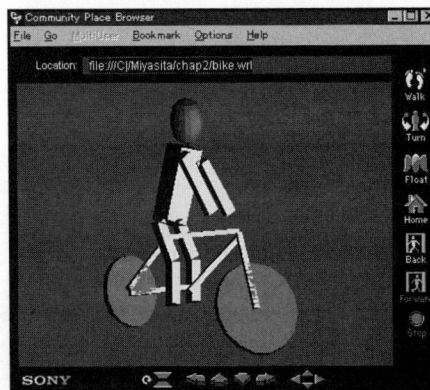

FIGURE 2.10

Bicycle and rider in a VRML 2.0 browser.

If you click on the bicycle, it will animate across the screen and back again.

OTHER THINGS TO TRY

Although this animation has introduced you to a lot of the power of the VRML 2.0 execution model, it is still rather simplistic from an animation point of view. The following are a few things you may want to try to increase your understanding of these fundamental nodes:

➤ Experiment with the cycleInterval time of the **TimeSensor** to see how different values affect the speed of animation.

➤ Experiment with the **PositionInterpolator** to have the bicycle travel a more complex path.

➤ Add an **OrientationInterpolator** to enable you to rotate the bicycle as it travels the more complex path.

ROUNDUP

This chapter introduced the basic execution model of VRML 2.0 and showed how to implement static behaviors by using sensors and interpolators. This approach enables you to write simple but nevertheless interesting animation. However, there are severe restrictions in the degree of flexibility that using event generators and routes alone provides. This lack of flexibility is caused by the inability to express any kind of logic using the execution model and the standard VRML 2.0 nodes. You can cause events to trigger only other events and link these together to animate sets of related objects.

Put simply, the VRML 2.0 nodes, plus the use of routes, enable you to do exactly what the designers of the nodes designed them to do. Although these nodes can result in quite sophisticated scene animation, they are not open. If this was all that VRML 2.0 had to offer (although it would have been a significant advance on VRML 1.0), it would not justify the interest generated.

Fortunately, VRML 2.0 has been designed in a way that enables arbitrary behavior to be written in any programming language and then to be connected into the scene by using the execution model.

The next chapter shows you how to use the power of the Java programming language to build complex behaviors and how to plug these into the scene by using the execution model described in this chapter.

CHAPTER 3

LETTING JAVA LOOSE

Chapter 2, "Adding Action to 3D Worlds," was a

rapid introduction to the VRML 2.0 execution model

and how it can be used to build animated 3D scenes.

Although it is clear that VRML 2.0 is a powerful 3D

language in its own right, the real power comes

from its capability to use a programming language

to build much more sophisticated, interactive

scenes. This chapter is all about using Java to do just

that.

WHAT THIS CHAPTER COVERS

In order to let Java loose on the 3D scene, you need a mechanism that enables you to combine the VRML world and the Java world. Chapter 2 showed that changing the VRML world is all about fields and using events to change their values. If Java is to be allowed to interact with VRML, it needs a mechanism to access fields, manipulate their values, and return the results to the VRML world. VRML 2.0 does that by extending its execution model into the Java world by using a special node that bridges the two worlds. That bridge is called the **Script** node. The **Script** node forms the basis of what, in the last chapter, was referred to as active behaviors.

In this chapter you will do the following:

➤ Learn about the **Script** node and how it fits into the VRML scene hierarchy

➤ Discover how the **Script** node acts as a bridge between the VRML and Java worlds, extending the VRML execution model into the Java world

➤ Look at the basic Java classes that are provided to interact with and manipulate VRML data

➤ Learn how to compile and run a Java program designed to interwork with the VRML 2.0 world

After you have a basic understanding of how VRML 2.0 and Java interact, you will be ready to move on to subsequent chapters where, while the Java and the VRML gets more powerful, the basic model of interaction between the VRML and Java worlds stays the same.

By the end of this chapter, you will understand how VRML and Java work together and how you can pass information from the VRML world to the Java world and back again. You will also understand all the components required to build simple Java programs that drive VRML 2.0 scenes.

In addition, you will have a good understanding of the underlying principles that are used to "marry" the two worlds. This understanding will help you to move rapidly toward creating complex Java programs that control dynamic, interactive 3D scenes.

DYNAMIC BEHAVIORS

The previous chapter began with the discussion of an example showing the need to be able to query state in the scene and then make decisions based on that state. The actual example used wanted to know the current color of the cube so that it could decide on a new color. In the remainder of Chapter 2, various examples showed the use of "static behaviors" to change aspects of the scene, but they never showed an example of this kind of decision logic. This was simply because there are no nodes in the VRML 2.0 specification that support such logic.

Clearly, there is a need for this type of functionality. Without it, the scene is restricted to routing predefined events along predefined routes between predefined nodes. If this was all that was available, it would not be possible to build anything more than predefined animation. Simple scenes that answered questions such as "if the door is open and the light is on"—or, in fact, any complex piece of logic—would be extremely difficult to build.

Decisions using complex data types form part of what was described as "dynamic behaviors." These behaviors are different from static behaviors because they are able to do more than just route events along predefined paths. Dynamic behaviors need the capability to query state, to make decisions based on that state, and to change the state of the scene based on these decisions. This is exactly what programming languages excel at. Because there are no predefined nodes in VRML 2.0 to do this kind of work, VRML 2.0 needs a way to reach out to a programming language to ask it to do it instead.

As briefly mentioned in the previous chapter, there is a way to do this. It involves "plugging" arbitrary programming logic into the scene, and the key to that is the **Script** node.

THE SCRIPT NODE

The **Script** node is similar to any other node in some respects, but is very special in others. This node is similar because, as with other VRML 2.0 nodes, you can place it anywhere in your scene hierarchies, you can name it with DEF, and you can route events to and from it. However, it differs in one key point: the fields of a **Script** node are user-extensible, and events arriving at those fields are automatically routed to the program associated with the **Script** node.

Listing 3.1 shows the specification of the **Script** node.

Listing 3.1   The Specification of the Script Node.

```
1  Script {
2      exposedField    MFString        url             [ ]
3      field           SFBool          directOutput    FALSE
4      field           SFBool          mustEvaluate    FALSE
5  # and any number of
6      eventIn         eventTypeName   eventName
7      field           fieldTypeName   fieldName       initialValue
8      eventOut        eventTypeName   eventName
8  }
```

The url field provides the link between the node and the program that will implement some behavior on behalf of this **Script** node. It enables the scene author to bind an arbitrary code fragment to the **Script** node. The field is named url because it is intended to hold a Universal Resource Locator and signifies that this field usually contains a string that points to a file containing the program that will be used by this **Script** node. This file can be local or anywhere on the Internet. The term "usually" is used because the url field can actually contain code itself.

When the url field contains a valid Universal Resource Locator that points to a file containing the program code, the type of file indicates which script language is inside the file. For example, see listing 3.2.

Listing 3.2   Setting Up a Script Node.

```
1  Script {
2  url [ "http://sony.com/demos/demo1.class",
3      "http://sony.com/demos/demo1.js",
4      "javascript:function start(value, timestamp) {...}"
5  ]
```

This tells the browser to try and use the Java byte code in demo1.class. If it can't resolve that URL, it tries the JavaScript in demo1.js; and if it can't resolve that URL, it uses the inline code in the final string.

Although VRML 2.0 enables any programming language to implement its behaviors, Java—because of its power and tight integration with the Internet—is used by the majority of serious VRML developers. Because this book is all about using Java to develop VRML, any future references to scripts or programs will imply Java.

NOTE

For various reasons, the VRML community decided that VRML 2.0 would not require any particular language. This decision was based, in part, on a wish to avoid "language wars" and also on the belief that no one language was capable of answering all the requirements of the VRML community. The drawback of this approach is that there is no guarantee that all browsers support the language you want. This inevitably leads to situations where content written for one browser won't work in another popular browser. Although this may be an inconvenience at first, it was felt by many that, eventually, browsers would converge to support one or more popular languages. Most likely, these languages would be dictated by the content creators. The VRML 2.0 specification provides annexes that explain how to support two popular languages: Java and JavaScript.

The second important feature of the **Script** node, and one that differentiates it from other nodes, is user-defined fields. These provide the link between state in the VRML scene and state in the Java program.

There can be any number of these fields, and they can be any legal VRML 2.0 type. They can also be one of the following: normal fields, eventIns, and eventOuts. However, they cannot be exposedFields.

Any events arriving at an eventIn field automatically cause the browser to pass the event to the program referred to in the url field of the **Script** node. How the browser does this really depends on the browser implementation and language being called. However, for a number of common languages—Java being one of them—the exact means by which events arrive in a Java program is specified. This mechanism is referred to as *event dispatching*. It describes the way the event is dispatched to the piece of code that will handle that event. Any browser that supports one of these common languages must implement this event dispatching mechanism so that code you write for one browser will work in any other browser that supports the same language.

After an event has been dispatched to the program, the program can do what it likes with that event. Eventually, the program will want to return some result from its computation. Again, the specification defines a way to enable a program to send information back to the **Script** node.

Such information is written back to fields in the **Script** node. Writing to a simple field does just that: update its value and finish. Writing an eventIn or eventOut has further effects. Writing to an eventIn in a **Script** node generates an event that is sent to the Java program. Writing to an eventOut field generates an event that will be sent to any nodes that are connected, via routes, to the eventOut field of the **Script** node.

Conceptually, you can think of this mechanism as shown in figure 3.1.

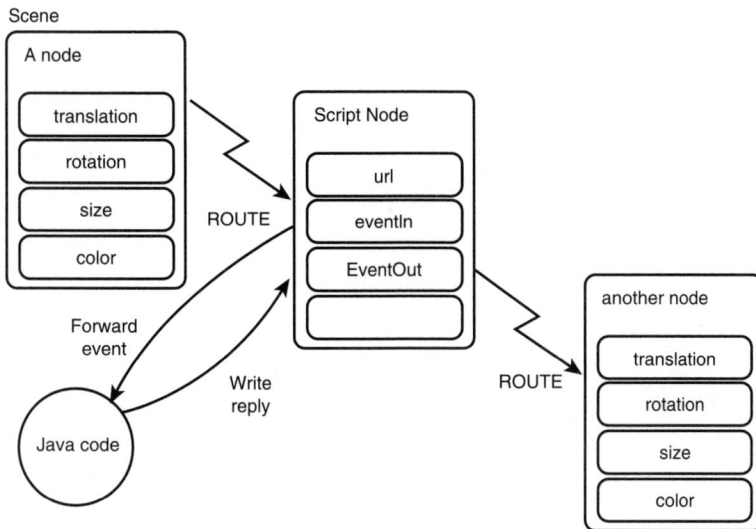

FIGURE 3.1

The Script node acts as a gateway to the script itself.

All that is happening in the model is that the **Script** node is acting as a messenger for the script itself. Any events sent to the **Script** node are packaged and delivered to the script. Any results written by the Java program update the **Script** node fields. Subsequently, the **Script** node will, if required, generate new events and automatically send them on.

This means that the **Script** node can be placed anywhere in the event cascade. Whenever you need to do a little extra processing as a result of an event, route the event to a **Script** node, handle it in the script, and send the results back to the **Script** node. If you want the results to also affect other entities in the scene, send the result back to an eventOut field and have the **Script** node ROUTE the event to the next node in the chain.

If you think back to the bicycle and rider example in Chapter 2, you can imagine an example where you want to check whether the rider is taking a lunch break, and if so, stop routing the bike translation events through to the rider.

To do this, insert a **Script** node in the scene. Route from BIKE.translation to a **Script** node eventIn field. Write some Java code to check that it wasn't lunch time, and if that's true, write the new position back into an eventOut field of the **Script** node that in turn has a ROUTE to the RIDER.translation field. Figure 3.2 shows this graphically.

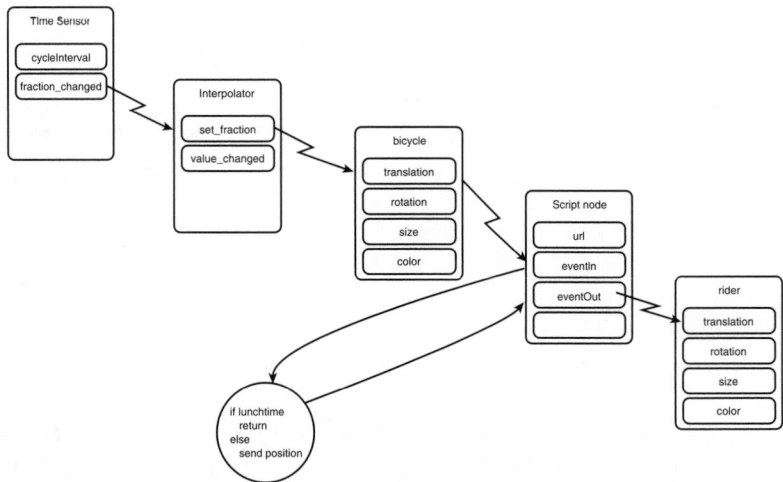

FIGURE 3.2

The Script node inserts extra logic into the event cascade.

COMMUNICATION BETWEEN SCRIPT NODE AND JAVA PROGRAM CODE

There are two aspects to the communication between the **Script** node and the program bound to it. The first concerns the means of using events to actually transfer data from the **Script** node into the Java program. The second aspect concerns the opposite case—how to get data from the Java program back to the VRML scene.

FROM SCRIPT NODE TO JAVA CODE

The best way to describe the sequence of events that enable data to be routed from a **Script** node to a Java program is using an example. Assume a VRML **Script** node, named DOIT, set up as shown in the following listing. DOIT points to a Java byte code program held in the file Test.class, which is on the fictional host sony.co.jp.

Listing 3.3   The DOIT Script Node.

```
1   DEF DOIT Script {
2       url "http://sony.co.jp/Test.class"
3       eventIn   SFBool start
4   }
```

The actual source code for Test.class is derived from the Java program in Test.java, which is shown in listing 3.4.

Listing 3.4   The processEvent() Method.

```
1   import vrml.*;
2   import vrml.field.*;
3   import vrml.node.*;
4
5   public class Test extends Script {
6   ...
7       // Thc following method is called when an event is
           ➥received
8       public void processEvent (Event e) {
9           /// ... do some processing ...
10      }
11  }
```

In this example, the eventIn, start, in the **Script** node, provides the data link between the VRML world and the Java world. When an event is routed to start, it is automatically directed to the program referenced in the url field of the **Script** node—in this case, Test.class.

Because the program bound to the **Script** node is Java, there needs to be a method available to receive the incoming event. Obviously this method must be associated with a class. This class is referred to as the "event-handler class" because it handles all events arriving from the **Script** node. Of course, it may then call other methods of other classes to do further processing, but the event-handler class is the first class that is involved in event handling.

Within the event-handler class, Test, the event is delivered to a special method called processEvent(). This method, which takes as its parameter an instance of the class Event, is the entry point for all events passed from the **Script** node to the associated Java program. The class Event defines the data structure into which a VRML event is converted when delivered to the Java program.

The name of the class is important and is derived from the name of the file specified in the url field of the **Script** node. In the current example, the url field specified a file called Test.class. This means that the class name has to be Test. If the file name had been Tako, the class name would need to be Tako. This naming convention is defined by the VRML to Java language binding, an annex of the VRML 2.0 specification. It is used by the browser to determine which class and which method must be used to handle the event. If the name of the file referenced in the url field of the **Script** node doesn't contain a class of the same name, the browser will be unable to decide which method to invoke and will flag an error.

Another important feature of the event-handler class is that it must be a subclass of the predefined class, Script, and it must be a public class. The Script class is actually defined in the vrml.node package and provides many calls to enable users to manage the interaction between the VRML nodes and the Java program. These calls, as well as other aspects of the imported packages, are discussed later in the chapter in the section "Other Java Classes."

The last important feature of this example is that there is no main method. This is because the event-handler class, in a similar way to a Java Applet, is being called in a special way. In the case of Sony's Community Place, the browser itself is the main program and it arranges to call the processEvent method when needed.

This works because Community Place contains a Java interpreter built into the browser. When the browser loads and parses the VRML file, it reaches the **Script** node, sees that it references a Java program, and looks for that program. When it locates the program, it invokes the Java class loader, which loads this class into the run-time environment. The browser then sets up the internal links between the **Script** node and the class entry point—processEvent().

At a later stage, when an event arrives at the **Script** node, the Community place browser converts this into an instance of the Java Event class and arranges to invoke the processEvent() method of the correct event-handler class.

Figure 3.3 shows the flow of events as they are dispatched to the event-handler class.

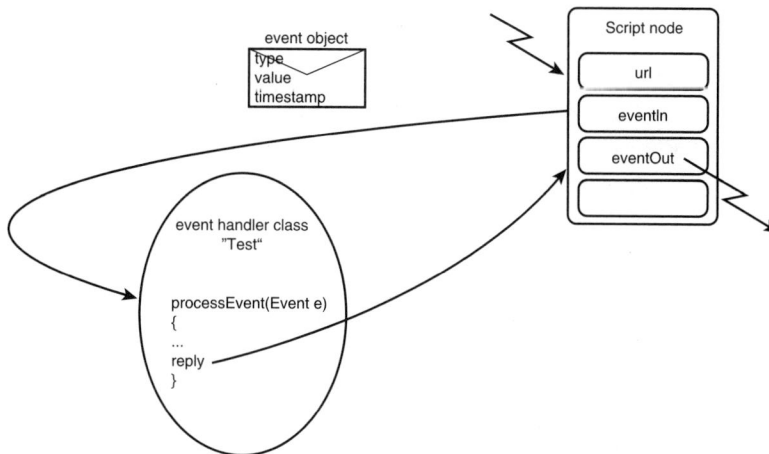

FIGURE 3.3

Event dispatching to the event-handler class.

THE EVENT CLASS

Because processEvent is a common entry point for all events sent to the event-handler class, it's important to be able to determine the type and value of the event so that the correct processing can take place. In the case of the DOIT **Script** node, there is only one eventIn field, so you know that any events arriving at processEvent() are from that field. However, in more complex situations it's common to have a **Script** node that is capable of sending one of several events. To get information about the incoming event, the Event class has the following methods (see listing 3.5).

Listing 3.5   The Event Class.

```
1   class Event {
2       public String getName();
3       public ConstField getValue();
4       public double getTimeStamp();
5   }
```

The method getName() returns the string name of the event, in other words, the name of the eventIn field of the **Script** node, which in this case is start. The call getValue() returns a reference to the VRML field that is mapped to a read-only instance of the Field class. The last call, getTimeStamp(), is used to get the time at which the event was generated within the VRML scene. This call enables you to decide on the order of events arriving at a particular **Script** node.

To determine whether the arriving event is the start event and what its value is, use listing 3.6.

Listing 3.6   Reading an Event's Value in processEvent().

```
1   public void processEvent (Event e) {
2       if(e.getName().equals("start")) {
3           ConstSFBool v = (ConstSFBool)e.getValue();
4           if(v.getValue() == true) {
5               // handle a TRUE start event
6           }
7       }
8   }
```

The variable "v" is an instance of a the class ConstSFBool. This class is predefined in the vrml.field package and represents the Java mapping for the VRML field type, SFBool. It is defined as a ConstSFBool rather than an SFBool because the code creates a reference to an event. Events, because they're messages from the VRML world to the Java world, can't be changed; there wouldn't be much point in doing so because they have already been delivered!

Once you have an instance of the ConstSFBool class, you can read its actual value by calling the method getValue(), which in this case returns the Boolean value of the eventIn, start. Note that the method getValue() is defined for both the Event class and the ConstSFBool class.

MAPPING VRML TYPES TO JAVA CLASSES

In listing 3.6, the value returned from the getValue() method called on the Event class was a ConstSFBool. It is an example of a Java read-only Boolean value mapped to the VRML type, SFBool.

All VRML types have a corresponding Java class that can be instantiated and used as a reference for the VRML field. The Java class is based on a generic class, Field, and supports a set of methods to read and write the field. Example classes include SFBool, which maps to the VRML type SFBool, SFColor for the VRML type SFColor, and so on.

The full set of VRML types and their associated classes are described in Appendix B, "Java Classes for VRML 2.0."

ACCESSING OTHER FIELDS OF THE SCRIPT NODE

The arrival of an event at the eventIn field of the **Script** node triggers the execution of the Java program and sends that event to the program. However, you aren't restricted only to receiving eventIns from the **Script** node as the sole means of determining its state. It's possible to actually get references to the fields of the **Script** node and to then query the value of those fields. To get a reference to a VRML field, the following calls are available:

➤ **Field getField(String fieldName).** This call returns a reference to the **Script** node's field named fieldName. The reference can be converted to the appropriate Java class mapping to that field type.

➤ **Field getEventOut(String eventName).** This returns a reference to an eventOut field and can be mapped to the correct Java class.

➤ **Field getEventIn(String eventName).** This final call returns a reference to an eventIn field value.

These calls are all methods of the Script class and can be used at any point in the event-handler class to access the fields in the **Script** node.

As mentioned earlier, all of these calls map an instance of a Java Field class to the corresponding VRML field. In this book, this instance is referred to as a reference to the VRML field. You can think of this Field class instance as a means of mapping between the Java world and the VRML world.

For example, the VRML type SFBool has a corresponding Java class. Once you have a reference for this field—in other words, an instance of the appropriate SFBool Field class—you can read the value it holds by using the getValue() method.

It's important to realize that accessing a field is a two-step process. The first step is to get a reference inside your Java program to the field held in the VRML scene. For this, an instance of a subclass of the generic class Field is used, depending on the type of the field you want to access. The second step is to read the value of that class instance.

You may have been a little confused by the use of getValue() in the previous example. getValue() was called once on the Event class to get a reference to a field class and then called again on the field class to get its value. Unfortunately, the designers of the VRML Java binding choose getValue() as a method name of both the Event and the Field class, but the semantics of the call are slightly different.

AN EXAMPLE: WRITING THE JAVA CONSOLE

In listing 3.7, an event in the VRML scene triggers a simple Java program that reads a value from the Java scene and writes it to the Java console.

You need to ensure that the Java console is visible so that you can see the result of this test. If you are using Sony's CP, select Java console in the Options menu.

Listing 3.7   Writing to the Java Console (Println.wrl).

```
1   #VRML V2.0 utf8
2   Transform {
3       children [
4           DEF TS TouchSensor {} # TouchSensor
5           Shape {
6               appearance Appearance {
7                   material DEF SphereColor Material { diffuseColor
                    ➡1 0 0 }#red
8               }
9               geometry Sphere {}
10          }
11      ]
12  }
13
14  DEF ColorScript Script {
15      url     "Println.class"
16      eventIn SFBool    clicked
17      field   SFString  sceneEnt    "Sphere"
18  }
19  # Routing
20  ROUTE TS.isActive TO ColorScript.clicked
```

Listing 3.8 shows the corresponding Java program. Remember that the source file is Println.java, and the corresponding Java byte code, produced by compiling Println.java, is Println.class.

Listing 3.8   The Event Handler Class (Println.java).

```
1   import vrml.*;
2   import vrml.field.*;
3   import vrml.node.*;
4
5   public class Println extends Script {
6   private SFString sceneEnt;
7
8     public void processEvent(Event e) {
9       ConstSFBool v = (ConstSFBool)e.getValue();
10      if(v.getValue()){  // got a touch event
11        sceneEnt = (3DString) getField("sceneEnt");
12        System.out.println("You've clicked a " +
          ➥sceneEnt.getValue());
13      }
14    }
15 }
```

This code is quite simple: whenever the red sphere in the VRML scene is clicked, the Java program prints a short message on the Java console telling you the type of object you've clicked.

It works by coding a string name, in this case "Sphere," into the sceneEnt field of the **Script** node. When the user clicks on the sphere, a **TouchSensor** sends an eventIn to the **Script** node. This triggers the execution of the event-handler class, Println, and the eventIn is delivered to the processEvent() method.

Within processEvent(), the event value is checked to see whether it is the Boolean true; if so, the sceneEnt field of the **Script** node is read using the method call, getField().

As discussed previously, this method returns a reference to the VRML field, whose actual value can be read by using the method getValue(). The code does just that, appending the result of the read onto the string "You've clicked a" and writes the whole string to the Java console using the method call, System.out.println().

As a result, the string "You've clicked a Sphere" appears on the Java console.

FROM THE JAVA PROGRAM TO THE SCRIPT NODE

After field values from the VRML scene have been read into the Java program, this data is available for further processing. When processing is finished, the Java program needs to be able to write the results back to the **Script** node. To achieve this, the Field class mentioned previously not only supports read methods, but a set of write methods as well. These include setValue(), which sets the VRML field to a specified value, and set1Value(), which sets an indexed element of a field.

The following are the methods of the Field class:

➤ **getSize().** Returns the number of elements in a MF field.

➤ **getValue().** Converts the VRML value into a Java value and returns it.

➤ **get1Value(int index).** Does the same as getValue() but accesses the value at index of a MF field.

➤ **setValue(value).** Sets the VRML field to the Java value.

➤ **set1Value(int index, value).** As setValue(), but sets an indexed field of an MF field.

➤ **addValue(value).** Adds a new value to the end of an MF field, thus adding a new element.

➤ **insertValue(int index, value).** Inserts a new element in an MF field with value.

➤ **deleteValue(int index).** Deletes the element denoted by index from the MF field.

➤ **clearValue().** Deletes all elements of the MF field.

After you have a reference to a field in a **Script** node, you can call any of the above methods to actually read and write the field directly.

Listing 3.9 is a simple example that alternates a sphere's color between red and blue each time it's clicked.

Listing 3.9   Accessing the Field of a Script Node (ChangeColor.wrl).

```
1    #VRML V2.0 utf8
2    Transform {
3      children [
4        DEF TS TouchSensor {} # TouchSensor
5        Shape {
6          appearance Appearance {
7            material DEF SphereColor Material { diffuseColor
             ➥1 0 0 } # red
8          }
9          geometry Sphere {}
10       }
11     ]
12 }
13
14   DEF ColorScript Script {
15
16     url "ChangeColor.class"
17     eventIn SFBool clicked
18     eventOut SFColor newColor
19     field SFBool on FALSE20    }
21   # Routing
22   ROUTE TS.isActive TO ColorScript.clicked
23   ROUTE ColorScript.newColor TO
       ➥SphereColor.set_diffuseColor
```

This VRML file sets up a single sphere, attaches a **TouchSensor**, and defines the color with a material node. The **TouchSensor** is routed to the eventIn field, clicked, of the **Script** node. The eventOut field, newColor, is routed to the diffuseColor field of the material node. The corresponding Java program is held in the file ChangeColor.java (see listing 3.10).

Listing 3.10   Java Code to Set an eventOut Field (ChangeColor.java).

```
1   // ChangeColor.java
2   import vrml.*;
3   import vrml.field.*;
4   import vrml.node.*;
5
6   public class ChangeColor extends Script{
7     private SFBool on;        // status of on/off
8     private SFColor newColor;
9     float red[]  =  { 1, 0, 0 };        // RGB(Red)
10    float blue[] = { 0, 0, 1 };        // RGB(Blue)
11
12    public void initialize(){
13      newColor = (SFColor) getEventOut("newColor");
14      on = (SFBool) getField("on");
15    }
16
17    public void processEvent(Event e) {
18      ConstSFBool v = (ConstSFBool)e.getValue();
19
20      if(v.getValue()){
21        if (on.getValue()) {
22          newColor.setValue(red);      // set red to 'newColor'
23        } else {
24          newColor.setValue(blue);      // set blue to 'newColor'
25        }
26        on.setValue(!on.getValue());
27      }
28    }
29 }
```

The goal of this program is to change the color of the sphere each time the user clicks on it. If it's blue, change it to red, and if it's red, change it to blue.

The **Script** node has an eventIn that is triggered from the **TouchSensor**. The **Script** node's eventOut field, newColor, is routed to the Material field of the sphere. An SFBool field, on, is used to hold the state of the sphere's color.

The Java program reads the current state of the on field, which is FALSE when the sphere is blue and is TRUE when it is red. The program then uses this Boolean value to set the sphere's new color.

The first thing to note is the use of a method called initialize(). Similar to processEvent(), initialize() is a special method and, when present, is always called when the browser sets up the mapping between the VRML **Script** node and the Java program containing the event-handler class. The browser guarantees that this method is called before any events are delivered to the Java program. In normal Java programs, you would use class constructors to initialize program variables. However, because of the relationship between VRML and Java, it is crucial that you use the initialize() method to initialize program variables that reference the VRML scene. This is because there is no guarantee that when a Java constructor is called, the VRML scene is created. However, you are guaranteed that when the initialize() method is called, the VRML scene is correctly set up. If you fail to follow this rule, you will at best get run-time errors and at worst, you will get undetermined results.

In the sphere color example, initialize() is used to set up an instance of an SFColor class, newColor, which is a reference to the **Script** node field, newColor. (The reference instance doesn't need to be named the same as the **Script** node field name.) This instance is initialized by using the getEventOut() method previously described. Then the SFBool instance, on, is set up using the getField() call.

Because this initialization takes place in the special method initialize(), you can be sure that this instance is correctly set up when you later come to write this field.

In the processEvent() method, the code queries the current state of the **Script** node field, on, by using on.getValue() and uses it to decide to which color the cube should be set. Setting the color is performed by using the setValue() method, which writes the new color value back to the VRML scene. Finally, the program sets the **Script** node field on to the new value, which is the opposite of its current value.

Because the newColor field is an eventOut field and has a route, after the value is written into the newColor field of the **Script** node, the value is sent as an event to the material field of the Sphere **Shape**.

This example shows a piece of Java code acting as a link between a cascade. The event arrives at the field clicked and causes the Java program to run. The result of the Java program is a write to the eventOut field newColor, which generates an event and continues the cascade.

ACCESSING FIELDS OF OTHER NODES

A third type of access, available to the scene nodes, is the most powerful. In the previous examples, interactions with the fields of the **Script** node that are bound to the event-handler class have been demonstrated. If you wanted to affect another node somewhere in the scene, you needed to set an eventOut in the **Script** node and then ensure that the eventOut was routed to the node you wanted to affect.

A more powerful and efficient way of achieving this is to directly read and write the fields of the node. To be able to do this, it is necessary to have access to that node.

With the **Script** node, the dispatch mechanism automatically arranges for the event-handler class to point to the **Script** node, enabling you to directly access fields of that node. To do this in an indirect manner requires that you are given a handle or "pointer" to the node you wish to manipulate.

This is achieved by using the SFNode type of VRML. An SFNode is a field type that acts as a pointer to a node. An SFNode field can point to any node in the scene. To make it available to a Java program, the SFNode field needs to be made accessible with a **Script** node. This enables the Java program to read the SFNode field and obtain a pointer to another node in the scene.

In listing 3.11, the Java program manipulates the translation field of the **Transform** node, MOVER. To do this, it accesses the node field of the MoveIt **Script** node, which holds a "pointer" to MOVER.

Listing 3.11   Accessing the File of Another Node (Mover.wrl).

```
1   #VRML V2.0 utf8
2   DEF MOVER Transform {
3      translation 10 0 0
4      children [
5        DEF TS TouchSensor {} # TouchSensor
6        Shape {
7          appearance Appearance {
8            material DEF SphereColor Material { diffuseColor
             ➥1 0 0 }#red
9          }
10         geometry Sphere {}
11       }
12     ]
13  }
14
15  DEF MoveIt Script {
16    url "MoveIt.class"
17     eventIn SFBool clicked
18     field SFNode node USE MOVER
19  }
20  # Routing
21  ROUTE TS.isActive TO MoveIt.clicked
```

Listing 3.12 shows the associated Java program.

Listing 3.12   Java Code to Manipulate an SFNode Value (MoveIt.java).

```
1   import vrml.*;
2   import vrml.field.*;
3   import vrml.node.*;
4
```

```
 5  public class MoveIt extends Script {
 6     private SFNode theNode ;
 7     private SFVec3f position;
 8
 9     public void initialize() {
10        theNode = (SFNode) getField("node");
11     }
12
13     public void processEvent(Event e) {
14        ConstSFBool v = (ConstSFBool)e.getValue();
15        Node node;
16        if(v.getValue()){
17           node = (Node)(theNode.getValue());
18           position =(SFVec3f)node.getExposedField
              ➡("translation");
19           position.setValue((position.getX() + 5), 0, 0);
20        }
21     }
22  }
```

Again, the special method, initialize(), was used to set up a
reference to the node field held in the **Script** node.

On receipt of the **TouchSensor** event, the processEvent() method
is called, setting the instance class, position, to the value of the
translation field of the **Transform** MOVER. It does so in two
stages. First the actual value of the instance, theNode, is read with
getValue(). This results in a reference to the node MOVER. Then a
reference to the exposedField, translation, of the node MOVER is
set up in position by using the getExposedField() method.

As you already know, this operation gives you an instance of the
class SFVec3f, whose actual value can be written with a setValue()
call.

The parameters of the setValue() call are the X, Y, and Z coordinates of the **Transform**. The code simply gets the current X value
and increments it by five.

If you load this example into the CP browser and try it out, every time you click on the red sphere it moves 5 meters in the X direction.

THE NODE CLASS

The example in listing 3.12 used the method getExposedField() on the instance variable theNode, which is based on the class Node. The Node class supports the following set of methods:

➤ **getType().** Returns the type of the VRML node—**Transform** or **Shape**.

➤ **getEventOut(String eventName).** Returns a reference to the eventOut field "eventname" which is part of the node type. The return value is an instance of the Field class.

➤ **getEventIn(string eventName).** Similar to getEventOut() except that it returns a reference to an eventIn field.

➤ **getExposedField().** Similar to getEventOut except it returns a reference to an exposedField.

➤ **getBrowser().** Returns a reference to a class instance that represents the browsers that are managing the node. The browser class provides a set of methods to access state managed by the browser on behalf of the VRML scene. This is discussed later in this chapter in the section "The Browser API."

This ability to read and write field values of any node as long as you have a handle for it is an extremely powerful tool. It means that a Java program can be placed into an existing event cascade and can also be used to start event cascades anywhere in the scene graph.

OTHER SPECIAL METHODS

In addition to the special methods, processEvent() and initialize(), which are called automatically by the browser, the following three methods are also available.

PROCESSEVENTS

Listing 3.13 is similar to processEvent() and receives incoming events triggered by eventIns in the **Script** node. It differs from processEvent() in that it handles multiple events. In the case where a **Script** node has more than one eventIn, it's possible for all the eventIns to receive an event at the same time. In that case, processEvents(), if defined, receives all these events in an array.

Listing 3.13   The processEvents() Method.

```
1  public void processEvents(int count Event events[])
2     for (int i =0; i < count; i++) {
3        processEvent( events[i] );
4        ...
5     }
6  }
```

The main benefit of this method is performance-related. The event dispatch mechanism that packages an eventIn sent to a **Script** node and delivers it to the Java program is expensive. If there are many eventIns for a **Script** node that are received at the same time, using processEvent() results in the browser constantly sending single events across to the Java program. However, if processEvents() is specified, the browser can package all the events into a single message and deliver them to the Java program in one invocation.

EVENTSPROCESSED

The eventsProcessed() method works in conjunction with the processEvents() method and is automatically called when processEvents() returns. It can be used to reduce the number of events that a script class generates. In some circumstances, not all events delivered to processEvents() generate a corresponding reply. For example, a set of incoming eventIns may be used to calculate a single return value to an eventOut. In that case, the eventsProcessed() method can be used to write a single reply.

SHUTDOWN

The third method is shutdown(). This method is automatically called when the corresponding **Script** node is deleted from the scene. This method is typically used to clean up the Java class associated with the **Script** node. A good example for this is the case when a Java program has created one or more threads and then needs to kill those threads gracefully before it exits.

SCRIPTS AND THE EXECUTION MODEL

The previous chapter discussed the VRML 2.0 execution model in some detail. However, it glossed over one aspect of that model— the relationship between events and time.

In a simple scene, where there is a single event cascade starting from a single source, the relationship between events is clear. In a more complex scene with many ROUTEs and **Script** nodes, the execution model needs some clarification.

The key feature of the execution model is that time advances in the scene in virtual units. These units may have little or no correspondence to physical time as measured by clocks or watches.

Each time unit in the scene has an associated time value, called a *timestamp*. The timestamp is attached to all events that occur during that period of time.

When an event cascade begins, a timestamp is created and attached to the event. As that event is routed between nodes, each successive event in the cascade is given the same timestamp. When the cascade ends, the virtual time unit is considered finished and the next virtual time unit is begun. Naturally, this new virtual time unit has a new timestamp whose value is greater than the previous timestamp.

The process then repeats itself; event-generating nodes are evaluated and new cascades are started, each with the attached timestamp.

When an event is delivered to a Java program, it has a copy of the timestamp that can be queried with the Event.getTimeStamp() method. Any writes from that Java program to eventOut fields in the scene cause new events to be generated. Each of these new events has the same timestamp as the eventIn that started the execution of Java program. As a result, it's possible to insert a **Script** node into an event cascade.

There is one slight complication to this. If a Java program writes to an eventIn in its own **Script** node that originally caused its execution, a loop is possible. The VRML 2.0 execution model doesn't allow such loops and breaks them by not forwarding the event back to the Java program.

At this point, you probably better understand the restriction on the **Script** node that stated that fields cannot be of the type, exposedField. If this was allowed, routing an event to a **Script** node that contained an exposedField would generate two events: one sent across to the Java program and the other sent along any routes from the exposedField. This would complicate the logic of the execution model.

DIRECTOUTPUT AND MUSTEVALUATE

You may remember that the **Script** node has two fields, directOutput and mustEvaluate, which haven't yet been discussed. The use of these fields is tied to the execution model and to how the browser exploits it for better performance.

In an ideal implementation of the execution model, no time would be required to process the event cascades, and the Java programs would execute in zero time. In the real world, things are a little less ideal and it is certain that the people who build VRML 2.0 browsers will need to work hard to ensure good performance. They will try to optimize the execution model by using such techniques as delaying execution of certain nodes until their results are needed or even deciding that certain scripts don't need to run because their results will never be seen.

Obviously, to be able to do this properly, the browser needs some clues to the nature of the Scripts. directOutput and mustEvaluate provide these clues.

directOut, when set to TRUE, tells the browser that the **Script** node's Java program will directly read and write other nodes in the VRML scene. Because the browser doesn't know which nodes are read/written, it should think carefully about trying to optimize this **Script** node.

mustEvaluate performs a similar function. When set to TRUE, it tells the browser that it must handle all events sent to this **Script** node at the proper time and immediately send them on to the Java program. If the field is set to false, the browser may decide that the results of the Java script are not yet needed and delay execution of the Java program.

THE JAVA CLASSES

The examples so far have introduced several predefined classes and their associated methods. These classes are provided in the three packages: vrml, vrml.field, and vrml.node. These are used to support the interaction between the scene entities and the Java world. The vrml package contains the base classes—Field, Event, Browser, and BaseNode—which are generally extended in the vrml.field and vrml.node packages. The vrml.field package contains a class definition for every VRML 2.0 type supporting both a Const version for events and a standard version for fields. The vrml.node package contains the Node and Script classes. Appendix B provides the full specification of these classes, including all supported methods.

POWER THROUGH SCRIPTING

At this point, you should have a clear idea of how VRML and Java work together. In a sense, the VRML execution model is extended via the **Script** node into the Java world. Within Java, you have access to the same notions of nodes, fields, and events. You can manipulate them and use them in turn to manipulate the scene itself.

This approach forms the basis of a very powerful tool, one that combines the 3D aspects of VRML and the programming facilities of the Java language.

WHY STATIC BEHAVIORS AREN'T ENOUGH

This chapter began by justifying the need for arbitrary decision logic in VRML worlds. However, it was clear from the previous chapter that the static behaviors available using VRML nodes are powerful enough to create interesting dynamic worlds. A legitimate question is "Do I really need Java?"

To answer that, it's necessary to understand the limitations of the static behavior model that VRML 2.0 supports internally:

➤ **No decision logic.** This issue has already been discussed, but it should be clear to any Java programmer that a language that doesn't support any form of decision making is an extremely weak one.

➤ **User-defined state.** In a similar manner, if the scene author is unable to create new types that represent his particular application data requirements, the development of anything other than simple applications will be extremely convoluted. This argument applies equally to a need to hold extra state about existing VRML 2.0 nodes. Again, a programming language that doesn't support flexibility in data management and user-defined types is a poor one.

➤ **No external access.** The built-in VRML 2.0 nodes are designed solely to support 3D scenes and have no notion of
the external world. The capability to carry out simple file I/O
is crucial for complex applications. More important, in
today's Web environment, the capability to call out from a
particular computer to others on the Internet is crucial for
the types of distributed programs that are increasingly being
developed.

Many other limitations of VRML 2.0 will become more evident as
you begin to use it. However, the word limitation has a negative
connotation that is not applicable in this case. VRML 2.0 was
designed knowing that external scripting languages would be
used and so was able to restrict its focus to supporting 3D scenes.
The designers accepted that any other options would be built by
using the external script languages. A better way to describe
VRML is to say that its true power comes when working with a
language such as Java.

Assuming that you are convinced that VRML needs Java and that
you now understand the way the two interact, the next step is
hands-on—how to compile and run your Java programs to drive
VRML.

COMPILING A JAVA SCRIPT

To be able to write, compile, and use Java for your VRML worlds,
you need to install the Java compiler on your machine. Obviously,
you can compile Java on any machine you have access to that
supports a Java compiler. For the purpose of this discussion, use
of a Windows 95 machine is assumed.

If your machine is not already set up to use Java, the first stage in
the process is to install the Java development kit (JDK), made
available from Sun Microsystems. At the time of writing, JDK 1.02
was the most stable and the version used in this book.

NOTE

The JDK can be found on the accompanying CD-ROM. Full instructions for installing it on your hard disk are provided in Appendix E, "What's On the CD-ROM?"

JDK 1.02 is also available directly from Sun and has been distributed with a number of Java text books. Some of these are referenced in Appendix C.

To download the JDK from Sun, go to http://java.sun.com/JDK and follow the instructions.

Once downloaded, the JDK needs to be installed and your environment set up so that the Java compiler (javac) is in your path and the environment variable, classpath, points to the installation directory of the Java class libraries.

All of the preceding installation is standard for Java. In addition to that, you need to tell the Java compiler where it can find the Java packages vrml, vrml.field, and vrml.node. You can do this in one of two ways: directly on the command line when you invoke the Java compiler or by adding the directory that contains these class libraries to your classpath environment variable.

In the case of Sony's Community Place, this path is as follows:

```
1  Command: set classpath=c:\Program Files\Sony\Community
Place Browser\lib\java;c:
➡\Program Files\Sony\Community Place Browser\lib\java\
classes.zip
```

See Appendix D, "Installing Community Place," for more information about the installation of the Java compiler.

To test that everything is working correctly, you should copy from the CD-ROM, or download, the examples used in this chapter and compile the Java source. The resulting Java byte code file (file.class) should be placed in the location specified in the url field of the **Script** node.

After the Java source has been compiled, load the corresponding VRML file into the Community Place browser, which in turn locates and loads the Java program. If all this works as expected, clicking on the test VRML object causes it to behave correspondingly.

OTHER JAVA CLASSES

The examples so far have covered all relevant aspects of the VRML 2.0 to Java interface. At this stage, you have enough knowledge to go ahead and build Java programs that animate VRML scenes.

Although this chapter has introduced you to the basic mechanisms for interacting with VRML scenes from Java, it has touched only on the range of possibilities. In particular, the examples have shown you only enough to get going. Many other method calls are available as part of the VRML packages, and these are explored further in subsequent chapters. Appendix B details all classes and methods available.

THE BROWSER API

This chapter finishes with one last example, showing the use of the browser class. This class is an extremely important one because it provides methods that enable you to manipulate the scene and to dynamically change the scene structure. All previous examples consisted of sending events or updating existing fields.

The browser class supports a set of methods that manipulate the browser state. Although the details on this can be found in Appendix B, two methods of interest are introduced here:

> **addRoute(node, fromField, node, toField).** Dynamically adds a route to the scene.

> **deleteRoute(node, fromField, node, toField).** Removes a node from the scene.

These methods enable a Java program to actually change the execution path of events in the scene. Coupled with the capability to start event cascades, this is yet another extremely powerful tool.

A simple program demonstrates this facility. The VRML scene consists of a cone, a sphere, and a light source (see listing 3.14). The sphere represents a light switch, but is not initially connected to the light source. Both the cone and the sphere have **TouchSensor**s to trigger their behaviors. When the user first clicks the sphere, nothing happens because there's no connection between the sphere and the light source. By clicking on the cone, a route is added to the scene that routes the light switch **TouchSensor** event to the light source, turning on the light. If the cone is clicked again, the new route is deleted. You can think of the cone as a route switch turning the route on and off.

Listing 3.14 shows the VRML source.

Listing 3.14   Dynamically Adding Routes (AddRoute.wrl).

```
1   #VRML V2.0 utf8
2   Transform {
3       children [
4       DEF RouteSwitch TouchSensor {}
5           Shape {  geometry Cone {} }
6       ]
7   }
8   Transform {
9       translation 3 0 0
10      children [
11      DEF LightSwitch TouchSensor {}
12          Shape {  geometry Sphere {} }
13      ]
14  }
15  DEF DL DirectionalLight { on FALSE }
16  NavigationInfo { headlight FALSE }
17  DEF SC Script {
18      url "AddRoute.class"
19      field SFNode lightswitch USE LightSwitch
20      field SFNode dl USE DL
21      eventIn SFTime touched
22  }
23  ROUTE RouteSwitch.touchTime TO SC.touched
```

The light source, DL, is initially turned off, as is the browser headlight. This makes the scene quite dark. The **Script** node has two SFNode fields, one referencing the LightSwitch (the sphere) and the other referencing the light source, DL. The **TouchSensor** of the cone—the route adding switch—is finally routed to the **Script** node. Listing 3.15 shows the Java code to add and remove the route.

Listing 3.15   Using the Browser Class (AddRoute.java).

```
1   import vrml.*;
2   import vrml.field.*;
3   import vrml.node.*;
4
5   public class AddRoute extends Script {
6     private boolean routed = false;
7     Browser b;
8     Node lightswitch, dl;
9
10    public void initialize () {
11      b = getBrowser();
12      dl = (Node)((SFNode)getField("dl")).getValue();
13      lightswitch = (Node)((SFNode)getField
        ➥("lightswitch")).getValue();
14    }
15
16    public void processEvent(Event e){
17      if(routed) {
18        b.deleteRoute(lightswitch, "isActive", dl , "on" );
19      }else{
20        b.addRoute(lightswitch, "isActive", dl, "on" );
21      }
22      routed = !routed;
23    }
24  }
```

In the initialize() method, references to the browser, the light source, and the light switch are set up. When an event arrives and the route has already been added, it has to be deleted. The method deleteRoute() on the browser class is used to specify the lightswitch node. The isActive field should be the source of the event. The light source node and the on event should be the target node.

Alternatively, if the route isn't established, the method addRoute is called with the same parameters.

These calls alternatively add and remove a route between the light switch **TouchSensor** and the light source so that, within the VRML scene, the light switch is alternately connected to and disconnected from the light source.

This example serves well to justify the need for external scripts. Without them, the scene author would be forced to design the scene and build the execution paths without ever changing them. However, given an external language and the ability to access the Browser class, the scene author can dynamically change the scene graph during execution to enable it to adapt to user input and evolve over time.

ROUNDUP

This chapter has shown you how to add behaviors to the VRML scene to support dynamic behaviors written in Java. Although the examples have not demonstrated all possibilities, the fundamental mechanisms have been introduced. At this stage, you have all the knowledge needed to build sophisticated 3D worlds.

The examples have shown how to get data into and out of the VRML world. After you have mastered these basic techniques, the VRML world is, as they say, "your oyster."

Because one of the best ways to learn something is by doing it, the rest of this book helps you do just that. The next four chapters introduce you to other features of VRML 2.0 and show you how to use simple Java programs to exploit these features. They then show you how to make advanced use of Java programs to build extremely sophisticated VRML worlds. To do that, each chapter relies heavily on the use of examples and each of those examples uses the mechanism discussed in this chapter and Chapter 2.

If at any point you are confused about how something is actually working, a quick reread of this chapter and Chapter 2 should resolve your confusion.

ADVANCED VRML

Chapter 2, "Adding Action to 3D Worlds," intro-

duced you to the basic VRML 2.0 execution model

and showed this model by using a series of ex-

amples. These examples gave you a brief taste of

some of the features provided by the built-in nodes

of the VRML 2.0 language. In Chapter 3, "Letting

Java Loose," you were shown the use of Java as a

language to build complex animation and interac-

tive worlds. Now it's time to combine the advanced

features of VRML with the power of Java.

WHAT THIS CHAPTER COVERS

This chapter is a practical overview of how to use some of the advanced features of VRML 2.0 from within the Java language. Because it's assumed that you're already aware of the basic features of VRML 2.0, the goal is not to give you a comprehensive set of examples showing all the nodes in VRML 2.0. Rather, it is to show, in some detail, certain nodes and how Java can be used to greatly expand their capabilities.

Instead of introducing you to a series of unrelated examples, this chapter builds up a complex 3D world by using a series of components. Each component is designed to show the use of a particular node in VRML 2.0 and how Java can be used to enhance the node's capabilities.

The example is based around a record store. Within the store are a set of objects you can interact with and a semi-intelligent agent, the store assistant, who will help you find the records you want. After you leave the store, you will be able to see other agents roaming the streets and take a taxi ride to a different part of town. In the examples you will do the following:

➤ Revisit some of the basic sensors that support user interaction

➤ Look at the issues of collision detection and **ProximitySensor**s

➤ Find out how to support large scenes using the Level of Detail (**LOD**) node

➤ Set up a predefined world tour and take users for a ride

➤ Explore the techniques available for extending VRML's built-in set of nodes

This chapter is designed to give you hands-on experience with some of the more interesting nodes in VRML 2.0. By working through the examples, you will understand some of the more sophisticated uses of the VRML 2.0 nodes and how their capabilities can be harnessed with Java. More important, you will have enough knowledge to successfully experiment with the various VRML 2.0 nodes.

By the end of the chapter, you will be sufficiently proficient in VRML 2.0 and its interaction with Java to enable you to tackle more complex Java examples.

SETTING THE SCENE: THE RECORD STORE

The scene is simple. It consists of a record shop in which you can interact with some objects. You can leave the shop and look around outside. If you're tired of walking, there's even a taxi to give you a free ride around the downtown area!

THE TOUCHSENSOR REVISITED

One of the most simple and most frequently used nodes for supporting user interaction is the **TouchSensor**. This node was introduced in Chapter 2 and used in Chapter 3. In this example you will see how to connect a **TouchSensor** to another VRML node, the **PointLight**, to provide a simple lamp object that can be switched on and off at will.

The **TouchSensor** is used to receive events concerning mouse movement and mouse button clicking. In the simplest example, you click a lamp shade and the lamp is turned on. If you click it again, the light is turned off. To realize this simple behavior, you need to use both the sending mechanism to dispatch events to a Java script and the return mechanism to write data back to the VRML world.

Although this is a simple example, it serves to recap the basic interaction mechanism between VRML and Java and shows a legitimate use of Java to maintain the light's state.

CAPTURING THE MOUSE EVENTS

In previous examples with the **TouchSensor**, the isActive field was used to determine the state of the **TouchSensor**. In this example, the touchTime field is used to inform the **Script** node at what time the **TouchSensor** was selected.

In the example VRML file (listing 4.1), a **TouchSensor** named LIGHT_ON_SWITH generates a touchTime event when you click the mouse button with the mouse cursor on a cone named LAMP_SHADE. This event is then routed through to the **Script** node, LIGHT_SCRIPT.

Listing 4.1   Switching a Light On and Off (lightOnOff.wrl).

```
1   # VRML V2.0 utf8
2   # turn the light on/off by touching the lamp shade.
3   Transform{
4      children[
5         DEF LIGHT PointLight{
6            on TRUE
7         }
8         Transform{
9            translation 0 1 0
10              children[
11                 DEF LAMP_SHADE Shape{  # lamp shade
12                    geometry Cone{
13                       height 2
14                       bottomRadius 4
15                       bottom FALSE
16                    }
17                 }
18              ]
19           }
20         # sensor to turn the light on / off
21         DEF LIGHT_ON_SWITCH TouchSensor{}
22      ]
23   }
24   Transform{    # dummy object to reflect the light.
25      translation 0 -5 0
26      children[
27         Shape{geometry Box{}}
```

```
28      ]
29    }
30    DEF LIGHT_SCRIPT Script{
31       url "LightOnOff.class"
32       eventIn SFTime touchTime
33       eventOut SFBool turnOnLight
34    }
35    ROUTE LIGHT_ON_SWITCH.touchTime TO LIGHT_SCRIPT.touchTime
36    ROUTE LIGHT_SCRIPT.turnOnLight TO LIGHT.on
```

SEND EVENTS BACK TO THE LIGHT

The Java code for this example is simple. The initialize function at line 13 is used, as usual, to set up the references to the VRML fields. In the example, only the turnOnLight field of the LIGHT_SCRIPT **Script** node is of interest.

When the LIGHT_ON_SWITCH **TouchSensor** is triggered by the user clicking on the light itself, the event is routed, via the **Script** node, to the event handler class, LightOnOff.

Listing 4.2   The Java Light Switch (lightOnOff.java).

```
1    //
2    // toggle the light state.
3    //
4    import vrml.*;
5    import vrml.node.*;
6    import vrml.field.*;
7
8    public class LightOnOff extends Script{
9       SFBool turnOnLight;
10      // light state.
11      boolean onOff = false;
12
13      public void initialize(){
14         // get the reference of the event out 'turnOnLight'.
15         turnOnLight = (SFBool)getEventOut("turnOnLight");
```

continues

Listing 4.2, CONTINUED.

```
16      }
17
18      public void processEvent(Event e){
19          if(e.getName().equals("touchTime") == true){
20              onOff = !onOff;       // toggle the light state.
21              turnOnLight.setValue(onOff);     // send the
                ➥event.
22          }
23      }
24  }
```

In the processEvent() method, the code uses a simple Boolean value, onOff, to record the state of the light. Each incoming event toggles this Boolean value. This new state is then sent to the **Script** node using the setValue() method (line 21), which writes the field, turnOnLight, in the LIGHT_SCRIPT. Because turnOnLight is an eventOut, the event is routed through to the **PointLight** node in the VRML scene, and the light switches on.

OTHER INFORMATION AVAILABLE IN THE TOUCHSENSOR

In some of the examples in Chapter 3, the **TouchSensor** was used to generate an isActive event when it was clicked. In contrast, the preceding example uses a **TouchSensor** to generate a touchTime event when the lamp is clicked. Both the isActive and touchTime events are discrete events that happen when the mouse is pressed and released over the entity.

A **TouchSensor** also generates a series of continuous events when you move the mouse cursor above geometry associated with the sensor. From the viewpoint of the cursor position, the event, isOver set to TRUE, is generated when the cursor first moves over the geometry. Then, while the cursor moves within the geometry, a series of hitNormal_changed, hitPoint_changed, and hitTexCoord_changed events are generated. The hitPoint event contains the actual coordinate position, on the surface of the geometry, over which the cursor is positioned. The hitTexCoord contains the texture coordinates for that hit point and the hitNormal field contains the surface vector.

With these fields, it's possible to determine where exactly on a scene entity the user has clicked and, if the surface has a texture map, the exact texture coordinates. In these simple examples, the **TouchSensor** was used to indicate that the user selected the object. However, a more sophisticated use may be to determine the exact geometry under the cursor so that a precise movement calculation can be made if, for example, the user is attempting to "push" the object through the 3D scene.

In a similar manner, the ability to determine the exact texture coordinates enables you to implement a 3D equivalent of the image map idea found in 2D browsers that can be used for a variety of purposes, including information retrieval.

When the cursor moves off the geometry, the isOver set to FALSE event is generated once the cursor is no longer over the geometry.

While the cursor is on the geometry, the isOver event is TRUE, and if the mouse button is held down, the isActive set to TRUE event is generated. When the mouse button is released, the isActive set to FALSE event is generated. By using these fields you can, for example, sense the period of time that the mouse is down and the user is attempting to drag an object.

However, the most useful event for ordinary cases is the touchTime event, generated when the mouse button is released. Because this event is the timestamp for when the button is released, you can directly route the event to any of the VRML nodes that require a startTime or stopTime for their operation. An example of this—controlling a **TimeSensor**'s startTime field or its stopTime field (and so directly controlling the start and stop time of the **TimeSensor**)—is discussed in the following section.

USING A TIMESENSOR AND JAVA

Chapter 3 has already shown how to realize simple animation by combining the **TimeSensor** and an interpolator. However, in the examples, the interpolator is constrained in the movements it can generate. This is because the interpolator is set up when the scene is created and because its keyValues, used to parameterize the interpolator, are already defined. After you have programmed it to interpolate positions between two coordinates in the keyValue set, it is difficult to change those coordinates and therefore difficult to use it to generate other positions.

In contrast, by using a **Script** node, you can describe arbitrary movements for an object and perform complex tracking. The new positions are calculated in the Java program and written back to the scene to control a scene entity.

In the following example, this facility is shown using an intelligent agent whose movement is initially randomly generated. Later in the chapter, the agent's movement is derived from the user's navigation through the store.

The example VRML file in listing 4.3 contains (in line 4) a **TimeSensor** that invokes a **Script** node named AGENT_SCRIPT every 0.1 seconds. This is an example of a repeating timer. Because the start and stop time have a default value of 0 and the loop field is set to TRUE, the timer runs continuously from the point when the world is loaded. Every 0.1 seconds it generates a cycleTime value, containing the current time, which is routed to the **Script** node. The associated Java program uses this event to randomly move the **Transform** node that includes the geometry representing the agent. As a result, the agent appears to be floating back and forth in a random fashion.

Because the geometry for the agent is relatively complex, it is not included directly in the file. Rather, it is included indirectly by using the **Inline** node (line 10), which points to another VRML file, in this case ManDetailed.wrl. The browser automatically reads in this description when needed.

Listing 4.3   The Random Agent (FloatingAgent..wrl).

```
1    #VRML V2.0 utf8
2    # an agent is floating randomly.
3    #
4    DEF AGENT_TIME TimeSensor{
5       loop TRUE
6       cycleInterval 0.1
7    }
8    DEF AGENT Transform{   # floating agent
9       children[
10          Inline{url "ManDetailed.wrl"}  # a model of agent.
11       ]
12    }
13    DEF AGENT_SCRIPT Script{
14       url "FloatingAgent.class"
15       eventIn SFTime interval
16       eventOut SFVec3f setAgentPosition
17    }
18    ROUTE AGENT_TIME.cycleTime TO AGENT_SCRIPT.interval
19    ROUTE AGENT_SCRIPT.setAgentPosition TO
      ➥AGENT.set_translation
```

By looking at the event handler class in listing 4.4 in detail, you can see that the initialize() method is used to create a reference to the **Script** node's setAgentPosition field. This field is used to receive the agent's new position when it's calculated. In addition, the agent's initial position is set up at line 18.

In the processEvent() method, moveAgent() is called, which subsequently calls generateRandomFloat() that generates a random number ranging from –0.1 to 0.1. The random number is generated by using the randomNumGenerator class that's part of the java.util package.

Listing 4.4   Java Code to Generate Random Movement (floatingAgent.java).

```
1    // an agent is floating randomly.
2    //
3    import java.util.*;
4    import vrml.*;
5    import vrml.node.*;
6    import vrml.field.*;
7
8    public class FloatingAgent extends Script{
9       SFVec3f setAgentPosition;
10       float agentPosition[] = new float[3];
11       Random randomNumGenerator = new Random();
12
13        public void initialize(){
14          // get the reference of the event-out
                 ➥'setAgentPosition'.
15          setAgentPosition =
16             (SFVec3f)getEventOut("setAgentPosition");
17          // initialize the agent position.
18          agentPosition[0] = 0.0f;
20          agentPosition[1] = 0.0f;
21          agentPosition[2] = 0.0f;
22        }
23        public void processEvent(Event e){
24           if(e.getName().equals("interval") == true){
25              moveAgent();
28           }
29        }
30        // generate random float value ranging between -0.1 to
              ➥0.1.
31        float generateRandomFloat(){
32           return(randomNumGenerator.nextFloat() * 0.2f - 0.1f);
33        }
34        // move the agent randomly.
35        void moveAgent(){
36           agentPosition[0] += generateRandomFloat();
37           agentPosition[1] += generateRandomFloat();
```

```
38              agentPosition[2] += generateRandomFloat();
39
40              // move the agent to the new position.
41              setAgentPosition.setValue(agentPosition);
42          }
43      }
```

By using this random number, the script moves the **Transform**
that represents the agent by setting its position coordinates to a
random position within a small distance of its current position.
This value is written back to the **Script** node and then routed
through to the agent's **Transform** node's translation field. This
kind of random movement, or a more complex behavior (for
example, changing the direction according to a state variable), is
impossible to realize with only a time sensor and an interpolator.

A ONE-SHOT TIMER

In many cases, the **TimeSensor** is used to realize repetitive
movement by specifying "loop TRUE" as in the previous example.
In some cases, you may want to realize a one-shot event where
the timer fires once and a single event occurs. To give you a
concrete example, let's develop some code, the aim of which is to
take one of the CDs in the shop and rotate it through 360 degrees
when you click on it.

The example actually shows you two things: how to set up and
use a one-shot timer to initiate a single event and, second, how to
dynamically reconfigure an interpolator by using Java. To do this,
a **TouchSensor** causes a script to run. The Java program updates
the interpolator's parameters and then causes a **TimeSensor** to
fire once. The **TimeSensor** is used to drive the interpolator, which
animates the CD based on its new set of parameters.

Listing 4.5   Spinning a CD (RollingCD.wrl).

```
1    #VRML V2.0 utf8
2    # a sample CD rolls 360 deg. about a random axis when
        ➥clicked
3
4    DEF CD_TIME TimeSensor{
5       loop FALSE      # not repetitive
6       cycleInterval 3
7    }
8    DEF CD_INTP OrientationInterpolator{
9       key [0, 0.25, 0.5, 0.75, 1.0]
10      # keyValue is set by Script.
11      }
12   DEF CD_TRANSFORM Transform{
13      children[
14         # a box representing a CD
15         Shape{geometry Box{size 1 1 0.1}},
16         # sensor to start the time sensor.
17         DEF CD_TOUCH TouchSensor{}
18      ]
19   }
20   DEF CD_SCRIPT Script{
21      url "RollingCD.class"
22      eventIn SFTime touched
23      eventOut MFRotation setCDrollingAxis
24      eventOut SFTime setCDstartTime
25      }
26
27   ROUTE CD_TOUCH.touchTime TO CD_SCRIPT.touched
28   ROUTE CD_SCRIPT.setCDrollingAxis TO CD_INTP.set_keyValue
29   ROUTE CD_SCRIPT.setCDstartTime TO CD_TIME.set_startTime
30   ROUTE CD_TIME.fraction_changed TO CD_INTP.set_fraction
31   ROUTE CD_INTP.value_changed TO CD_TRANSFORM.set_rotation
```

You should note that the **TimeSensor** (line 4) is set up with its loop field initialized to FALSE and a cycleInterval field of three seconds. This means that when the sensor becomes active, it stays active for only one cycle.

The other key aspect of this example is that the **OrientationInterpolator**, CD_INTP, is initialized with a set of five keys, but not keyValues (line 8). This means that it has not yet been told what coordinates it should interpolate between.

When you click the CD, the **Script** node receives the touched event, which is passed through to the event handler class.

The event handler class, shown in listing 4.6, has two main tasks. The first task is to decide on the axis of rotation for the CD, and the second task is to set up the orientation interpolator. Both of these tasks are performed in the setRollingParameters() method.

The initialize() method sets up the two eventOuts that will be written back to the VRML scene. The setCDstartTime, used to begin the animation, and the setCDrollingAxis are the keyValues for the **OrientationInterpolator** used to actually perform the animation in the scene. initialize() also sets up the initial rotation value for the five keyValues that will be written to the interpolator. These values are held in the rollingParameters structure, which is an array of 20 floats. Each SFRotation is four floats: three for the rotation vector and one for the rotation angle. Therefore, the index fields 3, 7, 11, 15, and 19 of the rollingParameters array are initialized with the correct degree of rotation at line 23. The values used are fractions of PI.

The method, setRollingParameters(), is then used to set the actual rotation vector values—in other words, the first three values of each SFRotation. This calculation is based on a random number used to calculate the X and Y values for each new rotation. These are then written (line 44) into the rollingParameters array using the for loop.

At line 50 these values are written to the **Script** node's field, setCDrollingAxis, which routes them to the keyValue field of the **OrientationInterpolator**.

The geometry of this example may seem complicated. If so, you may want to look at Appendix A, "VRML and 3D Principles," which has an overview section on 3D geometry and VRML 2.0.

Listing 4.6   Java Code to Spin the CD (RollingCD.java).

```
1    // a sample CD rolls 360 deg when clicked.
2    //
3
4    import java.util.*;
5    import vrml.*;
6    import vrml.node.*;
7    import vrml.field.*;
8
9    public class RollingCD extends Script{
10    MFRotation setCDrollingAxis;
11    SFTime setCDstartTime;
12    float rollingParameters[] = new float[4 * 5];
13    Random randomNumGenerator = new Random();
14
15        public void initialize(){
16            // get the reference of the event-out
                   ➥'setCDrollingAxis'.
17            setCDrollingAxis =
18                (MFRotation)getEventOut("setCDrollingAxis");
19            // get the reference of the event-out
                   ➥'setCDstartTime'.
20            setCDstartTime =
                ➥(SFTime)getEventOut("setCDstartTime");
21            // initialize the rotation parameters as angles
22            // axis is set later in setRollingParameters().
23            rollingParameters[3]  =  0.0f;
24            rollingParameters[7]  =  1.57f;
25            rollingParameters[11] = 3.14f;
26            rollingParameters[15] = 4.71f;
27            rollingParameters[19] = 6.28f;
28        }
29        public void processEvent(Event e){
30            if(e.getName().equals("touched") == true){
31                setRollingParameters();
32                // invoke the time sensor to roll the CD.
33                setCDstartTime.
```

```
34                    setValue(((ConstSFTime)e.getValue()).getValue());
35              }
36          }
37          // set the rolling axis randomly.
38          void setRollingParameters(){
39              // angle ranging between 0 to 2PI.
40              double angle =
41                  randomNumGenerator.nextDouble() * Math.PI * 2.0;
42              double axisX = Math.cos(angle);
43              double axisY = Math.sin(angle);
44              for(int i = 0; i < 5; i++){
45                  rollingParameters[i * 4 + 0] = (float)axisX;
46                  rollingParameters[i * 4 + 1] = (float)axisY;
47                  rollingParameters[i * 4 + 2] = 0.0f;
48              }
49              // set keyValue field of the OrientationInterpolator.
50              setCDrollingAxis.setValue(4 * 5, rollingParameters);
51          }
52      }
```

This example again exposes a powerful use of Java in conjunction with VRML. One possibility, to achieve the goals of rotating the CD, is to drive the animation purely from the Java code. However, because VRML already has built-in nodes that support key-frame animation, a more intelligent programming strategy is to use Java to reset the interpolator with a new set of keyValues but let the interpolator do the hard work of the animation.

There are many occasions where this approach is possible. By looking out for these occasions, it is possible to significantly reduce the programming burden and to make use of browser-supported functionality.

SOUND AND AUDIOCLIP

Because our basic scene is a record shop, it certainly needs some multimedia data. To begin, a simple talk feature is added to the intelligent agent that enables it to talk to you whenever it is clicked.

To realize sound in the 3D world, the **Sound** node and the **AudioClip** node are used. The role of the **Sound** node is to describe the spatial features of the sound. This includes the intensity and direction of the sound.

THE SOUND NODE

```
Sound {
    exposedField  SFVec3f  direction    0 0 1
    exposedField  SFFloat  intensity    1
    exposedField  SFVec3f  location     0 0 0
    exposedField  SFFloat  maxBack      10
    exposedField  SFFloat  maxFront     10
    exposedField  SFFloat  minBack      1
    exposedField  SFFloat  minFront     1
    exposedField  SFFloat  priority     0
    exposedField  SFNode   source       NULL
    field         SFBool   spatialize   TRUE
}
```

The **Sound** node is actually quite complicated and can be used to provide directional or ambient sound. The key fields for these purposes are the direction field, which defines the direction the sound is played into, the intensity field, which basically says how loud it is, and the maxBack and maxFront fields, which control the shape and size of the sound area.

In the simplest case, maxBack and maxFront are equal. The sound area is a sphere, with its center at the position specified in the location field and the radius equal to the maxFront field (or maxBack). If maxFront and maxBack aren't equal, the sound area becomes an ellipse, and the central axis is defined by the direction.

Figure 4.1 shows this graphically. The diagram on the left shows a spherical sound area; the diagram on the right shows an ellipse.

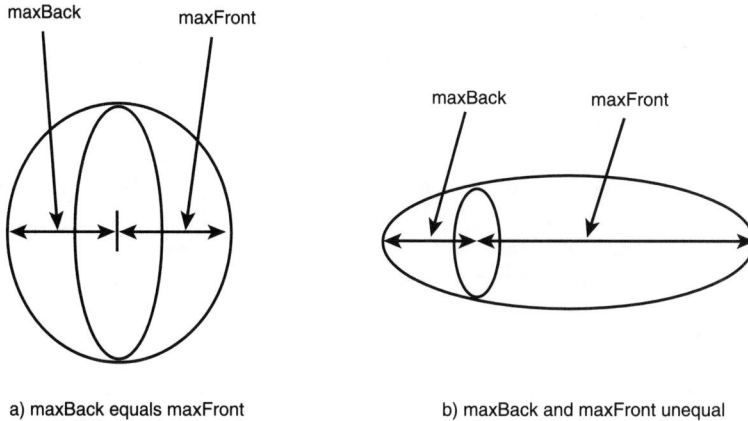

a) maxBack equals maxFront   b) maxBack and maxFront unequal

FIGURE 4.1

Defining the area in which a sound source is heard.

Within these sound areas, the intensity of the sound drops off proportionally as you move toward the boundary.

The minFront and minBack fields define an inner area inside the maxFront and maxBack, within which the sound is heard at full intensity.

Last, the spatialize field is used to "locate" the sound. If TRUE, a user within the sound area is able to locate the source of the sound by turning left and right.

Given that the spatial characteristics of the sound have been defined, the last thing necessary is the actual source of the sound. This is specified in the source field and points to another VRML 2.0 node.

The only types of nodes that the **Sound** node can legally point to are the **AudioClip** node and the **MovieTexture** node.

THE AUDIOCLIP NODE

The following shows the **AudioClip** node:

```
AudioClip {
    exposedField    SFString description       ""
    exposedField    SFBool    loop             FALSE
    exposedField    SFFloat   pitch            1.0
    exposedField    SFTime    startTime        0
    exposedField    SFTime    stopTime         0
    exposedField    MFString  url              []
    eventOut        SFTime    duration_changed
    eventOut        SFBool    isActive
}
```

The **AudioClip** node actually looks and operates similar to a **TimeSensor**. The startTime and stopTime fields specify when the AudioClip should be active. During that period, if the loop field is set to FALSE, the audio file pointed to by the field url is played. If the loop field is set to TRUE and the duration of the audio file is less than the total active period, the audio file is played continuously.

You can use the pitch field to set the pitch and the speed at which the audio is played. For example, a value of 2.0 plays the audio an octave higher and twice as fast.

You can find out the current status of the **Sound** node by using the isActive or duration_changed fields. The isActive field is set to TRUE when the sound is playing. duration_changed generates an event when the duration of the sound clip changes. This happens only if the url field is updated to point to another sound file.

A TALKING AGENT

Listing 4.7 uses two **AudioClip**s to describe two sound sources that start playing when startTime is reached. The sound clip isn't repeated because the loop field (line 22) is set to FALSE. The agent randomly chooses one of the two predefined phrases when clicked and starts to speak the phrase.

Listing 4.7   Using Sound Nodes a for Talking Agent (TalkativeAgent.wrl).

```
1    #VRML V2.0 utf8
2    # an agent talks when you click him.
3    #
4    Transform{
5      children[
6        Inline{url "ManDetailed.wrl"},
7          DEF AGENT_TOUCH TouchSensor{}
8      ]
9    }
10   Sound{
11      maxFront 100
12      maxBack 100
13      source DEF AGENT_VOICE1 AudioClip{
14         loop FALSE
15         url "agent_voice1.wav"
16      }
17   }
18   Sound{
19      maxFront 100
20      maxBack 3
21      source DEF AGENT_VOICE2 AudioClip{
22         loop FALSE
23         url "agent_voice2.wav"
24      }
25   }
26   DEF AGENT_SCRIPT Script{
27      url "TalkativeAgent.class"
28      eventIn SFTime invoked
29      eventOut SFTime startTalking1
30      eventOut SFTime startTalking2
31   }
32   ROUTE AGENT_TOUCH.touchTime TO AGENT_SCRIPT.invoked
33   ROUTE AGENT_SCRIPT.startTalking1 TO
     ➥AGENT_VOICE1.set_startTime
34   ROUTE AGENT_SCRIPT.startTalking2 TO
     ➥AGENT_VOICE2.set_startTime
```

Line 32 routes the touchTime through to the **Script** node and so on to the Java program. The Java program chooses which phrase to speak and then writes to either startTalking1 or startTalking2 of the **Script** node. These are then routed (lines 33 and 34) to the set_startTime of the chosen **Sound** node, causing them to play.

The example sets up the two **Sound** nodes in different ways. The first **Sound** node (line 10) defines a spherical sound area 200 meters in diameter. The actual sound file for this node is held in the WAV file, agent_voice1.wav.

The second **Sound** node (line 18) defines an elliptical sound area because the maxBack field is only 3 meters, whereas the maxFront field is set to 100 meters. This creates a large sound area in front of the agent but a small area behind the agent, similar to what you experience in the real world.

If you load this example into a VRML 2.0 browser, you should be able to navigate behind the agent and experiment with the sound values as you click it.

The Java code for this example (listing 4.8) is relatively straightforward. When the touch event is received, a random number is generated (line 23) and used to decide which sound clip to play. To start the chosen sound clip, the time of the **TouchSensor** event is written into the **Script** node, which routes it on to the startTime field of the **Sound** node. As discussed previously, the startTime field recognizes that the startTime has now passed and begins to play the associated **AudioClip**.

Listing 4.8   Selecting a Sound Node at Random (TalkativeAgent.java).

```
1    // an agent talks when you click him.
2    import java.util.*;
3    import vrml.*;
4    import vrml.node.*;
5    import vrml.field.*;
6
7    public class TalkativeAgent extends Script{
8       SFTime startTalking1;
9       SFTime startTalking2;
10       Random randomNumGenerator = new Random();
```

```
11
12      public void initialize(){
13          // get the reference of the event out
                ➥'startTalking1'.
14          startTalking1 = (SFTime)getEventOut("startTalking1");
15          // get the reference of the event out
                ➥'startTalking2'.
16          startTalking2 = (SFTime)getEventOut("startTalking2");
17      }
18      public void processEvent(Event e){
19          if(e.getName().equals("invoked") == true){
20              double touchTime =
21                  ((ConstSFTime)e.getValue()).getValue();
22              // select one of two phrases randomly.
23              if(randomNumGenerator.nextDouble() > 0.5){
24                  // start the agent talking phrase1.
25                  startTalking1.setValue(touchTime);
26              }else{
27                  // stop the agent talking phrase2.
28                  startTalking2.setValue(touchTime);
29              }
30          }
31      }
32  }
```

You can use this code fragment to experiment in a number of ways. One thing you may want to try is to associate the **Sound** node with the spinning CD from the previous example and play a track of music as the CD spins.

Another extension is to use the sound track from a **MovieTexture** rather than an **AudioClip**.

A third possible extension is to have the choice of **AudioClip** based on your location in the shop. For example, when you're in the jazz section and you click the agent, it plays this week's featured jazz artist, and when you're in the classical section, it plays the corresponding classical piece. To do this, you need to know the location of the user. The next example shows how to find information about the user's location in the scene.

LOCATING THE USER IN THE SCENE: THE PROXIMITYSENSOR

One of the basic requirements in interactive 3D scenes is the ability to locate the user in the scene. In some cases you will want to know whether a user is near a scene entity such as a door, and if so, automatically open the door. In other cases you may want to track the user's movement through the entire scene.

There are many examples for this kind of requirement. One would be a situation in a game-type scene in which you place game information (such as scores) on a semitransparent visor that is always displayed in front of the user. You would track the user and update the visor to always be displayed in front of the user's eye position.

To get the current position of the navigator, VRML 2.0 provides a node, **ProximitySensor**. It generates events, reporting the navigator's new position and orientation every time that information changes. By routing the eventOut fields of the **ProximitySensor** to **Script**s or other nodes, the scene author can track a user's movement in the scene and react accordingly.

The following is the format of the **ProximitySensor**:

```
ProximitySensor {
    exposedField SFVec3f    center      0 0 0
    exposedField SFVec3f    size        0 0 0
    exposedField SFBool     enabled     TRUE
    eventOut     SFBool     isActive
    eventOut     SFVec3f    position_changed
    eventOut     SFRotation orientation_changed
    eventOut     SFTime     enterTime
    eventOut     SFTime     exitTime
}
```

The key parameter field for the **ProximitySensor** is the size field, which defines the operating boundary of the sensor as a box around the center field. Outside this boundary, the **ProximitySensor** will not sense changes; inside the boundary, the sensor tracks movement.

As a user enters into the **ProximitySensor**'s box, the isActive field generates a TRUE event and the time of entry is generated in enterTime. Thereafter, the position_changed and orientation_changed fields generate events each time the user moves.

When the user exits the sensor's box, the isActive field is set to FALSE and the time of exit is generated in exitTime.

ProximitySensor has several possible uses. One is to fire off a set of events when a world is initially loaded. To do this you need to set the **ProximitySensor** to be as big as the world. When initially loaded, the sensor generates an isActive event. This can then be routed to any **Script** nodes that you want to use for initialization.

Another use has almost the opposite effect. If you confine your **ProximitySensor** to a small bounding box around a distinct scene entity, you can use it to check when the user approaches that object.

In listing 4.9 the **ProximitySensor** is set up to be the same size as the record store and so tracks the user as he navigates through the store.

The goal of the example is to use the **ProximitySensor** to determine the user's position and then use that information to update the position of the intelligent agent. By using this technique, you are able to have the agent track the user's position in the record store and "hover" nearby—just like real store assistants.

```
1    #VRML V2.0 utf8
2
3    # initial viewpoint
4    Viewpoint{
5       position 0 2 0
6    }
7    DEF PROX_SENSOR ProximitySensor{
8       size 100 100 100  # you are always in the sensor field.
9    }
10   Transform{      # floor
11      translation 0 -0.5 0
12      children[
13         Shape{geometry Box{size 100 0.1 100}}
14      ]
15   }
16   # stable object to make you realize the world coordinate.
17   Shape{geometry Box{}}
18
19   DEF AGENT Transform{ # following agent
20      children[
21         Inline{url "ManDetailed.wrl"}
22      ]
23   }
24   DEF PROX_SCRIPT Script{
25      url "FollowingAgent.class"
26      eventIn SFVec3f currentPosition
27      eventOut SFVec3f setAgentPosition
29   }
30   ROUTE PROX_SENSOR.position_changed TO
31                             PROX_SCRIPT.currentPosition
32   ROUTE PROX_SCRIPT.setAgentPosition TO
     ➥AGENT.set_translation
```

The **ProximitySensor** is set up to cover virtually the entire world and generates events when the navigator moves around the world.

The position event of the **ProximitySensor** is routed in line 30 to the **Script** node and passed on to the Java program. Within the event handler class (listing 4.10, line 28), the current user's position is read from this event into the variable yourPosition.

The agentPosition variable is then calculated, in moveAgent(), as a fixed offset from yourPosition. The new position for the agent is subsequently written back to the **Script** node (line 44) and routed to the agent translation field.

Listing 4.10   Handling ProximitySensor Events for Position Tracking in Java (Following Agent.java)

```
1    //
2    // an agent is always following you.
3    //
4
5    import vrml.*;
6    import vrml.node.*;
7    import vrml.field.*;
8
9    public class FollowingAgent extends Script{
10       SFVec3f setAgentPosition;
11       float yourPosition[] = new float[3];
12       float agentPosition[] = new float[3];
13
14       // the agent's position when you are at (0, 0, 0).
15       final float agentDefaultPositionX = 2.0f;
16       final float agentDefaultPositionY = -1.4f;
17       final float agentDefaultPositionZ = -6.0f;
18
19       public void initialize(){
20          // get the reference of the event out
                ➥'setAgentPosition'.
21          setAgentPosition =
22             (SFVec3f)getEventOut("setAgentPosition");
23       }
24
25       public void processEvent(Event e){
26          if(e.getName().equals("currentPosition") == true){
27          // record your current position.
28             ((ConstSFVec3f)e.getValue()).getValue(yourPosition);
```

continues

Listing 4.10, CONTINUED.

```
30              // move the agent.
31              moveAgent();
32          }
33      }
34      // move the agent just around you.
35      void moveAgent(){
36          // translate the agent according to your current
                ➥position.
37          agentPosition[0] =
38              yourPosition[0] + agentDefaultPositionX;
39          agentPosition[1] =
40              yourPosition[1]+ agentDefaultPositionY;
41          agentPosition[2] =
42              yourPosition[2]+ agentDefaultPositionZ;
43          // move the agent to the new position.
44          setAgentPosition.setValue(agentPosition);
45      }
46  }
```

FINE-GRAINED TRACKING WITH THE PROXIMITYSENSOR

In the preceding example, the **ProximitySensor** was used to locate the position of the user in the scene. Another use of the **ProximitySensor** is to find out when the user enters or exits a certain well-defined area.

For example, if you wish to implement an automatic door in your scene that opens as a user approaches the door, the **ProximitySensor** is ideal. The door entity has a **ProximitySensor** attached to it, whose size extends a short distance around the door itself. As the user navigates toward the door, the sensor fires and generates an entry time event. This can be used to animate the door.

Listing 4.11 uses a conditional situation. The goal is to realize an automatic door that opens when you go near it, but only if the room light is turned on.

In the case of the store scene, this type of requirement makes sense. If the light is on, the store is open and the door should work. When the store is closed, the lights are off and you can't open the door. Again, conditional situations are exactly where Java code becomes important.

Listing 4.11   Using a ProximitySensor for an Automatic Door (AutomaticDoor.wrl).

```
1    #VRML V2.0 utf8
2    # automatic door
3    # when light turned on, the door opens / closes
        ➥automatically.
4    NavigationInfo{   # turn off the browser default headlight
5        headlight FALSE
6    }
7    Viewpoint{   # initial viewpoint
8        position 0 2 5
9    }
10   Shape{   # room
11       geometry IndexedFaceSet{
12           solid FALSE      # double face
13           coord Coordinate{
14               point[    2 0 -10,        #0
15                  10 0 -10,      #1
16                  10 0  10,      #2
17                 -10 0  10,      #3
18                 -10 0 -10,      #4
19                  -2 0 -10,      #5
20                   2 3 -10,      #6
21                  10 3 -10,      #7
22                  10 3  10,      #8
23                 -10 3  10,      #9
24                 -10 3 -10,      #10
25                  -2 3 -10  ]       #11
26           }
27           coordIndex[   6, 0, 1, 7, -1,        #0
28               7, 1, 2, 8, -1,       #1
29               8, 2, 3, 9, -1,       #2
30               9, 3, 4, 10, -1,      #3
```

continues

Listing 4.11, CONTINUED.

```
31              10, 4, 5, 11, -1,    #4
32              4, 3, 2, 1       #5 (floor)
33          ]
34          color Color{
35              color[ 1 1 0, 0 0.2 1.0 ]    #0 (wall) #1 (floor)
36          }
37          colorPerVertex FALSE
38          colorIndex[ 0, 0, 0, 0, 0, 1]
39      }
40  }
41  DEF LIGHT1 DirectionalLight{
42      on FALSE
43  }
44  DEF LIGHT2 DirectionalLight{
45      direction 0 0 1
46      on FALSE
47  }
48  Transform{
49      translation 0 4 0
50      children[
51          # lamp shade
52          DEF LAMP_SHADE Shape{
53              geometry Cone{
54                  height 2
55                  bottomRadius 2
56              }
57          }
58          # sensor to turn the light on / off
59          DEF LIGHT_ON_SWITCH TouchSensor{}
60      ]
61  }
62  Transform{
63      translation 0 1.5 -10.1
64      children[
65          DEF DOOR Transform{    # door
66              children[
67                  Shape{geometry Box{size 4 3 0.1}}
68              ]
69          }
```

```
70          DEF PROX_SENSOR ProximitySensor{
71          size 8 3 15
72          }
73       ]
74    }
75    DEF DOOR_OPEN_TIME TimeSensor{
76       cycleInterval 2
77    }
78    DEF DOOR_OPEN_INTP PositionInterpolator{
79       key [ 0, 1]
80       keyValue [0 0 0, 3.5 0 0]
81    }
82    DEF DOOR_CLOSE_TIME TimeSensor{
83       cycleInterval 2
84    }
85    DEF DOOR_CLOSE_INTP PositionInterpolator{
86       key [ 0, 1]
87       keyValue [3.5 0 0, 0 0 0]
88    }
89    DEF DOOR_SCRIPT Script{
90       url "AutomaticDoor.class"
91       # light control
92       eventIn SFTime touched
93       eventOut SFBool turnOnLight
94       # door control
95       eventIn SFTime enterArea
96       eventOut SFTime openDoor
97       eventIn SFTime exitArea
98       eventOut SFTime closeDoor
99    }
100
101   ROUTE LIGHT_ON_SWITCH.touchTime TO DOOR_SCRIPT.touched
102   ROUTE DOOR_SCRIPT.turnOnLight TO LIGHT1.on
103   ROUTE DOOR_SCRIPT.turnOnLight TO LIGHT2.on
104
105   ROUTE PROX_SENSOR.enterTime TO DOOR_SCRIPT.enterArea
106   ROUTE DOOR_SCRIPT.openDoor TO DOOR_OPEN_TIME.set_startTime
107   ROUTE DOOR_OPEN_TIME.fraction_changed TO
108                              DOOR_OPEN_INTP.set_fraction
```

continues

Listing 4.11, CONTINUED.

```
109   ROUTE DOOR_OPEN_INTP.value_changed TO DOOR.set_translation
110
111   ROUTE PROX_SENSOR.exitTime TO DOOR_SCRIPT.exitArea
112   ROUTE DOOR_SCRIPT.closeDoor TO
      ➥DOOR_CLOSE_TIME.set_startTime
113   ROUTE DOOR_CLOSE_TIME.fraction_changed TO
114                                   DOOR_CLOSE_INTP.set_fraction
115   ROUTE DOOR_CLOSE_INTP.value_changed TO
      ➥DOOR.set_translation
```

This is a complex VRML scene that uses an **IndexedFaceSet**. Generally, the examples in this book have either used inlines to access complex models or avoided them for the sake of brevity. Because this example is sufficiently small to be comprehensible, it has been included to show the use of the **IndexedFaceSet**.

The coord field holds a set of coordinates—in this example, 12— which are defined as a set of vertices (lines 13–26). These vertices can then be used to define the faces (polygons) of various entities in the scene. Again, in listing 4.11, the coordIndex field defines six polygons (lines 27–33), based on the indices defined in coord. These six polygons describe the floor and walls for the CD store.

Two other scene entities are defined: the light (line 48), which is the familiar lamp shade from listing 4.1 and has an associated light switch, and the automatic door (line 62) with a small **ProximitySensor** attached.

In addition, a **TimeSensor** and two **PositionInterpolator**s control the opening and closing of the door. The first (line 78) moves the door during a two-second period from 0,0,0 to 3.5,0,0 and the second (line 85) moves it back to 0,0,0.

The route section has three parts. Lines 101–103 set up the light routing to enable the script to switch on and off the light and to record its current state. The second section, lines 105–109, sets up the route to open the door. The last section, lines 111–115, sets up the routine to close the door.

When you enter the area near the door, the **ProximitySensor** sends an enterTime event to the **Script** named DOOR_SCRIPT. The Java program in listing 4.12 then checks whether the room light is on or off (line 28). If the light is on, line 29 starts the **TimeSensor** (named DOOR_OPEN_TIME) by writing the current time back to the **Script** node. Referring back to listing 4.11 line 106, you see that the **Script** node then drives the DOOR_OPEN_INTP interpolator to animate the door.

When you leave the area, the sensor sends exitTime to the **Script** node. This causes the Java program (listing 4.12, line 34) to write the currentTime back to the **Script** node, which then causes the DOOR_CLOSE_INTP interpolator to close the door.

Listing 4.12   AND Logic within a Java Script (AutomaticDoor.java).

```
1    //
2    // toggle the light state. and control the automatic door.
3    //
4
5    import vrml.*;
6    import vrml.node.*;
7    import vrml.field.*;
8
9    public class AutomaticDoor extends Script{
10        SFBool turnOnLight;
11        SFTime openDoor;
12        SFTime closeDoor;
13        boolean onOff = false;    // light state.
14
15        public void initialize(){
16            // get the reference of the event out 'turnOnLight'.
17            turnOnLight = (SFBool)getEventOut("turnOnLight");
18            // get the reference of the event out 'openDoor'.
19            openDoor = (SFTime)getEventOut("openDoor");
20            // get the reference of the event out 'closeDoor'.
21            closeDoor = (SFTime)getEventOut("closeDoor");
22        }
23        public void processEvent(Event e){
```

continues

Listing 4.12, CONTINUED.

```
24        if(e.getName().equals("touched") == true){
25          onOff = !onOff;                // toggle the light
            ➥state.
26          turnOnLight.setValue(onOff);    // send the event.
27        }else if(e.getName().equals("enterArea") == true){
28          if(true == onOff){   // open the door if light is
            ➥on.
29            openDoor.setValue(((ConstSFTime)e.
30                                 getValue()).getValue());
31          }
32        }else if(e.getName().equals("exitArea") == true){
33          // close the door.
34          closeDoor.setValue(((ConstSFTime)e.
35                                 getValue()).getValue());
36        }
37      }
38    }
```

ANIMATING THE INTELLIGENT AGENT: THE SWITCH NODE

The agent is now talkative and always floats around you. The agent would be more alive, however, if it had an animation feature such as raising its hand in reaction to your clicking. By using a new node, the **Switch** node, a simple animation can easily be realized.

The **Switch** node is an example of a grouping node and is defined as follows:

```
Switch {
  exposedField    MFNode  choice    []
  exposedField    SFInt32 whichChoice -1
}
```

The purpose of the **Switch** node is to allow more than one child node to be attached and then to allow one of the child nodes to be active at any one time.

The child nodes are contained in the choice field. The whichChoice field specifies which of the children to use at a certain point in time, with the first choice having an index of 0, the second choice an index of 1, and so on.

This feature can be used to animate the agent by associating two different geometries with the **Switch** node: the normal agent and the agent in a greeting posture. This type of animation technique differs from those shown previously, where the use of interpolators actually moved an entity within the scene—in other words, translated its position. The **Switch** node enables you to rapidly shift between several predefined models. So rather than changing an existing model, a new model replaces it.

In the following example (listing 4.13) the agent has only two postures, but this could obviously be extended to support an arbitrary number of postures. All you have to do is define several models, and the **Script** node decides which model to show at any particular time.

The two models are put in a **Switch** node named AGENT_SWITCH. One is a model for a normal agent (line 10); the other is for an agent raising its hand (line 12). A script named AGENT_SCRIPT switches between the two models when the user clicks on the agent.

Listing 4.13   Simple Animation Using a Switch Node (SwitchAgent.wrl).

```
1    #VRML V2.0 utf8
2    # an agent raises his hand when you click him.
3
4    Transform{
5        children[
6        DEF AGENT_SWITCH Switch{
```

continues

Listing 4.13, CONTINUED.

```
7           whichChoice 0
8           choice[
9              # normal posture
10              Inline{url "ManDetailed.wrl"},
11              # hello posture
12              Inline{url "ManHello.wrl"}
13           ]
14        }
15     DEF AGENT_TOUCH TouchSensor{}
16        ]
17   }
18
19   DEF AGENT_SCRIPT Script{
20      url "SwitchAgent.class"
21      eventIn SFTime touchTime
22      eventOut SFInt32 setAgentImage
23   }
24
25   ROUTE AGENT_TOUCH.touchTime TO AGENT_SCRIPT.touchTime
26   ROUTE AGENT_SCRIPT.setAgentImage TO
      ➥AGENT_SWITCH.set_whichChoice
```

The two models used in the **Switch** node are again inlined for brevity. The **Script** node uses a simple field, setAgentImage, to enable the Java program (listing 4.14) to define which model to choose. The result of this choice is written back to the **Script** node at either line 21 or line 24. The result of the choice is then routed through to the whichChoice field of the **Switch** node (listing 4.13, line 26).

Listing 4.14   Controlling a Switch Node from Java (SwitchAgent.java).

```
1    // an agent raises his hand when you click him.
2    import vrml.*;
3    import vrml.node.*;
4    import vrml.field.*;
5
6    public class SwitchAgent extends Script{
7       SFInt32 setAgentImage;
```

```
8      boolean normalPosture = true;
9
10     public void initialize(){
11         // get the reference of the event out
               ➥'setAgentImage'.
12         setAgentImage = (SFInt32)getEventOut
               ➥("setAgentImage");
13     }
14
15     public void processEvent(Event e){
16         if(e.getName().equals("touchTime") == true){
17         // toggle the state.
18         normalPosture = !normalPosture;
19         if(true == normalPosture){
20             // set the agent to its normal posture.
21             setAgentImage.setValue(0);
22         }else{
23         // set the agent to its hello posture.
24             setAgentImage.setValue(1);
25             }
26         }
27     }
28 }
```

An easy and useful extension of this example is adding a
TimeSensor to control the duration of the switch. Currently, a
single click event switches between postures. It would be more
realistic to have the normal posture as the default and the hello
posture to be a short duration before switching back to the
normal posture.

One way to achieve this is to use a one-shot timer, which is
initialized when the agent is clicked, and which, after a preset
time, fires and sends a timer event to the script that could return
the agent to the normal posture.

You may want to write this example yourself based on the preceding code.

COLLISION DETECTION

By now, you have created a record shop where you can turn lights on and off and have an intelligent agent that is always ready to help you shop. Now it's time to go outside the shop! Assume this store has a semitransparent door that you can use to exit.

In VRML 2.0, the default behavior for scene entities is to be solid. This means that if the navigator attempts to pass through an object, a collision occurs. In the majority of cases, this is exactly the behavior you want. However, there are some cases where you need to be able to pass through objects; so there needs to be a means to turn off the collision detection. VRML 2.0 introduces the **Collision** node, a group node, that can turn the collision property of its children on or off. The default setting of collision is ON, so you usually use the **Collision** node to turn OFF the collision property—the opposite of what you'd expect from the **Collision** node's name.

```
Collision {
   eventIn       MFNode    addChildren
   eventIn       MFNode    removeChildren
   exposedField MFNode    children        []
   exposedField SFBool    collide         TRUE
   field         SFVec3f   bboxCenter      0 0 0
   field         SFVec3f   bboxSize        -1 -1 -1
   field         SFNode    proxy           NULL
   eventOut      SFTime    collideTime
}
```

The children field is obviously one of the key fields because it enables you to define the scene entities that have their collision checking turned off. Any child of the **Collision** node inherits the collision property.

The bbox (bounding box) fields are used, as described in previous chapters, as optimization hints by the browser.

The collideTime generates an event when a collision between the user and one of the children of the **Collision** node occurs.

The proxy field is interesting because it enables you to define any other VRML node to act as the child of this node for the purposes of collision detection. This is useful when the actual geometry of the node is extremely complicated. Rather than asking the browser to perform the collision detection on such a complex piece of geometry, this field can be used to point to a simple piece of geometry. For example, if you have a complex model of a tree, rather than checking for collision with each branch and leaf, you can use the proxy field to point to a simple **Sphere** node. This enables the browser to perform a simple collision check on a large sphere that "surrounds" the tree.

In listing 4.15 two half-transparent walls are located between you and a car. If you try to go through the red wall, you bump into the wall even though you can see the car through it. If you try to go through the green wall, you can reach the car without colliding with the wall. This is the result of setting up the **Collision** node's collide field as FALSE (line 34).

Listing 4.15   Using the Collision Node (Transparency.wrl).

```
1    #VRML V2.0 utf8
2
3    # window which you cannot go through.
4    Transform{
5    translation 0 -5 0
6       children[
7          Shape{
8             geometry IndexedFaceSet{
9                coord Coordinate{
10                   point[
11                      0 0 0,        #0
12                      10 0 0,       #1
13                      10 10 0,      #2
14                      0 10 0,       #3
15                   ]
16                }
17                coordIndex [0, 1, 2, 3, -1]
```

continues

Listing 4.15, CONTINUED.

```
18                  }
19                  appearance Appearance{
20                      material Material{
21                          diffuseColor 1 0 0
22                          transparency 0.7
23                      }
24                  }
25              }
26          ]
27      }
28
29  # window which you can go through.
30  Transform{
31      translation -10 -5 0
32      children[
33          Collision{
34              collide FALSE
35              children[
36                  Shape{
37                      geometry IndexedFaceSet{
38                          coord Coordinate{
39                              point[
40              0 0 0,        #0
41              10 0 0,       #1
42              10 10 0,      #2
43              0 10 0,       #3
44                          ]
45                          }
46                      coordIndex [0, 1, 2, 3, -1]
47                      }
48                      appearance Appearance{
49                          material Material{
50                              diffuseColor 0 1 0
51                              transparency 0.7
52                          }
53                      }
54                  }
55              ]
56          }
```

```
57      ]
58   }
59
60   # put a car on the other side of the window.
61   Transform{
62      translation 0 0 -8
63      rotation 0 1 0 0.75
64      children[
65         Inline{url "CarBody.wrl"}
66      ]
67   }
```

HANDLING LARGE SCENES USING LEVEL OF DETAIL

Compared to the inside of the shop, the outside world is likely to be much larger and full of objects. One of the main issues facing VRML designers is performance. Chapter 6, "Hints and Tips for Effective and Efficient VRML," discusses the factors that affect a scene's performance and offers some hints for improving the performance of your scenes. However, in this example, a new node, the **LOD** (Level Of Detail) node, is introduced to tackle one of the main causes of performance slowdown.

The rendering speed of any scene is directly proportional to the number of polygons in the scene. So from the viewpoint of rendering speed, it's important to "cull out" objects that are far enough away from the navigator to make it unnecessary to render them in detail. The **LOD** node is introduced to support this kind of culling and, more important, to give the user control over this issue.

To illustrate the use of the **LOD** node, listing 4.16 shows a man walking in the street outside the record shop. There are two models for this man, one of which is modeled in detail and used when the man is near enough to the user to make details important. The other is a rough model that is used when the user is farther away. The **LOD** node is a group node that holds several

models and switches between them automatically, according to
the distance between you and the **LOD** node. In fact, it's similar
to the **Switch** node discussed previously but uses spatial distance
to automatically switch between different children nodes.

```
LOD {
   exposedField MFNode   level    []
   field        SFVec3f  center   0 0 0
   field        MFFloat  range    []
}
```

The threshold for switching is determined by the range field.
When the user is farther from the node than the largest range
value, the lowest level of detail is used. As the user approaches the
node's center, the browser calculates the distance between the
two. This value is then used to determine which range value is
appropriate. That range value acts as an index into the level field,
enabling the browser to choose the correct model.

The level field contains a set of nodes, including geometry, that
are used for each corresponding range.

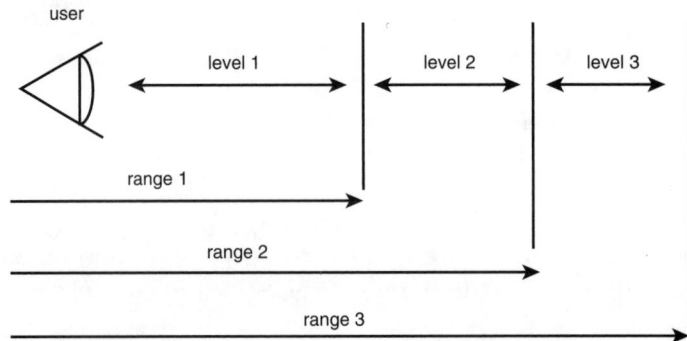

FIGURE 4.2

Mapping between LOD range values and levels.

SWITCHING BETWEEN MODELS USING THE LOD

Listing 4.16 shows how the **LOD** node works. There are two inlined models, one specifying the detailed model of a man and the other specifying the simple model of the man. The models represent the two possible choices for the **LOD** node.

Listing 4.16   Using Level of Detail—LOD Node (LodMan.wrl).

```
1   #VRML V2.0 utf8
2   DEF MAN Transform{
3      children[
4         LOD{
5            level[
6               Inline{url "ManDetailed.wrl"},
7               Inline{url "ManRough.wrl"}
8            ]
9            range[5]
10         }
11      ]
12   }
13   DEF MAN_TIME TimeSensor{
14      loop TRUE
15      cycleInterval 3
16   }
17   DEF MAN_POSINT PositionInterpolator{
18      key [0, 1]
19      keyValue [0 0 0, 0 0 10]
20   }
21   ROUTE MAN_TIME.fraction_changed TO MAN_POSINT.set_fraction
22   ROUTE MAN_POSINT.value_changed TO MAN.set_translation
```

The range value for the **LOD** node is set to 5 meters. When you're more than 5 meters away from the man, he appears as the simple model; at less than 5 meters, the **LOD** automatically switches to the more complex model.

Figure 4.3 shows the long-distance model for the man. Note how simple it is and how few polygons are required.

FIGURE 4.3

The long-distance man model for the LOD node.

To put this example into action, a **TimeSensor** and interpolator that move the man from his start position toward you are added. As the man approaches, you should see how the **LOD** node automatically activates and switches between the two models.

In figure 4.4 you can see the result of the **LOD** causing a model switch and the browser loading the more complicated man model.

FIGURE 4.4

The detailed man model for the LOD node.

You can use the **LOD** node to switch between any number of levels of detail, enabling you to build complex scenes that still perform well.

One thing to be aware of is that different browsers implement the **LOD** in different ways. In some browsers, a lot of work may have to be carried out to switch the models. In that case, if you design your world with a large number of objects that all have the same **LOD** range, the browser may slow down significantly as you navigate into another part of the scene and cause all of the **LOD**s to activate. Pay careful attention to the range values and define them so that they switch at different distances. This enables the browser to maintain its performance.

TELEPORTATION USING THE VIEWPOINT NODE

Using the **ProximitySensor**, a scene author can know the current position of the navigator within the scene. As previous examples have shown, this enables the scene author to build entities, such as the intelligent agent, that track the user. A natural extension of this facility is the capability to update the user's current position. In other words, you may want to move the user's position regardless of the user's navigation in the browser. This capability can be used, for example, to teleport a user from one part of the scene to another as he approaches and enters a teleportation booth.

VRML 2.0 introduces a concept called the **Viewpoint**, which acts like a prelocated camera position in the scene. Scene creators can command the user's viewpoint to jump to the position of one of those **Viewpoint** nodes.

```
Viewpoint {
  eventIn       SFBool     set_bind
  exposedField  SFFloat    fieldOfView    0.785398
  exposedField  SFBool     jump           TRUE
  exposedField  SFRotation orientation    0 0 1  0
  exposedField  SFVec3f    position       0 0 10
  field         SFString   description    ""
  eventOut      SFTime     bindTime
  eventOut      SFBool     isBound
}
```

At any particular point in time, a single **Viewpoint** is said to be bound to the user's view. In other words, the user's view is based on that **Viewpoint**. Any changes to the **Viewpoint**, such as changing its translation field, cause the user's view to change accordingly.

When a set_bind TRUE event is sent to a **Viewpoint** node, that **Viewpoint** becomes bound, and if the **Viewpoint** node's jump field is TRUE, the user's **Viewpoint** is adjusted to the **Viewpoint**'s position and orientation. This has the effect of "teleporting" the user to the position and orientation of the **Viewpoint**.

In Listing 4.17, when you click the sphere in front of you, your **Viewpoint** switches from a position in front of the car to a position beside the car.

Listing 4.17   Quick Teleportation Using the Viewpoint Node (Viewpoint.wrl).

```
1    #VRML V2.0 utf8
2
3    DEF FRONT_VIEW Viewpoint{
4        position 0 1 10
5        description "Front view"
6    }
7    DEF SIDE_VIEW Viewpoint{
8        position 10 1 0
9        orientation 0 1 0 1.57
10        description "Side view"
11    }
12    Inline{url "CarBody.wrl"}
13    Transform{
14        translation 0 4 0
15        children[
16            Shape{geometry Sphere{radius 0.5}},
17            DEF TOUCH TouchSensor{}
18        ]
19    }
20
21    DEF SCRIPT Script{
22        url "Viewpoint.class"
```

```
23        eventIn SFTime touched
24        eventOut SFBool bindFrontView
25        eventOut SFBool bindSideView
26    }
27    ROUTE TOUCH.touchTime TO SCRIPT.touched
28    ROUTE SCRIPT.bindFrontView TO FRONT_VIEW.set_bind
29    ROUTE SCRIPT.bindSideView TO SIDE_VIEW.set_bind
```

The two **Viewpoint** nodes (lines 3 and 7) define two positions:
one for the front view and one for the side view. A simple sphere
contains a **TouchSensor** that is used to call the **Script** node. You
can see this graphically in figure 4.5.

FIGURE 4.5

Viewpoints can be used to navigate around a scene.

When the associated Java program is invoked (listing 4.18), it
toggles the user's view between the two **Viewpoint**s and sends the
chosen view back to the **Script** node. The **Script** node then
forwards the event to the chosen **Viewpoint** node's set_bind field.

You can use this mechanism to define an arbitrary set of viewpoints in the scene and to move users between those points. An
example of this is a guided tour between different attractions in a
virtual museum. Or you could use it as a means to move users
around a car model in a virtual car showroom.

In the Community Place browser, the bookmark mechanism is based on this use of **Viewpoint**s, although it is augmented to support teleporting between different scenes.

Listing 4.18   Java Code to Rebind the Current Viewpoint (Viewpoint.java).

```
1   //
2   // change the viewpoint.
3   //
4
5   import vrml.*;
6   import vrml.node.*;
7   import vrml.field.*;
8
9   public class Viewpoint extends Script{
10      SFBool bindFrontView;
11      SFBool bindSideView;
12      // toggle.
13      boolean toggle = false;
14
15      public void initialize(){
16          // get the reference of the event out
                ➥'bindFrontView'.
17          bindFrontView = (SFBool)getEventOut("bindFrontView");
18          // get the reference of the event out 'bindSideView'.
19          bindSideView = (SFBool)getEventOut("bindSideView");
20      }
21
22      public void processEvent(Event e){
23          if(e.getName().equals("touched") == true){
24              toggle = !toggle; // toggle the state.
25              if(false == toggle){
26                  bindFrontView.setValue(true);
27              }else{
28              bindSideView.setValue(true);
29              }
30          }
31      }
32  }
```

GOING FOR A RIDE: ADVANCED USE OF THE VIEWPOINT NODE

Using only the **Viewpoint**'s jump mechanism, you can teleport between a set of predefined **Viewpoint** nodes. However, you have no control over the way you move between those **Viewpoint**s, and you can move only from one set point to another.

There are cases where what you really want to be able to do is move the user through a continuous set of points. To do this, the **Viewpoint** node also can be used. But rather than simply binding to a new **Viewpoint** every time you want to move, you actually change the position and orientation fields of the currently active, or bound, **Viewpoint** node.

In listing 4.19, the user's view becomes bound to the **Viewpoint** associated with the car. When the user clicks on the car, he is bound to that **Viewpoint**. However, because the car is a moving object, you can move the **Viewpoint** node within it and take the user along.

Listing 4.19   Attaching a Viewpoint Node to a Moveable Object (Car.wrl).

```
1    #VRML V2.0 utf8
2    # a car running on the street.
3    # you get on/off the car by clicking it
4
5    # inline scenery to make you realize your Viewpoint is
       ➥moving.
6    Transform{
7       translation -20 0 0
8       rotation 0 1 0 1.57
9       children[
10          Inline{url "world.wrl"}
11       ]
12   }
13   # your default viewpoint.
14   DEF DEFAULT_VIEWPOINT Viewpoint{
15      position 5 2 20
```

continues

Listing 4.19, CONTINUED.

```
16      orientation 0 1 0 1.0
17    }
18    DEF CAR Transform{
19      children[
20        Inline{url "CarBody.wrl"}, # car itself.
21        # touch sensor to get on/off the car.
22        DEF CAR_TOUCH TouchSensor{},
23        # viewpoint located at the driver's seat.
24        DEF CAR_VIEWPOINT Viewpoint{
25          position 0 2 0
26          orientation 0 1 0 3.14
27        }
28      ]
29    }
30    DEF CAR_TIME TimeSensor{
31      loop TRUE
32      cycleInterval 6
33    }
34    DEF CAR_POSINT PositionInterpolator{
35      key [0, 0.5, 1]
36      keyValue [0 0 0, 0 0 20, 0 0 0]
37    }
38    DEF CAR_SCRIPT Script{
39      url "Car.class"
40      # get on/off the car.
41      eventIn SFTime touched
42      eventOut SFBool bindCarViewpoint
43      eventOut SFBool bindDefaultViewpoint
44    }
45    ROUTE CAR_TIME.fraction_changed TO CAR_POSINT.set_fraction
46    ROUTE CAR_POSINT.value_changed TO CAR.set_translation
47    # get on/off the car.
48    ROUTE CAR_TOUCH.touchTime TO CAR_SCRIPT.touched
49    ROUTE CAR_SCRIPT.bindCarViewpoint TO CAR_VIEWPOINT.set_bind
50    ROUTE CAR_SCRIPT.bindDefaultViewpoint TO
51                                DEFAULT_VIEWPOINT.set_bind
```

The **TimeSensor** and **PositionInterpolator** are used to move the car within the scene. Line 24 of listing 4.19 defines the **Viewpoint** node as a child node of the CAR **Transform** node. As a result, any update to the translation field of this **Transform** automatically affects the position of the **Viewpoint** node. Line 46 then sets up a route from the **PositionInterpolator**, CAR_POSINT, to the CAR's translation field so that the car is continually moving and the **Viewpoint** is continually moving with it.

When the car is clicked, the event is forwarded to the event handler class (listing 4.20), which holds the current state of the user. When not riding in the car, the click event causes the Java program to write to the bindCarViewpoint eventOut field of the **Script** node (line 26). Otherwise, the Java program writes to the bindDefaultViewpoint eventOut field. In the first case, this event is then routed through to the CAR_VIEWPOINT, making it the currently bound **Viewpoint**. However, because this **Viewpoint** is continuously being moved as the car moves, the effect is that the user moves with the car. The second case binds the user to the other **Viewpoint** node, DEFAULT_VIEWPOINT, which is a static position near the car.

If you try this example in the Community Place browser, you will see that after you click the car, you can't navigate in the ordinary way. This is because your current view is bound to the **Viewpoint** defined as part of the car's **Transform** node, and you are forced to move along with the car. This technique can be used to realize any kind of virtual tour, or as in the current example, as the basis for a virtual taxi cab.

Listing 4.20   Animating the Car and the Viewpoint (Car.java).

```
1    // a car running on the street.
2    // you get on/off the car by clicking it.
3
4    import vrml.*;
5    import vrml.node.*;
6    import vrml.field.*;
7
8    public class Car extends Script{
9       SFBool bindCarViewpoint;
```

continues

Listing 4.20, CONTINUED.

```
10      SFBool bindDefaultViewpoint;
11      boolean onCar = false;
12
13      public void initialize(){
14          // get the reference of the event out
                ➡'bindCarViewpoint'.
15          bindCarViewpoint =
16              (SFBool)getEventOut("bindCarViewpoint");
17          // get the reference of the eout
                ➡'bindDefaultViewpoint'.
18          bindDefaultViewpoint =
19              (SFBool)getEventOut("bindDefaultViewpoint");
20      }
21
22      public void processEvent(Event e){
23          if(e.getName().equals("touched") == true){
24              onCar = !onCar;   // toggle the state.
25              if(true == onCar){
26                  bindCarViewpoint.setValue(true);
27              }else{
28                  bindDefaultViewpoint.setValue(true);
29              }
30          }
31      }
32  }
```

DO IT YOURSELF: THE PROTO NODE

The last thing needed to complete this chapter's scenario is to include several people walking on the street outside. Listing 4.16, which explained the **LOD** node, has already shown a man who walks autonomously on the street outside. It makes sense to reuse that example and replicate it several times to create several people walking about.

You have already seen how to use the **Inline** node to reuse an existing VRML model contained in another file, and this would seem the logical way to solve the problem here. However, the expressive power of **Inline** node is quite restricted because you can't change the fields of nodes included in an inlined VRML file.

If you were to use the inline technique, although you could set up several men walking in different directions, they would all be synchronized because the internal details of their movement are replicated by each instance. To realize asynchronous people walking, it's necessary to set different values to each **TimeSensor**'s cycleInterval field in the inlined file (listing 4.16, line 15). This is impossible because each instance is an exact copy of the inlined file.

What is needed is a mechanism to parameterize a set of nodes that make up a model and to be able to make a copy of those nodes but be able to specify different parameters for each copy. In the example, you want to parameterize the cycleInterval of the **TimeSensor** node.

This type of requirement is evident to a Java programmer. Time and time again, a data structure is reused but parameterized for the job at hand.

What is needed is a way to define parameterized data structures in VRML 2.0. In essence, this is a means to extend the built-in VRML 2.0 nodes with a set of new nodes. VRML 2.0 has a means to do this, and it's based on a language mechanism called *prototyping*.

A prototype is defined within a VRML file by using the keyword PROTO. The syntax is as follows:

```
PROTO prototypename [ eventIn        eventtypename name
                      eventOut       eventtypename name
                      exposedField fieldtypename name
                      ➡defaultValue
                      field          fieldtypename name
                      ➡defaultValue
                      ... ] {
   Zero or more routes and prototypes
   First node (defines the node type of this prototype)
   Zero or more nodes (of any type), routes, and
   ➡prototypes
}
```

The PROTO declaration consists of three parts: the name of the new node type, a declaration of the parameters of this new node, and a definition of the node itself. The definition of the node can consist of any legal VRML 2.0 built-in nodes and may also include any previously defined prototypes.

Within the definition, the keyword IS can be used to specify which of the parameters should be used to define the field values of the definition nodes.

The following is a simple example of a prototype:

```
PROTO mySquatCone [ field  SFFloat size 5.0] {
   Cone {
      bottomRadius IS size
      height IS size
   }
}
mySquatCone { size 10}
```

The PROTO declaration defines a new node type called **mySquatCone** with a parameter field size. Within the definition, a **Cone** node is used whose height and bottomRadius fields are set by the value of the parameter size.

Later in the file, the instantiation of this node with a size field of 10 creates an instance within the scene graph. If no parameter was specified, the **mySquatCone** defaults to the field value specified in the declaration part of the prototype—that is, 5.0.

Because the first and—in this case—only node within the prototype definition is a **Cone** node, this prototype has as its type, **Cone**. This means that this prototype node can be used wherever a **Cone** node can be used.

This PROTO mechanism is exactly what is needed to provide a parameterized version of the walking man in our street scene. In listing 4.21, a new node, **WalkingMan**, is defined using a PROTO (line 3). The PROTO contains both the **LOD** information and the **TimeSensor** and **PositionInterpolator** needed to animate the man.

The **WalkingMan** node is defined with three parameters: a translation that defines the start position, a rotation that defines the start direction, and a walkingCycle that defines the period taken for the man to move between the start and finish positions.

Within the definition of the prototype, these three parameters are used to set the field values for the **Transform** node that contains the man's geometry and for the **TimeSensor** that drives the **PositionInterpolator**. As discussed previously, the IS syntax is used to bind an internal field within the prototype definition to a parameter in the prototype's declaration section. Lines 7, 8, and 24 use this syntax.

After this PROTO has been defined, lines 47, 52, and 57 instantiate three different versions of the prototype. All three have different parameters and define three asynchronous walkers.

Listing 4.21   Walking Men Using PROTOs (ProtoMan.wrl).

```
1    #VRML V2.0 utf8
2
3    PROTO WalkingMan[   exposedField SFVec3f translation 0 0 0
4         exposedField SFRotation rotation 1 0 0
5         exposedField SFTime walkingCycle 1]{
6      Transform{
7         translation IS translation
8         rotation    IS rotation
9         children[
10
11           DEF MAN Transform{
12              children[
13                LOD{
14                   level[
15                       Inline{url "ManDetailed.wrl"},
16                       Inline{url "ManRough.wrl"}
17                   ]
18                   range[10]
19                }
20              ]
21           }
22           DEF MAN_TIME TimeSensor{
23              loop TRUE
24              cycleInterval IS walkingCycle
25           }
26           DEF MAN_POSINT PositionInterpolator{
27              key [0, 1]
28              keyValue [0 0 0, 0 0 10]
29           }
30           DEF MAN_SCRIPT Script{
31              url "ProtoMan.class"
32              eventIn SFTime cycleEnd
33              eventOut MFVec3f setPath
34           }
35         ]
36      }
37      ROUTE MAN_TIME.fraction_changed TO
       ➥MAN_POSINT.set_fraction
38      ROUTE MAN_POSINT.value_changed TO MAN.set_translation
```

```
39      ROUTE MAN_TIME.cycleTime TO MAN_SCRIPT.cycleEnd
40      ROUTE MAN_SCRIPT.setPath TO MAN_POSINT.set_keyValue
41   }
42
43   Viewpoint{
44      position 0 0 3
45   }
46
47   WalkingMan{
48      translation 0 0 -5
49      walkingCycle 3
50   }
51
52   WalkingMan{
53      translation 3 0 -8
54      walkingCycle 5
55   }
56
57   WalkingMan{
58      translation -3 0 -5
59      rotation 0 1 0 0.78
60      walkingCycle 7
61   }
```

Line 30 defines a **Script** node that calls a Java program to set up the distance each man walks per cycle. The **Script** node is part of the prototype declaration and is also replicated.

In listing 4.22, the initialize() function sets up the default walk distance for each walker as 10 meters in the Z axis. At the end of each cycle period, a new walk distance is calculated and sent to the **Script** node (line 34). This, in turn, is routed through to the keyValue field of the **PositionInterpolator** for that instance of the walking man. In this way, the start position, walking direction, and walking duration are set up using the instance parameters of the prototype instances. The distance walked per cycle is set up dynamically in the Java program.

Listing 4.22   Using Java to Customize a PROTO (ProtMan.java).

```
1   //
2   // Walking man in prototype.
3   //
4
5   import java.util.*;
6   import vrml.*;
7   import vrml.node.*;
8   import vrml.field.*;
9
10    public class ProtoMan extends Script{
11       MFVec3f setPath;
12       float path[] = new float[3 * 2];
13       Random randomNumGenerator = new Random();
14
15       public void initialize(){
16          // get the reference of the event out 'setPath'.
17          setPath = (MFVec3f)getEventOut("setPath");
18          // initialize the path.
19          path[0] = 0.0f;           // start position
20          path[1] = 0.0f;
21          path[2] = 0.0f;
22          path[3] = 0.0f;           // end position
23          path[4] = 0.0f;
24          path[5] = 10.0f;
25       }
26
27       public void processEvent(Event e){
28          if(e.getName().equals("cycleEnd") == true){
29             // decide how far the man goes in the next cycle.
30             // the distance is between 10.0 and 20.0
31             path[5] = 10.0f +
32                randomNumGenerator.nextFloat() * 10.0f;
33             // send the event.
34             setPath.setValue(3 * 2, path);
35          }
36       }
37    }
```

SHARING YOUR WORK: EXTERNPROTO

The PROTO mechanism gives you the ability to extend the VRML 2.0 node set with any number of new nodes. Further, it enables flexible parameterization of the new nodes, enabling you to reuse basic types in a variety of ways. A natural extension of this is to provide a mechanism to share PROTOs among several VRML files. For example, if you are creating several scenes, modeling cities such as Tokyo or Manchester, you would need many common models, such as the walking man, the car, buildings, and so on.

The mechanism to do this is the EXTERNPROTO, a way to share PROTOs. The EXTERNPROTO operates in the same way as the PROTO in that it enables the user to extend the set of nodes. However, it's designed to use external files for the definition part of the prototype.

The syntax is shown in the following code:

```
EXTERNPROTO extern prototypename [ eventIn eventtypename
➥name
                                eventOut eventtypename
                                ➥name
                                field fieldtypename
                                ➥name
                                exposedField
                                ➥fieldtypename name ]
    "URL/URN" or [ "URL/URN", "URL/URN", ... ]
```

The first part of the syntax is the same as the PROTO syntax and specifies the parameters that this new node will take.

The key difference is that the EXTERNPROTO syntax defines the prototype name and declaration. The actual definition of the prototype is loaded from the specified URL.

In listing 4.23, a PROTO definition for **WalkingMan** isn't specified; only the EXTERNPROTO interface is given. This interface specifies the actual file (ExProtoManDef.wrl), which contains the full PROTO definition of the **WalkingMan**. This definition is the same as in listing 4.21.

Lines 9, 14, and 20 use this prototype definition in the same way as listing 4.21.

Listing 4.23   Walking Men Using EXTERNPROTO (ExProtoManUse.wrl).

```
1    #VRML V2.0 utf8
2    #
3    # use EXTERNPROTO
4    #
5    EXTERNPROTO WalkingMan[    exposedField SFVec3f translation 0
     ➥0 0
6          exposedField SFRotation rotation 1 0 0 0
7          exposedField SFTime walkingCycle 1]"ExProtoManDef.wrl"
8
9    WalkingMan{
10         translation 0 0 -5
11         walkingCycle 3
12    }
13
14    WalkingMan{
15         translation 3 0 -8
17         walkingCycle 5
18    }
19
20    WalkingMan{
21         translation -3 0 -5
22         rotation 0 1 0 0.78
23         walkingCycle 7
24    }
```

All that has really happened is that the definition of the prototype has been moved to a separate file, which is then available to be included in any VRML file. In this way, **WalkingMan** PROTO becomes a common library definition. The common definition is shown in listing 4.24.

Listing 4.24   The PROTO Definition Used by an EXTERNPROTO (ExProtoManDef.wrl).

```
1    #VRML V2.0 utf8
2
3    PROTO WalkingMan[    exposedField SFVec3f translation 0 0 0
4           exposedField SFRotation rotation 1 0 0 0
5           exposedField SFTime walkingCycle 1]{
6       Transform{
7           translation IS translation
8           rotation    IS rotation
9           children[
10              DEF MAN Transform{
11                  children[
12                      LOD{
13                          level[
14                              Inline{url "ManDetailed.wrl"},
15                              Inline{url "ManRough.wrl"}
16                          ]
17                          range[10]
18                      }
19                  ]
20              }
21              DEF MAN_TIME TimeSensor{
22                  loop TRUE
23                  cycleInterval IS walkingCycle
24              }
25              DEF MAN_POSINT PositionInterpolator{
26                  key [0, 1]
27                  keyValue [0 0 0, 0 0 10]
28              }
29          ]
30      }
31      ROUTE MAN_TIME.fraction_changed TO
        ➥MAN_POSINT.set_fraction
32      ROUTE MAN_POSINT.value_changed TO MAN.set_translation
33   }
```

This mechanism provides a way for users to build up a library of useful types and make them available, both for themselves and for other developers to reuse.

It's likely that as VRML becomes more widely used, such libraries will become commonly available, making the task of scene developers easier as time passes.

ROUNDUP

This chapter concentrated on some of the more interesting nodes in VRML 2.0 and has shown how Java can be used to extend their capabilities. In many cases, the examples were restricted in functionality so that the essential features of the node could be shown. However, you are encouraged to experiment with the use of Java with these and other nodes.

After working through the examples and experimenting on your own, you should be familiar with the use of Java in conjunction with VRML 2.0.

As the examples have shown, there are endless possibilities for the control of VRML scene entities via Java. This chapter built up a set of interrelated examples that describe a store and street scene. In all cases, the examples provided the minimum needed to show how to use a particular node. You are encouraged to experiment with these skeleton examples and extend both the richness of the scene entities and the functionality they possess.

As already mentioned, some interesting extensions are as follows:

➤ Extend the shop to include several different sections and use some interesting textures to decorate the walls

➤ Experiment with other audio to add music to the scene and use **ProximitySensor**s to play different music in different sections

➤ Build a set of predefined models for an actual walking man and use a switch node to give the impression of real movement

➤ Extend the outside scene and make the taxi cab take a real tour through your new scene, showing off highlights of the city

Chapter 5, "Advanced Java," continues the use of practical examples to show how to use Java to manage VRML scenes. However, the emphasis switches to using Java to merge the virtual world in your 3D scene and the real world that your computer exists in.

ADVANCED JAVA

In the previous chapter, "Advanced VRML," the emphasis was on the use of Java to augment the functionality of VRML's built-in nodes. This chapter switches focus and looks at how to use Java to bridge from the 3D world of VRML to the real world. This is really where the power of Java over a more simple scripting language shines through. With Java, it's easy to read and write to local disks, enabling you to access and display local information using VRML. Building a user interface to your VRML worlds is made possible by using Java's windowing facility. However, probably most important of all, the capability of Java to work with the Internet means your VRML worlds can be tightly coupled with the World Wide Web.

WHAT THIS CHAPTER COVERS

This chapter works through a series of examples showing how VRML can access and use different types of real-world data. This chapter includes the following issues:

➤ How to access the local file system

➤ How to build interfaces by using Java's Abstract Windowing Toolkit

➤ How to use client/server-based networking

➤ How to make use of Java's multithreading capabilities

Each example area starts with a simple program explaining the basic concept, followed by a more complex piece of Java code to apply the basic ideas.

By the end of this chapter, you'll be able to build Java programs that access and manipulate various input/output streams. These include the ability to access and write data on your local disk, which you can then use within your VRML scene; the ability to build simple user interfaces that interact with the user and can be used to directly manipulate the VRML scene; and the understanding of how you can use Java's networking facilities to build distributed client/server, network-based applications that work with your VRML scenes. To show off this capability, you'll experiment with a simple multiuser server that supports shared VRML scenes.

JAVA, FILE ACCESS, AND VRML

File access, although a simple and necessary part of any programming language, is obviously not a part of the VRML 2.0 language. Hence, it's necessary to use Java for accessing files on behalf of the VRML scene. There are many cases where this capability is needed.

One such case is the issue of scene persistence. When a VRML file is loaded, the scene is initialized to a certain start state defined by the VRML file. Any subsequent interactions with the user or Java programming scripts will change the state of the scene. However, because VRML 2.0 has no way to store those changes, when the user quits the scene, the changes are lost. When you reload the scene from the VRML file, you are returned to the original state. One solution to this is to write the changes as updates to the original VRML file. When the scene is reloaded, the changes are part of the new VRML file and so are not lost.

Another example that combines VRML and file access is to actually visualize data that can be found on the local disk. This can be used to visualize database data for easier assimilation or to use the VRML browser as a 3D interface to data or files on the local disk.

This last possibility is actually quite intriguing. As you're probably aware, current trends in desktop computing reveal HTML browsers that view network and local data. It's possible that in three years, using VRML to view the structure of local disks in 3D will become the next desktop interface model. In this section, you're going to get a taste of that future by building a simple disk visualization example that, although fairly simplistic, provides a good basis for your own experiments.

Before starting these examples, however, you need to be aware of the security policy Community Place uses. Although this discussion concentrates on Community Place, the ideas are relevant to any VRML browser. In fact, in much the same way you expect a 2D browser such as Netscape or Internet Explorer to protect you from malicious Java code, you should expect your 3D browser to do the same. If your 3D browser doesn't have a well-defined, flexible security mechanism, it may be worth investigating alternatives.

COMMUNITY PLACE'S SECURITY POLICY

The accompanying CD-ROM contains two versions of Community Place: a plug-in version that runs as a plug-in to Netscape Navigator and a stand-alone version that runs as a helper application to Netscape Navigator.

These two versions have different security policies. The plug-in version uses the default policy of Netscape Navigator whereas the helper version uses a more flexible security policy. You will need to use the helper version of Community Place for the examples in the rest of this chapter.

In Netscape, Java applets can't read or write files. However, Sun's AppletViewer provides a little more flexibility and allows applets to read or write files in the directories that are specified in an access control list (ACL).

These access control lists are found in the following file: ~/.hotjava/properties. In the following text, this file will be referred to as the properties file.

The helper version of Community Place implements a security policy similar to Sun's AppletViewer and uses the same properties file to enable you, the user, to control what Java programs can and can't do when they are run as part of a VRML scene.

If you specify the HOME environment variable in your AUTOEXEC.BAT file, you'll need to create the .hotjava directory under the directory specified in HOME environment variable. This file is also created automatically when you use Sun's AppletViewer. For instance, if your HOME is set to \ma2da, the properties file is \ma2da\.hotjava\properties.

Use of the properties file gives you control over the following features:

➤ Checking for the existence of the file and its file type

➤ Reading, writing, and renaming the file

➤ Listing a directory or creating a new one

➤ Listing the files in this file (as if it were a directory)

➤ Checking the file's size and when last modified

➤ Accessing the network

Because Community Place's security policy is based on the AppletViewer's policy, you'll need to set up the properties file if you want to allow VRML contents that use Java to read/write or access local files on your hard disk.

For example, if you don't set up the properties file appropriately and then try to load some VRML contents that use Java to try to read or write files, the Community Place browser displays "Cannot open file" in its Java console window.

SETTING UP THE ACCESS CONTROL LISTS

To enable VRML contents to read or write files in the Community Place browser, you need to set up the access control lists by using acl.read and acl.write properties (acl is an acronym for Access Control List).

For example, if you want to enable the VRML contents to read all files in the directory \tmp, you need to add the following lines to the properties file. Do this now. Because the properties file is a standard text file, you can use your favorite text editor (Notepad, for example). Add the following lines:

```
acl.read=c:\tmp
acl.read=c:\tmp;c:\var\tmp
```

You can use ; to specify multiple directories to the list.

If you want to allow the VRML contents to write files, you also need to add the following line to the file:

```
acl.write=c:\tmp
```

Again you can use ; to specify multiple directories to the list.

SIMPLE FILE I/O EXAMPLE (MESSAGE OF THE DAY)

This example is a VRML scene that displays the message of the day (motd). It checks to see whether the motd file exists in the \tmp directory. If the file exists and the user clicks on the sphere in the scene, the contents of the file are displayed as a message.

NOTE

> Don't forget that before executing this example, you need to add permission to the properties file as follows:
>
> ```
> acl.read=c:\tmp
> ```
>
> Otherwise, the Community Place browser throws an exception.
>
> You will also need to ensure that the directory \tmp exists and that the motd file exists within it. You should create a simple text file motd with any message you want inside it.

Listing 5.1 Displaying Text Read from a Local File (Motd.wrl).

```
1    #VRML V2.0 utf8
2    # Motd.wrl
3    Transform {
4        children [
5            DEF TS TouchSensor {}
6            Shape { geometry Sphere {}}
7        ]
8    }
9    DEF Motd Script {
10       url "Motd.class"
11       eventIn SFBool clicked
12   }
13   # Routing
14   ROUTE TS.isActive TO Motd.clicked
```

The VRML example is trivial. It defines a simple sphere with a **TouchSensor**. The **TouchSensor** routes its isActive field to the **Script** node, which causes the event handler class, Motd, to be executed.

Listing 5.2   Reading from the Local File System (Motd.java).

```
1    // Motd.java
2    // This program displays the contents of the Motd file.
3    import vrml.*;
4    import vrml.node.*;
5    import vrml.field.*;
6    import java.io.*;
7
8    public class Motd extends Script {
9    String myFile = "/tmp/motd"; // message of today
10        Browser b;
11        DataInputStream in;
12        String message;
13
14        public void initialize() {
15            b = getBrowser(); // to display error message
16        }
17
18        public void processEvent(Event ev){
19            File f = null;
20            // open file
21            if(ev.getName().equals("clicked")){
22                try {
23                    f = new File(myFile);
24                    in = new DataInputStream(new FileInputStream(f));
25                } catch (Exception e){
26                    b.setDescription("can not open file: " + myFile);
27                    e.printStackTrace();
28                }
29
30                // if it exists, read it
31                try {
32                    if(f.exists()){
33                        message = in.readLine();
34                        // display the message of today.
35                        b.setDescription(message);
36                    } else {
37                        b.setDescription("file doesn't exist:
                        ➥"+myFile);
38                    }
39                } catch (Exception e){
```

continues

```
40                    e.printStackTrace();
41              }
42          }
43      }
44  }
```

HOW THIS EXAMPLE WORKS

The first thing to note is that the example includes the package java.io.*, which is necessary when you want to use any file I/O.

The initialize() function sets up an instance of the Browser class. This class, introduced in the previous chapter, provides a set of methods that enable Java programs to manipulate browser-related features. In this example, we will be using the method setDescription(), which enables a program to display a textual string in the browser's window. This differs from displaying a **Text** node in the VRML scene and is purely a means for the browser to report status or error messages. In Community Place, this message is scrolled along the bottom of the screen.

In the main processEvent() method, when the clicked event is delivered from the VRML **Script** node, the program attempts to open the file and set up an input stream for reading that file (lines 23–24). Note that the attempt to open the file is bracketed by a try-catch construct—that is, any failure to open the file will be caught at line 25.

EXCEPTIONS AND THE VRML JAVA API

As a Java programmer, you're no doubt aware of the exception model in Java. Certain calls are capable of generating an error—throwing an exception—and need to be treated with care. Generally, these calls are bracketed by a try-catch construct that says, "try this call." If it throws an exception, catch it and do something about it.

The VRML Java API classes are no exception to this model, and many of the method calls are capable of generating exceptions. When you're using classes from the VRML-related packages (vrml, vrml.field, and vrml.node), you have to be aware of any potential exceptions and arrange to catch them.

Appendix B, "Java Classes for VRML 2.0," gives full details on which methods can throw which exceptions.

To return to the example, assuming that the attempt to open the file doesn't fail, the code at line 32 reads the first line of the file with the readline() call and then uses the method setDescription() on the Browser class to write a message to the browser screen. In Community Place, this results in the message of the day being displayed as scrolling text across the bottom of the screen.

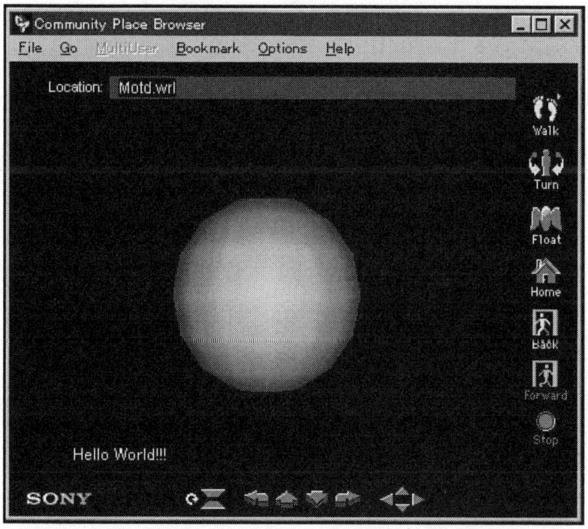

FIGURE 5.1
The message of the day is scrolled in the browser window.

Although this example is simple, it shows the basis needed for any interaction between the VRML world and the real world. There are many places where the ability to read and write files is necessary to build more complex VRML scenes. For example, being able to read files enables you to read in new VRML data from your hard disk and dynamically add it to the scene you're viewing. Alternatively, being able to write files enables you store the result of changes caused by user actions within the VRML scene.

As a concrete instance of this type of functionality, the following example extends the basic read and write capability to enable you to dynamically read the contents of your hard disk and display its structure.

DIRECTORY BROWSER EXAMPLE

As a VRML user, you know that using 3D graphics to present complex data is one of the most efficient ways of conveying such information. Data visualization is seen in a variety of applications, presentation graphics, financial and scientific data visualization, and computer-aided design. In recent years, with the growth of the World Wide Web, there has been a trend toward visualization of more mundane data.

Simple presentations of data on Web pages—directory listings, 2D graphics, or even simple 3D graphics—have become commonplace. In that context, there has been an unexpected growth in the number of ways Web browsers are used. Not only are they being used to display preformatted data pages, but they are being employed to display automatically generated directory and file listings. Traditional file management facilities for local disks are increasingly being merged into this model, so that the distinction between what's out there on the Web and what's on your local disk is becoming blurred.

Although the current trend is to use a 2D HTML browser to visualize the local disk, this example uses VRML to provide a simple visualization of the local disk structure. It's designed to enable users to interactively browse their local disks. Files and directories are represented with 3D entities, a directory is shown as a sphere, and files within a directory are shown as cubes. Selecting a directory object explodes the next level as a set of 3D objects. Entity size and color give an indication of file size. Each entity, when the mouse is left over the entity, displays the name of the file or directory in scrolling text that appears along the bottom of the browser. What's more, certain files can also be selected and viewed in a 2D browser.

The code shown in listing 5.3 consists of a simple VRML file that generates the Start directory as well as a more complex Java program that enables you to recursively descend into your hard disk directories and display their contents in a 3D form.

Because the display metaphor for the directory structure is truly 3D, line 3 sets the navigation mode of the browser to FLY. This mode enables users to navigate in three axes and doesn't force them to stay on the ground plane.

The example works by dynamically generating new VRML nodes based on the directory structure on the disk. These VRML nodes are then added to the existing VRML scene.

A **Switch** node with one child is defined at line 15. This node is the root of the 3D representation of the directory; the node is also the point in the VRML scene that the Java code will begin adding new VRML entities to represent the directories on the disk.

Within the **Script** node, there are three fields that are updated as the scene is dynamically built. The SFNode field dirnode holds a reference to the node where new VRML should be added. As the user descends into directories, new VRML is added to the scene, beginning at the ROOT transform. Each time VRML is added, the field is updated to point to the latest transform added. The SFNode field, swnode, contains a reference to a **Switch** node. Again, this is initialized to the top level **Switch**, and as VRML is added to the scene, this refers to the latest **Switch**, which is chosen as the insertion point. The last field is an SFString field, dirname, which holds the name of the currently active directory—that is, the directory that is being viewed at this point in time.

Listing 5.3   A 3D Directory Browser (DirBrowser.wrl).

```
1    #VRML V2.0 utf8
2    Viewpoint { position 20 0 3 orientation 0 1 0 1.0 }
3    NavigationInfo { type "FLY" }
4    Transform {
5       children [
6          Transform {
7             children [
8                DEF TS TouchSensor {}
9                Shape {
10                  appearance Appearance { material Material
                    ➥{diffuseColor 1 0 0 }}
11                     geometry Sphere { radius 1}
12                }
13             ]
14          }
15          DEF SW Switch {
16             whichChoice 0
17                choice [
18                   DEF ROOT Transform { translation 0 0 -10 }
19                ]
20          }
21       ]
22    }
23
24    DEF DirBrowser Script {
25       url "DirBrowser.class"
26       eventIn  SFBool   clicked
27       field SFNode dirnode USE ROOT
28       field SFNode swnode USE SW
29       field SFString dirname "/tmp" # this is the directory to
         ➥open
30    }
31    ROUTE TS.isActive TO DirBrowser.clicked
```

The directory browser Java program in listing 5.4 is quite long. Most of its length comes not through complexity but through the need to generate VRML dynamically based on the directory structure, which is then added to the scene.

As shown in listing 5.4, the overall structure of the program is as follows: lines 23–108 are string definitions that describe VRML.

When the scene is loaded, a simple sphere is created to represent the root directory—in this case, /tmp as defined by line 29 of listing 5.3. When the user clicks on this sphere, the event causes the openDirectory() method to be called. This method reads the list of files in the directory (line 152) and then uses this information to create a set of VRML entities, one for each file or directory. These entities are arranged in a spherical order whose size depends on the number of files in the directory. Lines 169–179 are responsible for determining the radius of the spherical display.

The program then has to create the VRML entities for each file and directory that it wants to display. This happens in lines 181–230. The VRML that represents the new entities to be added to the scene are built as a large string. This string is then used as a parameter to the createVrmlFromString() method call at line 235. This method tells the browser to use the string as a piece of VRML and to create the corresponding set of VRML nodes. These nodes are then added to the VRML scene at line 237 by adding them as children nodes at the current insert point.

Listing 5.4   Java Code to Dynamically Create VRML (DirBrowser.java).

```
1    // DirBrowser.java
2    // simple 3D directory browser
3    import vrml.*;
4    import vrml.node.*;
5    import vrml.field.*;
6
7    import java.io.*;
8
9    public class DirBrowser extends Script {
10       private Browser b;                    // to display error
         ➥message
11       private File dir;
12       private SFString dirname;
13       private MFNode addChildren = null;    // to add sub
         ➥directory/files
14       private SFInt32 whichChoice = null;   // to show/hide
         ➥sub directory
15
16       public final static int NOTOPENED = 0;
```

continues

Listing 5.4, CONTINUED.

```
17      public final static int OPENED = 1;
18      public final static int HIDE = 2;
19      private int opened = NOTOPENED;
20
21      public final static float FILESIZE = 1000.0f; // 1K byte
22
23      final String HEADER =  "#VRML V2.0 utf8\n";
24      final String ROOT1R =  "Transform { \n" +
25                          "   children [ \n" +
26                          "       Transform { translation 0 0 5
                            ➥\n" +
27                          "         children [ \n" +
28                          "          Shape { \n " +
29                          "           appearance DEF MAT
                            ➥Appearance{ \n" +
30                          "               material Material{
                            ➥\n" +
31                          "               diffuseColor 0.4
                            ➥0.4 0.8 \n" +
32                          "               ➥emissiveColor 0.1
                            0.1 0.4 \n" +
33                          "               transparency  0.5
                            ➥\n" +
34                          "               } \n" +
35                          "             } \n" +
36                          "           geometry Box { size 0.2
                            ➥0.2 10.0 }}] \n" +
37                          "       } \n" +
38                          "       Transform { \n" +
39                          "         rotation 1 0 0 1.57 \n" +
40                          "         children [ \n " +
41                          "          Shape { \n " +
42                          "           appearance USE MAT \n" +
43                          "           geometry Cylinder {
                            ➥radius ";
44      final String ROOT2E =
                            ➥" height 0.01 } }\n" +
45                          "             ] \n" +
46                          "       }\n";
47
```

```
48      final String TAILER1R = "   ]\n";
49      final String TAILER2E = "}\n";
50
51      final String ROUTING1T = "ROUTE ";
52      final String ROUTING2S =            ".isActive TO ";
53      final String ROUTING3E =
        ➥".clicked \n";
54
55      final String DIROBJ1XY = "Transform { \n translation ";
56      final String DIROBJ2U =
                                ➥" 0 \n" +
57                              "    children [ \n" +
58                              "      Transform { \n" +
59                              "        children [ \n" +
60                              "          Anchor { \n" +
61                              "            url \"";
62      final String DIROBJ3T =                    "\" \n" +
63                              "            children [ \n" +
64                              "              DEF ";
65      final String DIROBJ4S =                 " TouchSensor
                                               ➥{} \n" +
66                              "               Shape { geometry
                                               ➥Sphere {}} \n" +
67                              "            ] \n" +
68                              "          } \n" +
69                              "        ] \n" +
70                              "      } \n" +
71                              "    DEF SW Switch {\n" +
72                              "      whichChoice 0 \n" +
73                              "      choice [\n" +
74                              "        DEF DIR Transform {
                                          ➥translation 0 0 -10 }
                                          ➥\n" +
75                              "      ] \n" +
76                              "    } \n" +
77                              "  ] \n" +
78                              "} \n" +
79                              "DEF ";
80      final String DIROBJ5F =        " Script { \n" +
81                              "  url \"DirBrowser.class\" \n" +
82                              "  eventIn SFBool   clicked \n" +
```

continues

Listing 5.4, CONTINUED.

```
83                          "    field SFNode dirnode USE DIR \n" +
84                          "    field SFNode swnode USE SW \n" +
85                          "    field SFString dirname \"";
86     final String DIROBJ6E =
       ➥"\" \n" +
87                              "} \n";
88
89     final String FILEOBJ1XYZ = "Transform { \n" +
90                          "    translation ";
91     final String FILEOBJ2U =   "    children [ \n" +
92                          "        Anchor { \n" +
93                          "            url \"";
94     final String FILEOBJ3H =               "\"" +
95                          "            children [ \n" +
96                          "              Shape { \n" +
97                          "                appearance
                                              ➥Appearance { \n" +
98                          "                  material
                                              ➥Material { \n" +
99                          "                    diffuseColor 1
                                                ➥1 0 \n" +
100                         "                  } \n" +
101                         "                } \n" +
102                         "                geometry Box { size
                                            ➥2.0 2.0 ";
103     final String FILEOBJ4E =
        ➥"}\n" +
104                         "              } \n" +
105                         "            ] \n" +
106                         "        } \n" +
107                         "    ] \n" +
108                         "}\n";
109
110     public void initialize() {
111        Node tmpnode;
112
113        b = getBrowser();
114
```

```
115        dirname = (SFString) getField("dirname");
116
117        // to add sub directory/files
118        tmpnode =
           ➥(Node)((SFNode)getField("dirnode")).getValue();
119        addChildren =
           ➥(MFNode)tmpnode.getEventIn("addChildren");
120
121        // to show/hide sub directory
122        tmpnode =
           ➥(Node)((SFNode)getField("swnode")).getValue();
123        whichChoice =
           ➥(SFInt32)tmpnode.getExposedField("whichChoice");
124    }
125
126    public void processEvent(Event ev){
127        if(ev.getName().equals("clicked")){
128            ConstSFBool v = (ConstSFBool)ev.getValue();
129
130            if(false == v.getValue()){
131                if(NOTOPENED == opened){
132                    openDirectory(dirname.getValue());
133                    opened = OPENED;
134                } else if(OPENED == opened){
135                    whichChoice.setValue(-1);
136                    opened = HIDE;
137                } else if (HIDE == opened) {
138                    whichChoice.setValue(0);
139                    opened = OPENED;
140                }
141            }
142        }
143    }
144
145    public void openDirectory(String directory){
146        String[] files;
147        int numfiles;
148        float angle;
149        float radius;
150
151        try {
152            dir = new File(directory);
```

continues

Listing 5.4, CONTINUED.

```
153        }catch (Exception e){
154            b.setDescription("Can not open " + directory);
155            e.printStackTrace();
156            return;
157        }
158
159        if(false == dir.isDirectory()){
160            b.setDescription("No such a directory: " +
               ➥directory);
161            return;
162        }
163
164        files = dir.list();
165        numfiles = files.length;
166
167        if(0 == numfiles) return;
168
169        if(2 < numfiles) {
170            angle = (float)(Math.PI * 2/numfiles);
171            radius = (float)(6.0/(2.0 * Math.sin(angle)));
172        } else if(2 == numfiles) {
173            angle = (float) Math.PI;
174            radius = 2.0f;
175        } else {
176            // if there is one file or directory ...
177            angle = 0.0f;
178            radius = 0.1f;
179        }
180
181        String vrmldir = HEADER + ROOT1R + radius + ROOT2E;
182        String routing = "";
183
184        for(int i = 0; i < numfiles; i++){
185            File f = null;
186            String filename = null;
187            float x, y;
188
189            if(0.0f != angle){
190                x = (float)(radius * Math.sin(angle * i));
191                y = (float)(radius * Math.cos(angle * i));
192            } else {
```

```
193                x = y = 0.0f;
194            }
195
196        try {
197            filename = directory + "/" + files[i];
198            f = new File(filename);
199
200            if(f.isDirectory()){
201                String touchsenor = "TS" + filename;
202                String script = "SC" + filename;
203
204                vrmldir = vrmldir + DIROBJ1XY + x + " " + y +
205                                    DIROBJ2U + filename +
206                                    DIROBJ3T + touchsenor +
207                                    DIROBJ4S + script +
208                                    DIROBJ5F + filename +
209                                    DIROBJ6E;
210
211                routing += ROUTING1T + touchsenor +
212                           ROUTING2S + script +
213                           ROUTING3E;
214            } else {
215                float height = (float)(f.length()/FILESIZE);
216
217                if(height < 0.000001f) height = 0.1f;
218
219                vrmldir += FILEOBJ1XYZ + x + " " + y + " " +
220            ➡(-(height/2.0)) + "\n" +
221                           FILEOBJ2U + filename +
                           FILEOBJ3H + (height) +
222                           FILEOBJ4E;
223            }
224        } catch (Exception e) {
225            b.setDescription("Can not open " + filename);
226            e.printStackTrace();
227            return;
228        }
229        }
230        vrmldir = vrmldir + TAILER1R + routing + TAILER2E;
231        // System.out.println(vrmldir);
232
233        // create VRML objects and add them to the scene
```

continues

Listing 5.4, CONTINUED.

```
234        try {
235            BaseNode nodes[] = b.createVrmlFromString(vrmldir);
236            if(null != nodes) {
237                addChildren.setValue(nodes);
238            }
239        } catch (Exception e) {
240            b.setDescription("can not create VRML node");
241            e.printStackTrace() ;
242        }
243    }
244  }
```

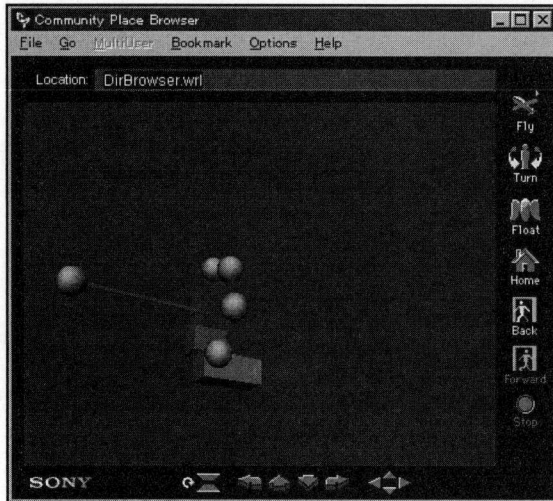

FIGURE 5.2

Browsing the initial directory.

In the following two figures, you can see shots of the 3D directory scene as it's explored. You can see in figure 5.2 how the Start directory, shown as a sphere on the left of the browser window, has been opened to show a set of subdirectories and files. Extending from the start directory sphere is a "subdirectory" marker line that opens out into a set of spheres and blocks. These are arranged in a circular pattern. Each sphere represents another subdirectory, which when clicked will display its contents. Each block represents a file. The size of the file is indicated by the length of the block. From figure 5.2 you can see that the start directory, tmp, has four subdirectories and three files. In figure 5.3, the user has descended two levels in the directory structure into the directory /tmp/Cop/doc. Again, you can see how the selected directory sphere has been visualized. In this case, the directory "doc" contains five files and seven subdirectories.

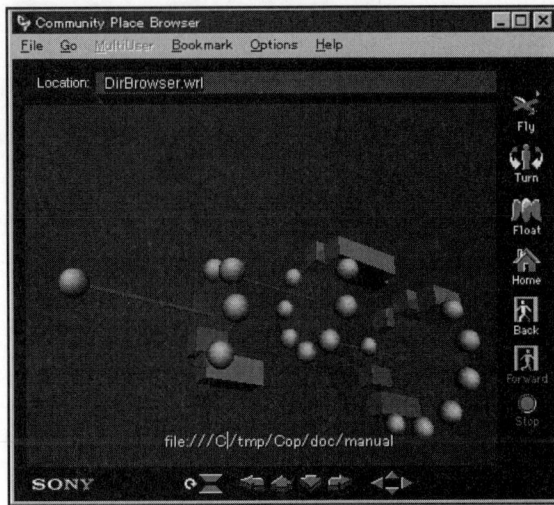

FIGURE 5.3

Descending deeper into the directory structure

You should also note how the file name is displayed in the scrolling text across the bottom of the browser window.

Last, figure 5.4 shows the user selecting an HTML file in the 3D browser window, the contents of which are then displayed in the associated HTML browser which can be seen, slightly obscured, behind the VRML browser window.

To enable you to understand how the VRML is dynamically created for each directory, the structure is shown in figure 5.5.

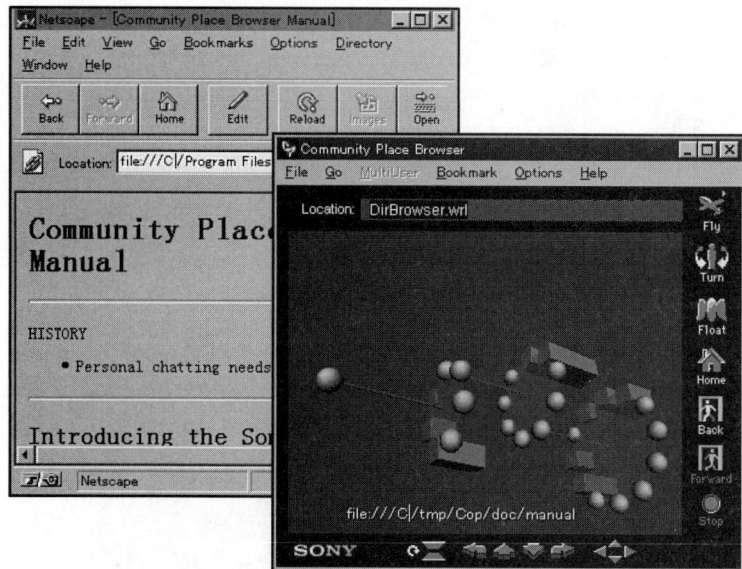

FIGURE 5.4

Viewing an HTML file from the 3D directory browser.

For each directory five parts are needed, including a HEADER part, which is the VRML 2.0 header string, and a ROOT part, which is the transform and child that shows the cone from the source directory to its files. Then a series of DIROBJs or FILEOBJs are added, one for each file or directory. Last, a ROUTE section is added and a TAILER section.

If you look at listing 5.4, you'll see that each section has a set of predefined versions—each named according to its type. For example, at line 24, ROOT1R defines a ROOT section, whereas line 65 defines a DIROBJ.

The Java code at lines 181–230 uses these predefined "chunks" of VRML to create the correct VRML for the directory currently being viewed.

HEADER	#VRML V2.0 utf8
ROOT	Transform { Children [
FILEOBJ	file object
DIROBJ	directory object
FILEOBJ	file object
	•••
TAILER	]
ROUTE	routing information
	}

FILEOBJ

DIROBJ

FIGURE 5.5

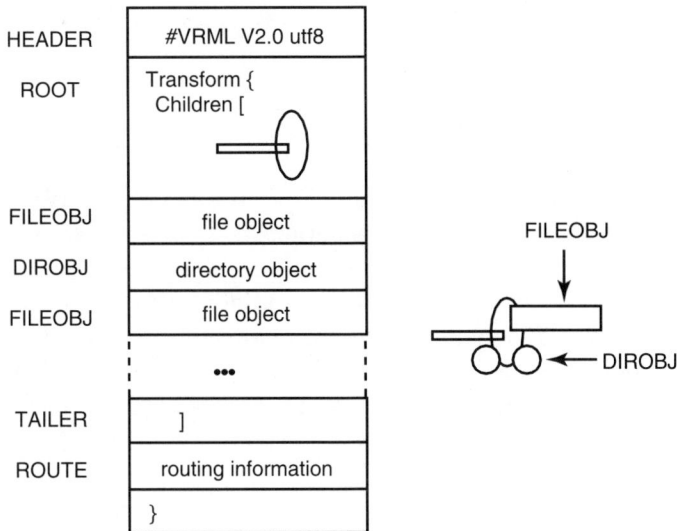

The structure of the dynamically created VRML.

This example shows several important features:

➤ Dynamically creating VRML

➤ Use of the createVrmlFromString() method of the browser

➤ Dynamically adding VRML nodes to a scene

However, the example is quite simplistic and can be improved in a number of ways. These include better use of 3D entities to describe objects and use of text nodes to name files and directories within the scene. However, the place where the example would most benefit from extra work is in the layout policy for the 3D scene.

An interesting extension to this code might be to experiment with different layout policies and possibly to offer users the choice of how they'd like the data laid out in the 3D scene. One possibility for this is to move away from the current approach and use a cityscape model. Directories are represented by buildings; entering a building would be like descending into the directory within which may be other buildings or rooms.

USING THE JAVA WINDOW SYSTEM (AWT)

Java supports its own windowing system, the Abstract Windowing Toolkit (AWT), to allow user interaction via a graphical user interface (GUI). In Java, there are two ways to use AWT as part of a Java program: as part of an applet or as part of a stand-alone application. Using applets provides a high-level interface to AWT functionality whereas writing stand-alone applications that use AWT requires that the programmer take care of handling window-related events. The Community Place browser uses the same mechanism as a Java application, and you need to be aware of events relating to AWT windows.

The following example presents a simple introduction to using AWT and VRML. The goal is to create a VRML version of "Ali Baba and the Forty Thieves" from the book *Arabian Nights*. Within the VRML scene, there is a door that, as you approach, queries you for a magic password. If you type the correct password, it opens; otherwise it remains closed.

SIMPLE WINDOWING EXAMPLE (OPEN SESAME!)

This example consists of three files: OpenSesame.wrl, which defines the basic scene, and two Java programs, OpenSesame.java and OpenDialog.java, which control the door opening and the dialog box.

THE VRML SCENE

Listing 5.5   Using an AWT Window (OpenSesame.wrl).

```
1   #VRML V2.0 utf8
2   Transform {
3      translation -2.5 0 0
4      children [
5         DEF POLE Shape {
6            appearance Appearance {
7               material DEF SphereColor Material {
8                  diffuseColor 0.6 0.8 0.6
```

```
 9                  }
10                }
11              geometry Cylinder { radius 0.5 height 5 }
12          }
13        ]
14    }
15    Transform {
16        translation 2.5 0 0
17        children [ USE POLE ]
18    }
19    DEF DOOR Transform {
20        children [
21            DEF PS ProximitySensor { size 7 5 12 }
22            Shape {
23                appearance Appearance {
24                    material DEF SphereColor Material {
25                        diffuseColor 0.5 0.5 0.7
26                    }
27                }
28                geometry Box { size 5 4 0.3}
29            }
30        ]
31    }
32    DEF OpenSesame Script {
33        url "OpenSesame.class"
34        eventIn SFBool entered
35        eventOut SFTime startTime
36    }
37    DEF TIME TimeSensor {
38        cycleInterval 30
39        stopTime 1
40        loop TRUE
41    }
42    DEF POSITION PositionInterpolator {
43        key [0 1]
44        keyValue [ 0 0 0, 5 0 0 ]
45    }
46    # Routing
47    ROUTE PS.isActive TO OpenSesame.entered
48    ROUTE OpenSesame.startTime TO TIME.startTime
49    ROUTE TIME.fraction_changed TO POSITION.set_fraction
50    ROUTE POSITION.value_changed TO DOOR.set_translation
51    ROUTE PS.exitTime TO TIME.stopTime
```

Again, this is a simple VRML file designed to give the basics of the scene. The key features are the door, which is defined from line 19 and contains a **ProximitySensor**, a **Script** node at line 32, and the door animation mechanism, which uses a **TimeSensor** and **Interpolator** at lines 37 and 42 respectively. The **ProximitySensor** is used as discussed in Chapter 4: as the user approaches the door, the **ProximitySensor** fires and sends its isActive event to the **Script** node. The **Script** node prompts the user for a password and then—if it is correct—sends a time event to the **Script** node. The **Script** node uses the time event to activate the **TimeSensor**, which generates the key values for the **PositionInterpolator**.

THE JAVA PROGRAM

The Java code for this example is separated into two class files. The first file (listing 5.6) is the event handler class, which initializes the dialog box and, in response to the user approaching the door, shows and hides the dialog box. The second class (listing 5.7) is responsible for managing the dialog box and for checking the password.

Listing 5.6   Using User Input to Change the Scene (OpenSesame.java).

```
1     // OpenSesame.java
2     // pop up dialog and open the door
3     import vrml.*;
4     import vrml.node.*;
5     import vrml.field.*;
6
7     import java.util.*;
8
9     public class OpenSesame extends Script {
10        OpenDialog myDialog;
11        SFTime startTime = null;
12        Date date = null;
13
14        public void initialize(){
15            myDialog = new OpenDialog(this);
16            startTime = (SFTime)getEventOut("startTime");
17            date = new Date();
```

```
18          }
19
20          public void processEvent(Event ev){
21              if(ev.getName().equals("entered")){
22                  ConstSFBool v = (ConstSFBool)ev.getValue();
23                  if(v.getValue()){
24                      myDialog.show();
25                  } else {
26                      myDialog.hide();
27                  }
28              }
29          }
30
31          public void openDoor(){
32            startTime.
33                      setValue((double)((date.getTime()/1000.0)+1.0));
34          }
35      }
```

Listing 5.6 shows the code of the event handler class for the **Script** node. Its initialization function is used to create an instance of the actual dialog box—a separate class that actually prompts the user and checks to see whether the reply is correct.

When the isActive event is received from the **ProximitySensor** in the VRML scene, the processEvent() method is called. This method simply calls the show() and hide() methods of the openDialog class—a subclass of frame—to show or hide the dialog box.

Listing 5.7 shows the code for the OpenDialog class, which displays the dialog box, prompts for user input, and if it's correct, calls back into the OpenSesame class (listing 5.6) to initiate the door opening sequence.

Listing 5.7   Managing an AWT Window (OpenDialog.java).

```
1    // OpenDialog.java
2    // pop up dialog and check user's input
3    import java.awt.*;
4
```

continues

Listing 5.7, CONTINUED.

```
5    public class OpenDialog extends Frame {
6       OpenSesame opensesame;
7       public final static String MAGICSPELL = "open sesame";
8       TextField passwd = null;
9
10       OpenDialog(OpenSesame owner){
11          super(MAGICSPELL); // Title name is the magic spell
12          setLayout(new FlowLayout());
13          add(new Label("Magic Spell?"));
14          passwd = new TextField(20);
15          passwd.setEchoCharacter('*'); // hides the real input
             ➥text
16          add(passwd);
17          pack();
18          opensesame = owner;
19       }
20
21       public boolean handleEvent(Event e){
22          switch(e.id){
23             case e.ACTION_EVENT:
24                if(passwd == e.target){
25                   if(((String)e.arg).equals(MAGICSPELL)){
26                      opensesame.openDoor();
27                      this.hide();
28                      return true;
29                   }
30                   passwd.setText("");
31                   return true;
32                }
33             break;
34          default:
35             break;
36          }
37          return false;
38       }
39    }
40
```

HOW THIS EXAMPLE WORKS

User input to the dialog box triggers execution at line 21 by delivering a window event to the method handleEvent. This method then checks to see whether the user input equals the predefined password (line 25). If it does, the openDoor method is called in the OpenSesame class at line 31 (listing 5.6), which sets the startTime in the **Script** node and causes the interpolator to run.

Be careful not to confuse the handleEvent method at line 21 with the processEvent method in OpenSesame.java. The handleEvent method deals with AWT events, not VRML events, and is waiting for user input.

However, it is interesting to note that the AWT library, like VRML, uses an event-based model.

> **NOTE**
>
> The use of AWT windowing and VRML requires the application programmer to take full responsibility for the AWT windows. One of the strengths of the relationship between VRML and Java is that Java is separated from the VRML scene and communicates actions only via the **Script** node. Although this gives the Java programmer great flexibility, it brings with it a certain degree of responsibility. In particular, because the browser is unaware of the AWT windows created by the Java programs, it can't be responsible for their management. Generally, this isn't an issue. However, one of the advanced features of Community Place brings problems to light.
>
> Community Place caches scenes and tries to maintain the scenes within the browser. When you load a new scene, usually the old scene is cached, and you can quickly switch back to it by using the back and forward feature of the GUI. This saves the scene load time when switching between scenes. In a complex CyberSpace that consists of several related—but separate—scenes, with anchors to enable you to move between them, this scene caching allows rapid scene change.
>
> Suppose that scene A is loaded and displays a dialog box. Assume the user then loads scene B. The browser caches the A scene and displays the B scene. However, the dialog box displayed by scene A will remain on the screen because nobody has told the script of the A scene that the scene has changed.
>
> *continues*

CONTINUED

To avoid this problem, the scene creator needs to check whether the browser has loaded a new scene. One way to achieve this is mentioned in Chapter 4 in the discussion of the uses of the **ProximitySensor**. This sensor, if set up with a size field as large as the scene, enables you to sense the user's position in the scene. If the user is no longer in the scene—that is, the isActive field becomes FALSE—you know that the user has stopped viewing that scene.

This mechanism is used, albeit in a different way, at line 26 of the OpenSesame.java (listing 5.6) program. The code is checking to see whether the user has moved away from the door. If so, the dialog box is removed. This technique should also be used in conjunction with a larger **ProximitySensor** to check whether the user has left the scene.

Remember that the special method shutDown() is called when a **Script** node is deleted—that is, when the browser no longer holds the VRML scene. You can use this method to destroy AWT windows associated with a VRML scene. To do that, call the dispose() method on the Frame class within your shutDown() method.

USING AWT TO BUILD A SIMPLE REAL-TIME VRML MANIPULATOR

The next example builds on the ideas shown in the previous example to build a simple real-time VRML manipulator. The goal is to use an AWT window to directly manipulate some aspects of the VRML scene. The example we chose enables a scene developer to create a VRML object and then manipulate its appearance properties (that is, its color via the AWT window).

This simple tool enables the scene developer to dynamically manipulate the scene and so enables him to play around with scene properties as he builds the VRML file. You can think of it as a post-processing tool. After the scene has been modeled in a VRML authoring tool, it's loaded into a VRML browser and aspects of it are fine-tuned.

VRML

The VRML scene loaded is quite simple and consists of a cone with an interpolator that constantly rotates the cone.

Listing 5.8   Manipulating VRML Fields Using an AWT
Window (ColorTester.wrl).

```
1    #VRML V2.0 utf8
2    DEF PS ProximitySensor { size 1000 1000 1000 }
3    DEF OBJ Transform {
4       children [
5          Shape{
6          appearance Appearance{material DEF TARGET Material{}}
7          geometry Cone{}
8             }
9          ]
10   }
11   DEF ColorTester Script{
12      url "ColorTester.class"
13      eventIn SFBool entered
14      field SFNode target USE TARGET
15   }
16   ROUTE PS.isActive TO ColorTester.entered
17   DEF TIME TimeSensor{
18      cycleInterval 13
19      loop TRUE
20      stopTime -1
21   }
22   DEF OI OrientationInterpolator{
23      key [0, 0.5, 1]
24      keyValue [0 1 1 0, 0 1 1 3.14, 0 1 1 6.24]
25   }
26   ROUTE TIME.fraction_changed TO OI.set_fraction
27   ROUTE OI.value_changed TO OBJ.set_rotation
```

Because the scene contains a **ProximitySensor** with a large size, the **ProximitySensor** generates the isActive event as soon as the scene is loaded.

The key aspect of this VRML is the USE of the cone entity, named TARGET, in the **Script** node. This provides the reference that is passed to the event handler class, which is shown in listing 5.9.

THE JAVA PROGRAMS
As in the previous example, there are two Java programs for this example. The first is the event handler class that is responsible for

reading the current status of the target object—in this case the Cone—and for setting the values. The second is the manager for the color panel.

The initialization method gets the reference to the target object and stores it in the variable, target. It then initializes the color manager panel at line 16. After this, it queries each of the appearance fields of the target entity and stores these in local variables.

Listing 5.9   Reading and Writing the Color Fields (ColorTester.java).

```
1    // ColorTester.java
2    import vrml.*;
3    import vrml.node.*;
4    import vrml.field.*;
5
6    public class ColorTester extends Script{
7       ColorPanel panel;
8
9       SFFloat a_field, s_field, t_field;
10       SFColor dc_field, ec_field, sc_field;
11
12       public void initialize(){
13          // get the reference to the target node.
14          Node target = (Node)((SFNode)getField
          ➥("target")).getValue();
15
16          panel = new ColorPanel(this);          // start the
                                                  ➥panel.
17
18          // get the references to exposed fields, event-in/outs.
19          a_field = (SFFloat)target.getExposedField
          ➥("ambientIntensity");
20          dc_field = (SFColor)target.getExposedField
          ➥("diffuseColor");
21          ec_field = (SFColor)target.getExposedField
          ➥("emissiveColor");
22          s_field = (SFFloat)target.getExposedField("shininess");
23          sc_field = (SFColor)target.getExposedField
          ➥("specularColor");
24          t_field = (SFFloat)target.getExposedField
          ➥("transparency");
25       }
```

```
26
27      public void processEvent(Event ev){
28         if(ev.getName().equals("entered")){
29            ConstSFBool v = (ConstSFBool)ev.getValue();
30
31            if(v.getValue()){ panel.map(); }
32            else { panel.hide(); }
33         }
34      }
35
36      public void shutdown(){ panel.dispose(); }
37
38          public float get_ambientIntensity(){
               ➥return(a_field.getValue()); }
39      public void set_ambientIntensity(float val){
        ➥a_field.setValue(val); }
40
41      public void get_diffuseColor(float[] rgb){
        ➥dc_field.getValue(rgb); }
42      public void set_diffuseColor(float[] val){
        ➥dc_field.setValue(val); }
43
44      public void get_emissiveColor(float[] rgb){
        ➥ec_field.getValue(rgb); }
45      public void set_emissiveColor(float[] val){
        ➥ec_field.setValue(val); }
46
47      public float get_shininess(){ return(s_field.getValue()); }
48      public void set_shininess(float val){
        ➥s_field.setValue(val); }
49
50      public void get_specularColor(float[] rgb){ sc_field.
        ➥getValue(rgb); }
51      public void set_specularColor(float[] val){ sc_field.
        ➥setValue(val); }
52
53      public float get_transparency(){
        ➥return(t_field.getValue()); }
54      public void set_transparency(float val){
        ➥t_field.setValue(val); }
55   }
```

Once initialized, the code waits for the first event, which is the isActive event generated by the **ProximitySensor** when the scene is loaded. This event causes the AWT panel to be displayed (or hidden) as required.

Lines 38–54 contain a set of simple methods, each one designed to get or set one of the properties of the target object. These methods are called from the panel manager, which is shown in listing 5.10.

The color panel manager is responsible for managing the AWT window and responding to the values typed by the user.

The class constructor (line 16) creates a new panel and adds a set of text fields for each of the appearance properties of the target object (diffuseColor, specularColor, and so on). The panel is not actually displayed at this point; the show and hide methods are called from the event handler class (listing 5.9) when the scene is loaded.

The AWT window event handler method (line 67) is called whenever the user types input into one of the fields of the color panel. Depending on the field, the event handler method calls a routine that reads the current values in the panel fields and uses them to call back into the event handler class (listing 5.9) to set the correct fields in the VRML scene.

When the user changes one of the R, G, or B color values of the diffuse color, for example, the AWT event handler is called at line 67, which determines that the field being manipulated was associated with the diffuse color property, and at line 69 calls the set_diffuseColor() method. This method (line 96) uses a helper method to read the R, G, and B values from the color panel (lines 86–88) and convert them into an array of three float values and then at line 98 calls into the event handler class (listing 5.9), which writes the diffuse color field of the target in the VRML scene.

Listing 5.10   Managing the Color Change AWT Panel (ColorPanel.java).

```
1   // ColorPanel.java
2   import java.awt.*;
3   import java.util.*;
4
5   public class ColorPanel extends Frame{
6       ColorTester tester;
7       float[] rgb = new float[3];
8       float val;
9
10      TextField a_txt, s_txt, t_txt;
11      TextField dc_txt_r, dc_txt_g, dc_txt_b;
12      TextField ec_txt_r, ec_txt_g, ec_txt_b;
13      TextField sc_txt_r, sc_txt_g, sc_txt_b;
14      Panel a_panel, dc_panel, ec_panel, s_panel, sc_panel,
        ➥t_panel;
15
16      ColorPanel(ColorTester owner){
17          super("ColorPanel"); // Title name
18
19          a_panel = new Panel(); a_panel.setLayout(new
            ➥FlowLayout());
20          a_txt = new TextField(10);
21          a_panel.add(new Label("amibientIntensity"));
22          a_panel.add(a_txt);
23
24          dc_panel = new Panel(); dc_panel.setLayout(new
            ➥FlowLayout());
25          dc_txt_r = new TextField(10); dc_txt_g = new
            ➥TextField(10); dc_txt_b = new TextField(10);
26          dc_panel.add(new Label("diffuseColor"));
27          dc_panel.add(dc_txt_r); dc_panel.add(dc_txt_g);
            ➥dc_panel.add(dc_txt_b);
28
29          ec_panel = new Panel(); ec_panel.setLayout(new
            ➥FlowLayout());
30          ec_txt_r = new TextField(10); ec_txt_g = new
            ➥TextField(10); ec_txt_b = new TextField(10);
31          ec_panel.add(new Label("emissiveColor"));
32          ec_panel.add(ec_txt_r); ec_panel.add(ec_txt_g);
            ➥ec_panel.add(ec_txt_b);
```

continues

Listing 5.10, CONTINUED.

```
33
34          s_panel = new Panel();   s_panel.setLayout(new
            ➡FlowLayout());
35          s_txt = new TextField(10);
36          s_panel.add(new Label("shininess"));
37          s_panel.add(s_txt);
38
39          sc_panel = new Panel(); sc_panel.setLayout(new
            ➡FlowLayout());
40          sc_txt_r = new TextField(10); sc_txt_g = new
            ➡TextField(10); sc_txt_b = new TextField(10);
41          sc_panel.add(new Label("specularColor"));
42          sc_panel.add(sc_txt_r); sc_panel.add(sc_txt_g);
            ➡sc_panel.add(sc_txt_b);
43
44          t_panel = new Panel();   t_panel.setLayout(new
            ➡FlowLayout());
45          t_txt = new TextField(10);
46          t_panel.add(new Label("transparency"));
47          t_panel.add(t_txt);
48
49          setLayout(new GridLayout(6, 1, 1, 1));
50          add(a_panel); add(dc_panel); add(ec_panel);
            ➡add(s_panel); add(sc_panel); add(t_panel);
51          pack();
52
53          tester = owner;
54      }
55
56      public void map(){
57          a_txt.setText("" + tester.get_ambientIntensity());
58          get_diffuseColor();
59          get_emissiveColor();
60          s_txt.setText("" + tester.get_shininess());
61          get_specularColor();
62          t_txt.setText("" + tester.get_transparency());
63
64          show();
65      }
66
67      public boolean action(Event ev, Object what) {
```

```
68          if(ev.ACTION_EVENT == ev.id){
69              if(a_txt == ev.target) { set_ambientIntensity(); }
70              else if(dc_txt_r == ev.target || dc_txt_g ==
                ➥ev.target || dc_txt_b == ev.target){
                ➥set_diffuseColor();   }
71              else if(ec_txt_r == ev.target || ec_txt_g ==
                ➥ev.target || ec_txt_b == ev.target){
                ➥set_emissiveColor(); }
72              else if(s_txt == ev.target) { set_shininess(); }
73              else if(sc_txt_r == ev.target || sc_txt_g ==
                ➥ev.target || sc_txt_b == ev.target){
                ➥set_specularColor(); }
74              else if(t_txt == ev.target) { set_transparency(); }
75          }
76        return true;
77      }
78
79      void set_rgb(float[] rgb, TextField r, TextField g,
        ➥TextField b){
80          r.setText("" + rgb[0]);
81          g.setText("" + rgb[1]);
82          b.setText("" + rgb[2]);
83      }
84
85      void get_rgb(TextField r, TextField g, TextField b,
        ➥float[] rgb){
86          rgb[0] = (float)Float.
                ➥valueOf(r.getText()).doubleValue();
87          rgb[1] = (float)Float.valueOf(g.getText()).
                ➥doubleValue();
88          rgb[2] = (float)Float.valueOf(b.getText()).
                ➥doubleValue();
89      }
90
91      void set_ambientIntensity(){
92          val = (float)Float.valueOf(a_txt.getText()).
                ➥doubleValue();
93          tester.set_ambientIntensity(val);
94      }
95
96      void set_diffuseColor(){
97          get_rgb(dc_txt_r, dc_txt_g, dc_txt_b, rgb);
98          tester.set_diffuseColor(rgb);
```

continues

Listing 5.10, Continued.

```
99        }
100
101       void set_emissiveColor(){
102          get_rgb(ec_txt_r, ec_txt_g, ec_txt_b, rgb);
103          tester.set_emissiveColor(rgb);
104       }
105
106       void set_shininess(){
107          val = (float)Float.valueOf(s_txt.getText()).
             ➥doubleValue();
108          tester.set_shininess(val);
109       }
110
111       void set_specularColor(){
112          get_rgb(sc_txt_r, sc_txt_g, sc_txt_b, rgb);
113          tester.set_specularColor(rgb);
114       }
115
116       void set_transparency(){
117          val = (float)Float.valueOf(t_txt.getText()).
             ➥doubleValue();
118          tester.set_transparency(val);
119       }
120
121       public void get_diffuseColor(){
122          tester.get_diffuseColor(rgb);
123          set_rgb(rgb, dc_txt_r, dc_txt_g, dc_txt_b);
124       }
125
126       void get_emissiveColor(){
127          tester.get_emissiveColor(rgb);
128          set_rgb(rgb, ec_txt_r, ec_txt_g, ec_txt_b);
129       }
130
131       void get_specularColor(){
132          tester.get_specularColor(rgb);
133          set_rgb(rgb, sc_txt_r, sc_txt_g, sc_txt_b);
134       }
135    }
```

Figure 5.6 shows the AWT color panel and associated VRML scene. This example, although written to manipulate the appearance properties of a cone, can be used to manipulate these properties for any object in the scene. All that is necessary is that the target field in VRML **Script** node points to another object in the scene.

In addition, it would be straightforward to take this example and build an equivalent version that manipulates the geometric properties of the VRML scene entities.

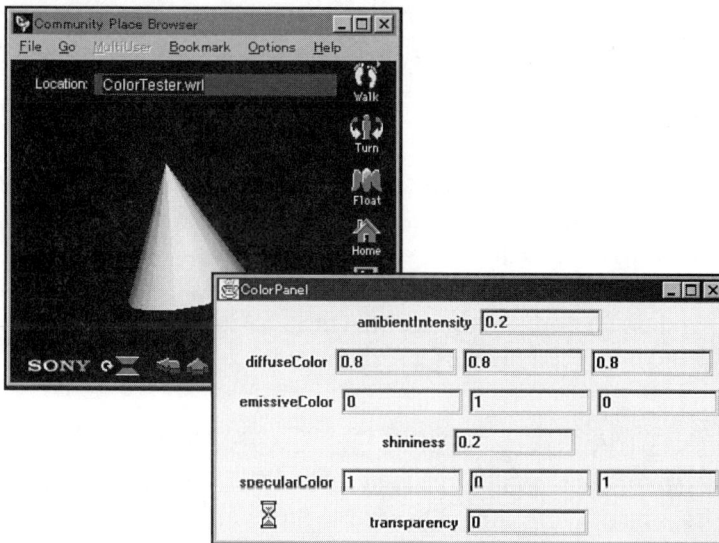

FIGURE 5.6

A simple dynamic VRML manipulation tool based on AWT.

USING NETWORKING

One of the main strengths of Java, and the reason it has gained so much attention recently, is its tight integration with the World Wide Web. This chapter finishes with a discussion of how to use the networking features of Java in conjunction with VRML.

Again, there are many possibilities for combining VRML and the World Wide Web. In much the same way as the file I/O examples, VRML can be used to visualize data—in this case, data that is remote and stored on a machine somewhere on the Internet. This can be VRML data located at a remote location, real-time data such as stock or weather data, but equally data held in a large commercial database or contained in some legacy application.

The structure for using this type of data is generic and consists of local client code that contacts a remote server to access the data and then uses VRML to display the results. If this is done continuously, it's easy to build such examples as real-time 3D stock data display or continuous tracking of aircraft movement.

This book began by discussing some of the driving forces behind the development of VRML and how the vision of CyberSpace, a shared 3D environment, has been a major motivation for its evolution.

The next example lays the foundation for a simple multiuser shared VRML world. It begins by building the client and server side code that will enable a client to send its position to a server and that will allow the server to use that position information to update an entity in the scene. These basic mechanisms will be used later for a multiuser server.

NETWORK ACCESS CONTROL

Network access, like local file access, is also part of the security regime of Community Place (and Sun's AppletViewer). Network security is handled in the same way as other security issues and is controlled via an ACL field in the security properties file.

The ACL in question is the appletviewer.security.mode and can be set with the following three keywords:

➤ **Unrestricted.** There is no limitation to network access from Java code associated with the VRML contents. The Java code can open network connections to any valid Internet host.

➤ **None.** No network access is allowed. Any attempt to open connections to other hosts will throw an exception.

➤ **Host** or **unspecified.** Provides limited network access by enabling the Java code to open connections to the network host from which the VRML file has been loaded. It enables a scene author to serve a VRML scene and have any associated Java code call back to the server machine.

These restrictions apply only if the VRML file is loaded from the network. If the file is loaded from the local scene, these settings are ignored and a default policy of unrestricted access is applied.

For the following examples, we will assume you are using the local disk. If not, add the following line to the properties file:

```
applet.viewer.security.mode=unrestricted
```

SIMPLE NETWORKING EXAMPLE (ROAD MIRAGE)

The first example is designed to show the basics of client-server Java networking and how server data can be sent to the client and used to manipulate the VRML scene.

The example is based on a simple road mirage. Often, when driving on long straight roads on hot days, you'll see what appears to be water on the road ahead. As you approach it, it seems to recede—always keeping the same distance. This phenomenon is actually a result of the heated air above the road ahead and caused by light being diffracted at different angles from different air densities. This example does not attempt anything as complicated as air diffraction calculations, but it does use a simple server to track the user's position and move a mirage object—in our case, the ubiquitous sphere—backward as we approach it.

THE POSITION SERVER

The Server program (listing 5.11) is a stand-alone Java application. Of course, you could write this server in any computer language (for example, C), but because Java's networking libraries are so powerful, it's simple to do it in Java.

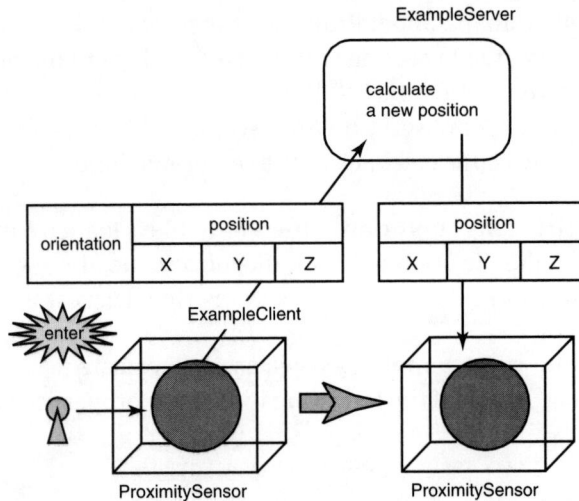

FIGURE 5.7

The architecture of "Road Mirage" VRML contents.

Listing 5.11   A Remote Server (ExampleServer.java).

```
1    // ExampleServer.java
2    // Simple Server Application
3    import java.net.*;
4    import java.io.*;
5    import java.util.*;
6
7    class ExampleServer{
8        public final static int PORT = 4130;
9
10       public static void main(String[] args){
11           ServerSocket server_socket = null;
12           Socket client_socket = null;
13           DataInputStream in = null;
14           DataOutputStream out = null;
15           float x = 0.0f, y = 0.0f, z = 0.0f, r = 0.0f;
16
17           System.out.println("Start server: " + PORT);
18
19           // open socket on PORT
20           try{
21               server_socket = new ServerSocket(PORT);
22           } catch(IOException e){
23               System.out.println("Could not create socket on: " +
```

```
24                                    PORT + ", " + e);
25                 System.exit(1);
26          }
27          System.out.println("Socket created: " + PORT);
28          System.out.println("Waiting for client...");
29
30          // accept client's request
31          try{
32              client_socket = server_socket.accept();
33          } catch(IOException e) {
34              System.out.println("Accept error: " + PORT + ", " + e);
35              System.exit(1);
36          }
37
38          System.out.println("Connection established: "
39                              + client_socket.getInetAddress());
40          System.out.println("Open input/output stream...");
41          try{
42
43              in = new DataInputStream(
44                          client_socket.getInputStream());
45              out = new DataOutputStream(
46                          client_socket.getOutputStream());
47          } catch (IOException e) {
48              System.out.println("Could not create input/output
                ➥stream on: "
49                                                          + PORT
                                                        ➥+ ", "
                                                        ➥+ e);
50              System.exit(1);
51          }
52          while(true){
53              System.out.println("Reading data from client...");
54              try {
55                  r = in.readFloat();
56                  x = in.readFloat();
57                  y = in.readFloat();
58                  z = in.readFloat();
59                  System.out.println("  rotation: " + r + " position:
    "
60                                                      + x + "," + y +
                                                    ➥"," + z);
61              } catch (IOException e) {
```

continues

Listing 5.11, CONTINUED.

```
62              System.out.println("Could not read data.");
63              System.exit(1);
64          }
65          try {   // calculate a new position
66              x -= Math.sin(r);
67              z -= Math.cos(r);
68
69              out.writeFloat(x);
70              out.writeFloat(y);
71              out.writeFloat(z);
72              System.out.println(" Sending new position to
                ➥client: "
73                                                      + x + "," +
                                                        ➥y + "," +
                                                        ➥z);
74          } catch (IOException e) {
75              System.out.println("Could not write data");
76              System.exit(1);
77          }
78      }
79   }
80 }
```

HOW THE POSITION SERVER WORKS

The position server is a good example of the basic structure of any network server written in Java. Its job is to sit and wait for incoming connections from clients. When it receives a connection request, it sets up a communication link to the client and waits for service requests. For each request, it handles them and returns the result to the client.

This model is so generic that usually the only difference between one server and another is that the processing for the service request is changes. By isolating this as a separate class and methods, you can reuse the example code for a variety of servers.

Because the server uses network code, it imports the Java network package at line 3. After basic initialization, lines 20–25 attempt to create a socket, server_socket, for clients to use. The creation attempt is bracketed by a try-catch construct to ensure that the code handles errors correctly. The socket used for the server is predefined as PORT and uses socket number 4130 by default.

After the socket is successfully created, the server goes into a waiting phase, which enables it to sit dormant until a connection request from a client is made. This phase is handled entirely by the Java networking libraries and occurs at line 32 with a call to the method accept().

When a connection request is accepted, this call returns the value of a new socket, which is to be used to communicate with the client. Lines 42–49 then set up the read and write streams on that socket.

The next section, lines 55–58, reads the position information being sent by the client program. The first value is the rotation field, and the subsequent three values are the X, Y, and Z coordinates.

In lines 66–71 the new position for the mirage sphere is calculated based on its current position and the user's orientation. The result is sent back to the client. The program then loops back, on the true condition at line 52, and waits for more client input.

When the client programs quits, the socket connection is broken and then a read or write system call will fail, causing the program to exit at line 63 or 76.

RUNNING THE SERVER

You can execute the server program as follows. The code you type is shown in bold; the lines following are displayed by the program.

```
> java ExampleServer
      Start server: 4130
      Socket created: 4130
      Waiting for client...
```

THE CLIENT SIDE PROGRAMS (EXAMPLECLIENT.WRL AND EXAMPLECLIENT.JAVA)

Obviously, the client side will consist of two programs: the VRML scene and the associated Java program that communicates with the server.

Listing 5.12 shows the VRML scene file, which consists of a simple sphere and **ProximitySensor**. The orientation information from the **ProximitySensor** is routed to the **Script** node.

Listing 5.12   The Client Side Program (ExampleClient.wrl).

```
1    #VRML V2.0 utf8
2    DEF TARGET Transform {
3       children [
4          DEF PS ProximitySensor { size 5 5 5 }
5          Shape {
6             geometry Sphere {}
7          }
8       ]
9    }
10   DEF ExampleClient Script {
11      url "ExampleClient.class"
12      eventIn SFRotation orientation
13      field SFNode target USE TARGET
14   }
15   # Routing
16   ROUTE PS.orientation_changed TO ExampleClient.orientation
```

The Java client code is shown in listing 5.13. Its role is to set up a connection to the server and then wait for the **ProximitySensor** to send it data via the **Script** node. It forwards this data to the server, which calculates the new position for the mirage entity, the sphere, and returns it. The client then uses this information to update the sphere's position in the scene.

Listing 5.13   The Java to Manage the Client Side
Program (ExampleClient.wrl).

```
1    // ExampleClient.java
2    // Send a current position to server and then get a new
        ➥position
3    // from the server
4    import vrml.*;
5    import vrml.field.*;
6    import vrml.node.*;
7
8    import java.net.*;
9    import java.io.*;
10    import java.util.*;
11
12    public class ExampleClient extends Script{
13       public final static int PORT = 4130;
```

```
14    public final static String HOST = "localhost"; // server
      ➥name
15
16    Socket socket = null;
17    DataInputStream in = null;      // input: server to client
18    DataOutputStream out = null;    // output: client to server
19    Browser b;                      // for error message to
      ➥user
20    Node target = null;
21    SFVec3f trans = null;
22    float[] coord = null;
23    float[] rotation = null;
24
25    public void initialize(){
26       b = getBrowser();
27       // get the reference to 'translation' field of 'target'
            ➥node
28       target = (Node)((SFNode)getField("target")).getValue();
29       trans = (SFVec3f)target.getExposedField("translation");
30       coord = new float[3];
31       rotation = new float[4];
32
33       try {
34          // open network and input/output stream
35          socket = new Socket("localhost", PORT);
36          in = new DataInputStream(socket.getInputStream());
37          out = new DataOutputStream(socket.
            ➥getOutputStream());
38       } catch (UnknownHostException e) {
39          b.setDescription("Unknown host: " + HOST);
40       } catch (Exception e) {
41          b.setDescription("Connection error");
42       }
43    }
44
45    public void processEvent(Event ev) {
46       // get rotation angle
47       ((ConstSFRotation)ev.getValue()).getValue(rotation);
48       try {
49          // get current position
50          trans.getValue(coord);
51
52          // send collision angle
```

continues

```
53              out.writeFloat(rotation[3]);
54
55              // send current position to server
56              out.writeFloat(coord[0]);
57              out.writeFloat(coord[1]);
58              out.writeFloat(coord[2]);
59
60              // receive new position from server
61              coord[0] = in.readFloat();
62              coord[1] = in.readFloat();
63              coord[2] = in.readFloat();
64
65              // display new position
66              b.setDescription("position: " + coord[0] + "," +
67                  coord[1] + "," + coord[2]);
68
69              // set new position
70              trans.setValue(coord);
71          } catch (IOException e) {
72              b.setDescription("IOException:  " + e);
73          }
74      }
75
76      public void shutdown(){ // closing stream and network
77          try {
78              out.close();
79              in.close();
80              socket.close();
81          } catch (Exception e) {
82              b.setDescription("Connection close error");
83          }
84      }
85  }
```

How the Client Side Works

In the initialize() method, the example program gets the reference
to the translation field of the target node. This is a reference to the
Transform node's translation field in listing 5.12.

The initialization function then tries to connect to the server and open input/output streams to/from the server. The connection host and port are predefined as localhost (that is, the same machine and the hardwired port 4130). Obviously, you can change these to reflect your current system setup. Any error messages are displayed in Community Place browser's window by using the setDescription() method of the Browser class.

In the processEvent() method, which is called when the user enters the **ProximitySensor** of the sphere, the current rotation and position of the user are read (lines 47 and 50 of listing 5.13).

These values are then sent to the server using the writeFloat() method's calls on the I/O stream, out, at lines 53–58. The client then immediately waits for the return values from the server, which are used at line 70 to set the translation field of the mirage sphere.

The shutdown() method is called when this **Script** node is deleted. This happens when the user exits the scene and causes the script to close the input/output streams and the socket.

RUNNING THE SERVER

You'll need to execute the server program (listing 5.11) before executing the client program. After you launch the server program, you should wait until you see the message "Waiting for client" printed by the server on its console. Because the server has to set up and initialize a fair amount of networking code, this may take a few moments. You should test this code by running both the server and the client on the same machine. After it successfully works, you can edit the host name (*localhost* at line 35 of listing 5.13) to enable you to place the server on another machine.

After the server is ready, load the VRML file into your browser and it will connect automatically.

You'll see the following set of messages generated by the server as it accepts an incoming client connection and begins to process the service requests. (The code you type is shown in bold; the lines following are the output.)

```
>java ExampleServer
     Start server: 4130
     Socket created: 4130
     Waiting for client...
     Connection established: 127.0.0.1
     Open input/output stream...
     Reading data from client...
     ......
```

BUILDING A MULTIUSER SYSTEM

The final example of networking code is an implementation of a simple, multiuser server for a shared VRML scene. In all the examples shown so far, users have a copy of the scene locally in their browser and can navigate around the scene. If 10 people have loaded the file from a Web server into their browsers—and they are all viewing the same scene—they are not aware of each other. This is exactly the same model as viewing an HTML Web page. You're never aware of other people who are viewing that HTML page.

The goal of CyberSpace, and of this example, is to change that—to make viewing a VRML file a social activity by adding a notion of presence to the scene.

Presence means that when you're viewing a VRML scene, you are represented in that scene (you have a presence in that scene). If several people are viewing the same scene, they all have a presence in the scene and are aware of each others' movement through the scene. The usual mechanisms to show a user's presence in the scene is to represent him with a 3D object—often called an *avatar*—that acts on the his behalf in the scene.

In more sophisticated systems, users would be able to communicate with each other by gestures or sending text or even live audio among their browsers.

This example implements a simple version of the shared multiuser VRML system. It works by using a simple server that tracks the location of each user in the scene and then sends that information to all other users who are viewing the scene.

To track user positions, each client, when it begins to view the scene, connects to the server and sends its position in the scene. Figure 5.8 shows the connections and messages being sent between clients and the server.

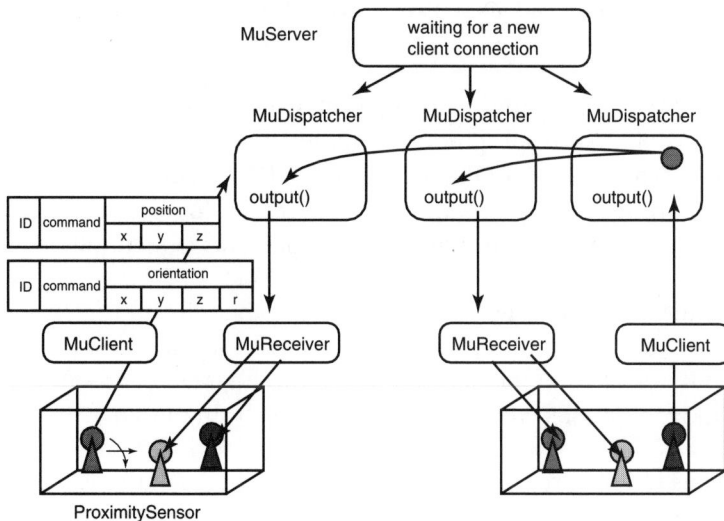

FIGURE 5.8

Client-server communications for a multiuser system.

As you can see, the system consists of four components. On the client side, the MuClient is responsible for communicating the position of the user to the server. The MuReciever is responsible for receiving information about other clients and for using that information to update the local scene.

On the server side, the MuServer program is designed to act as the contact point for clients. Each client connects to MuServer when first loading the world. The MuServer then creates a separate thread for that client and launches it at the entry point for

MuDispatcher. Thus, the server creates one instance of MuDispatcher per client and creates one thread to handle that client.

MULTITHREADING

The example uses multiple threads to manage the connections from the clients. Networking is one of the areas where multiple threads are frequently used in Java and other programming languages. Although it isn't the goal of this book to teach such fundamental aspects of Java, a short introduction to threading is useful.

A *thread* represents an abstraction of a process, or a locus of control. In most programming languages, a single thread is created on behalf of the program that is launched at the program's entry point, (main() in C or C++, for example) and which then steps through the program code sequentially.

Multithreaded languages provide the capability for the programmer to create multiple threads of control—each running in a different part of the program. Each thread is conceptually running in parallel with the other threads within the single program.

This type of programming is useful is several situations, but one example is in which the programmer wants to perform several tasks, all of which may block on I/O. In a single-threaded language, the programmer is forced to wait for the operation to finish and then go on to the next or try the operation and if it blocks, skip it and go on to the next operation.

The use of multiple threads enables a programmer to start a thread of control for each operation. If any of them block, the system ensures the others can continue in parallel. This usage is ideal for building a network server that accepts several incoming connections from clients. A thread is created for each client and can be programmed to wait for requests from that client. When there are no requests, the thread blocks and waits; other threads are able to run and handle requests.

SERVER-SIDE CODE

Listing 5.14 shows the main server. Its job is to wait for client requests and, when they arrive, create a new thread to handle the client.

Listing 5.14   A Multiuser Server (MuServer.java).

```
1    // MuServer.java
2    // Server Application for multiuser system
3    import java.net.*;
4    import java.io.*;
5    import java.util.*;
6
7    class MuServer{
8        static Vector clients = new Vector();
9
10       public static void main(String[] args){
11           ServerSocket server_socket = null;
12           Socket client_socket = null;
13           int id;
14
15           // open socket on PORT
16           try{
17               server_socket = new ServerSocket(MuProtocol.PORT);
18           } catch(IOException e){
19               System.out.println("create socket fail: " +
                 ➥MuProtocol.PORT + ", " + e);
20               System.exit(1);
21           }
22
23           System.out.println("Waiting for client connection...");
24
25           while(true){
26               // accept client's request
27               try{
28                   client_socket = server_socket.accept();
29               }catch(IOException e){
30                   System.out.println("Accept failed: " +
                     ➥MuProtocol.PORT + ", " + e);
31                   System.exit(1);
32               }
```

continues

Listing 5.14, CONTINUED.

```
33              System.out.println("Connection established: "
34                              + client_socket.
                                ↪getInetAddress());
35
36              // create one thread for client request and
37              // store it in 'clients' for client management
38              id = clients.size();
39              clients.insertElementAt(new MuDispatcher
                ↪(client_socket, clients, id), id);
40              System.out.println(" id=" + id);
41          }
42      }
43  }
```

This server works in much the same way as the server for the road mirage example (listing 5.11). It sets up a communications socket and waits for clients to connect. However, the crucial difference is its use of multithreading. Line 8 creates an instance of the Vector class, clients, which is used to hold the references to the thread created for each new client.

When an incoming connection is accepted from a new client at line 28, a new identifier is assigned to it at line 38 and then a new thread is created at line 39. This thread is inserted into the Vector class and initialized to start in the class MuDispatcher, which is derived from the Thread class. The MuServer then returns to waiting for new connections.

MuDISPATCHER
The MuDispatcher class (listing 5.15) receives position updates from the clients and sends them to all the other connected clients. It's initialized with three pieces of information:

➤ The socket, s, that the client has been assigned by the accept call in MuServer

➤ The Vector class, c, that holds the list of MuDispatcher instances

➤ The identifier, id, assigned to this client

The first task of the MuDispatcher class is to set up a communication link to the client browser. It does this in lines 18–23, creating an input and an output stream. It then sends the identifier associated with this client to the client itself so that the client knows its own identifier.

After initialization, the thread is launched by using the start() method, which causes the thread to start execution at the run() method (line 30).

Listing 5.15   Server Side Dispatching (MuDispatcher.java).

```
1    // MuDispatcher.java
2    // dispatch a client's message to other clients
3    import java.net.*;
4    import java.io.*;
5    import java.util.*;
6
7    class MuDispatcher extends Thread {
8        DataInputStream in = null;
9        DataOutputStream out = null;
10        Vector clients;
11
12        MuDispatcher(Socket s, Vector c, int id){
13            super("MuDispatcher");
14
15            clients = c;
16
17            try {
18                // create input/output streams from/to client
19                in = new DataInputStream(s.getInputStream());
20                out = new DataOutputStream(s.getOutputStream());
21
22                out.writeInt(id); // send id to client
```

continues

```
23
24              this.start();        // start this thread
25          } catch (IOException e) {
26              e.printStackTrace();
27          }
28      }
29
30      public void run(){
31          int id;
32          int command;
33          float x=0f, y=0f, z=0f, r=0f;
34
35          try{
36              while(true){
37                  // read message from a client
38                  id = in.readInt();
39                  command = in.readInt();
40                  x = in.readFloat();
41                  y = in.readFloat();
42                  z = in.readFloat();
43                  if(MuProtocol.ROTATION == command){ r =
                      ➥in.readFloat();}
44
45                  // dispatch message to other clients
46                  for(int i = 0; i < clients.size(); i++){
47                      if(i != id){
48                          if(MuProtocol.ROTATION == command){
49                              ((MuDispatcher)clients.elementAt(i)).
                                  ➥output(id, command, x, y, z, r);
50                          }else{
51                              ((MuDispatcher) clients.elementAt(i)).
                                  ➥output(id, command, x, y, z);
52                          }
53                      }
54                  }
55              }
56          }catch (IOException e){
57              e.printStackTrace();
58          }
59      }
60      // following two methods actually do the
```

```
61        // output, one for movement, other for movement+rotation
62
63        // send MOVE message to client
64         public synchronized void output(int id, int command,
65                                              float x, float y, float
                                         ↪z){
66            try{
67                out.writeInt(id);
68                out.writeInt(command);
69                out.writeFloat(x);
70                out.writeFloat(y);
71                out.writeFloat(z);
72            }catch (IOException e){
73                e.printStackTrace();
74            }
75        }
76      // send ROTATE message to client
77         public synchronized void output(int id, int command,
78                                              float x, float y,
                                         ↪float z, float
                                         r){
79            try{
80                out.writeInt(id);
81                out.writeInt(command);
82                out.writeFloat(x);
83                out.writeFloat(y);
84                out.writeFloat(z);
85                out.writeFloat(r);
86            }catch (IOException e){
87                e.printStackTrace();
88            }
89        }
90    }
```

After it is up and running, the thread's task is simple. It needs to receive position updates from its client and send those to all other clients. In addition, it is responsible for sending the position updates of other clients to its client so that its client is aware of the position changes of others.

Lines 37–42 are responsible for receiving the updates from its own client. They arrive in a simple format consisting of one of two messages. The first possible message is the MOVE message, consisting of two integers and three floats. The first integer is the identifier of the sending client; the second is the type of message (in this case, the MOVE message, which has a type value of 1), and finally, three floats for the X, Y, and Z coordinates.

The second possible message is the ROTATE message, with type value 2, consisting of the X, Y, and Z coordinates and a rotation angle. In this case, the X, Y, and Z coordinates define a vector about which the rotation angle is specified.

After these values are successfully received, the MuDispatcher has to dispatch them to all the other connected clients. To do this, it uses the output() method.

However, it doesn't need to send these positions back to itself. Therefore, it isn't using the output() method in itself. Rather, it needs to call the output() method on the other instances of MuDispatcher. This is where the Vector class, clients, is used.

clients is initialized at line 15 to refer to the Vector class passed as a parameter to MuDispatcher. It holds a reference to each instance of MuDispatcher created by MuServer. At lines 49 or 51, the output() method of these other instances of MuDispatcher is called by indexing into the Vector class, clients. These calls are within a for loop that performs this call for each MuDispatcher in the Vector class.

In this way, a MuDispatcher for client one can receive position information from its client and dispatch it to all other clients by calling their output() method.

In a similar manner, whenever another browser sends a position update to its MuDispatcher, that dispatcher (dispatcher two, for example) performs exactly the same operation and calls into the output() method of client one to inform the browser belonging to client one that client two has moved.

The output() method is overloaded with two implementations, one for sending MOVE messages and the other for sending ROTATION messages. The only difference is that ROTATION messages contain an extra float value.

Last, note that the two output methods are synchronized methods. That's because they are called by threads running in other instances of MuDispatcher, which can result in a situation where several threads call the output() method at the same time. To ensure that if this happens—only one thread executes the method at any one time—the method is protected by the fact that it is a synchronized method.

CLIENT SIDE CODE

On the client side, there are also two classes. MuClient is responsible for tracking the user's movement in the scene and for sending it to the corresponding MuDispatcher. MuReciever is responsible for receiving messages from MuDispatcher, informing it about movements of other clients. It then passes this information to MuClient to update the position of other users' avatars.

To understand the manipulation of avatars in the scene, the VRML file is presented prior to the MuClient and MuReciever.

THE MULTIUSER VRML SCENE AND ITS AVATARS

In listing 5.16, you can see that the main VRML scene is actually inlined at line 2. The rest of this file describes the avatars that represent the users.

Lines 5–32 define a PROTO node, AVATAR, that is used to represent the avatar. The PROTO specification section uses two fields, color and translation, which are the parameters for the avatar. The rest of the PROTO definition specifies a simple avatar consisting of a head, a body, and arms.

Line 33 sets up a **ProximitySensor** that covers the entire world. This is used to track the user's navigation position in the scene as discussed in the previous chapter.

Lines 34–36 instantiate three copies of the avatar PROTO node: a red, a green, and a blue version. This enables the browser to see and manage at most three clients connected to the server. This limitation is imposed to reduce the complexity of the example code.

The MuClient **Script** node is then defined and specifies the MuClient class as the Java program associated with this node. The **Script** node holds information about the user's current position in the world, including the position and orientation of the user. In addition, it holds references to the three avatars that are manipulated by the MuClient class.

Last, three **ROUTE**s are set up. The first routes the isActive field of the **ProximitySensor** to the **Script** node. The second and third route the position and orientation of the user, as read by the **ProximitySensor**, through to the **Script** node.

Listing 5.16   The Multiuser Client Scene (MuClient.wrl).

```
1    #VRML V2.0 utf8
2    Inline { url "Background.wrl" }
3    Viewpoint { position 0 0 20 }
4    # Prototype of avatar
5    PROTO AVATAR [
6        field    SFColor color  1 1 1
7        field    SFVec3f translation 0 0 0
8    ]
9    {
10    Transform {
11       translation IS translation
12       children [
13          Transform {
14             translation 0 -1.0 0
15             children [
16                Transform {
17                   translation 0 1.2 0
18                   children [ Shape { geometry Sphere {} } ] #
                   ➥head
19                }
20                Transform {
21                   translation 0 0.1 0
22                   children [ Shape { geometry Box { size 3.0 0.1
                   ➥0.1 } } ] # hand
23                }
24                Shape {
25                   appearance Appearance { material Material {
                   ➥diffuseColor IS color } }
26                   geometry Cone {} # body
```

```
27              }
28          ]
29        }
30     ]
31  }
32  }
33  DEF PS ProximitySensor { size 1000 1000 1000 }
34  DEF AVATAR0 AVATAR { color 1 0 0 }
35  DEF AVATAR1 AVATAR { color 0 1 0 }
36  DEF AVATAR2 AVATAR { color 0 0 1 }
37
38  DEF MuClient Script {
39     url "MuClient.class"
40     eventIn SFBool entered
41     eventIn SFVec3f myPosition
42     eventIn SFRotation myOrientation
43
44     field SFNode avatar0 USE AVATAR0
45     field SFNode avatar1 USE AVATAR1
46  field SFNode avatar2 USE AVATAR2
47  }
48  # Routing
49  ROUTE PS.isActive TO MuClient.entered
50  ROUTE PS.position_changed TO MuClient.myPosition
51  ROUTE PS.orientation_changed TO MuClient.myOrientation
```

Because the isActive field of the **ProximitySensor** fires when the user enters the area managed by the sensor and because the sensor has been defined to be as large as the scene, this sensor always fires when the scene is loaded. After the isActive event is generated, it is delivered to the MuClient class.

MuClient

The MuClient class is responsible for informing the server of the user's position in the scene and managing the avatars that represent other users in the scene (listing 5.17). At initialization time, it sets up an internal structure that holds the position and rotation of the three avatars that can be managed for the scene by reading the fields in the **Script** node (lines 31–43).

As discussed previously, the loading of the scene causes an isActive event to be generated and received at processEvent(). This first event acts as an initialize event and causes the code in lines 49–67 to be executed. Thereafter, this code is executed only when the user reloads the scene. During this phase, the code creates the socket connection to the server (line 52) and sets up the input and output streams.

At line 58, a new thread is created for an instance of the class MuReciever. This class is responsible for reading data from the server. It is set up as a separate thread because the current thread has been created in response to the isActive event generated by the VRML scene. While this thread is active, the VRML scene is effectively blocked, waiting for processEvent() to return. By creating a new thread to handle communications from the server, the current thread is able to exit processEvent() and enable the VRML scene and the current event cascade to continue.

Listing 5.17   The Java to Manage the Client (MuClient.java).

```
1    // MuClient.java
2    //
3    import vrml.*;
4    import vrml.field.*;
5    import vrml.node.*;
6
7    import java.net.*;
8    import java.io.*;
9    import java.util.*;
10
11   public class MuClient extends Script{
12       public final static String HOST = "localhost"; // server
         ➥host name
13       public final static int AVATARS = 3;
14
15       Socket socket = null;
16       DataInputStream in = null;        // input stream from server
         ➥to client
17       DataOutputStream out = null;      // output sream from client
         ➥to server
18       Browser b;                        // for displaying error
         ➥message to user
19       SFVec3f avatarPosition[] = new SFVec3f[AVATARS];
```

```
20      SFRotation avatarRotation[] = new SFRotation[AVATARS];
21      float[] coord;
22      float[] rotation;
23      int id;
24      boolean connected = false;
25
26      public void initialize(){
27          b = getBrowser();
28          Node avatar = null;
29
30          // get the reference to 'translation' field of 'avatar'
                ➥node
31          for (int i=0; i < AVATARS; i++){
32              try {
33                  avatar = (Node)((SFNode)getField("avatar" +
                        ➥i)).getValue();
34                  avatarPosition[i] = (SFVec3f)avatar.
                        ➥getExposedField("translation");
35                  avatarRotation[i] = (SFRotation)avatar.
                        ➥getExposedField("rotation");
36              } catch (Exception e) {
37                  b.setDescription("can not get avatar");
38                  return;
39              }
40          }
41          coord = new float[3];
42          rotation = new float[4];
43      }
44
45      public void processEvent(Event ev) {
46          if(ev.getName().equals("entered")){
47              ConstSFBool v = (ConstSFBool)ev.getValue();
48
49              if(v.getValue() && (!connected)){
50                  // open network and input/output stream
51                  try {
52                      socket = new Socket(HOST, MuProtocol.PORT);
53                      in = new DataInputStream
                            ➥(socket.getInputStream());
54                      out = new DataOutputStream
                            ➥(socket.getOutputStream());
55                      id = in.readInt();
```

continues

```
56
57                          // create a thread to wait for data from
                                ➥server
58                          new MuReceiver(in, this);
59                          connected = true;
60                      } catch (UnknownHostException e) {
61                          b.setDescription("Unknown host: " + HOST);
62                          return;
63                      } catch (Exception e) {
64                          b.setDescription("Connection error");
65                          return;
66                      }
67                  }
68              } else if(ev.getName().equals("myPosition")){
69                  ((ConstSFVec3f)ev.getValue()).getValue(coord);
70
71                  try {
72                      // send my id and my current position to server
73                      out.writeInt(id);
74                      out.writeInt(MuProtocol.MOVE);
75                      out.writeFloat(coord[0]);
76                      out.writeFloat(coord[1]);
77                      out.writeFloat(coord[2]);
78                  } catch (IOException e) {
79                      b.setDescription("Fail to send position to
                            ➥server:  " + e);
80                      return;
81                  }
82              } else if(ev.getName().equals("myOrientation")){
83                  ((ConstSFRotation)ev.getValue()).getValue(rotation);
84
85                  try {
86                      // send my id and my current position to server
87                      out.writeInt(id);
88                      out.writeInt(MuProtocol.ROTATION);
89                      out.writeFloat(rotation[0]);
90                      out.writeFloat(rotation[1]);
91                      out.writeFloat(rotation[2]);
92                      out.writeFloat(rotation[3]);
93                  } catch (IOException e) {
94                      b.setDescription("Fail to send orientation to
                            ➥server:  " + e);
```

```
95                  return;
96              }
97          }
98      }
99
100     public void updatePosition(int id, float x, float y,
        ⇒float z){
101         avatarPosition[id].setValue(x, y, z);
102     }
103
104     public void updateOrientation(int id, float x, float y,
        ⇒float z, float r){
105         avatarRotation[id].setValue(x, y, z, r);
106     }
107
108     public void shutdown() {
109         try {
110             out.close();
111             in.close();
112             socket.close();
113         } catch (Exception e) {
114             b.setDescription("Connection close error");
115         }
116     }
117 }
```

Once processEvent() returns after handling the initial isActive event, the Java program is ready to receive position update events from the VRML scene.

When these arrive, they're dispatched to processEvent() in the usual fashion. There are two possible events: a position update and a rotation update. These are generated by the **ProximitySensor** and handled at line 68 or 82. In both cases, the event handler code sends a MOVE or ROTATE message to the server.

Two methods are also defined on this class: updatePosition() and updateOrientation(), which are used to set the translation and rotation values of the avatar objects. These methods aren't called from within MuClient; they're called from within MuReceiver when it receives new data from the server.

MURECEIVER
The code for MuReceiver is shown in listing 5.18. Its job is to receive messages from the server, determine whether they are MOVE or ROTATION messages, and call the relevant method in MuClient.

Listing 5.18   Client Side Java to Monitor the Network (MuReciever.java).

```
1    // MuReceiver.java
2    // waiting for avatars' position from server and update them
3    import vrml.field.*;
4
5    import java.net.*;
6    import java.io.*;
7    import java.util.*;
8
9    class MuReceiver extends Thread {
10       DataInputStream in = null;
11       MuClient muclient;
12
13       MuReceiver(DataInputStream i, MuClient muc){
14          super("MuReceiver");
15
16          in = i;
17          muclient = muc; // to call methods of MuClient class
18          this.start();    // start this thread
19       }
20
21       public void run(){
22          int id;
23          int command;
24          float x, y, z, r;
25
26          while(true){
27             try {
28                // receive client's id and its    position from
                   ➥server
29                id = in.readInt();
30                command = in.readInt();
31                x = in.readFloat();
32                y = in.readFloat();
33                z = in.readFloat();
```

```
34
35              if(Protocol.MOVE == command){
36                  // update position
37                  muclient.updatePosition(id, x, y, z);
38              }else{
39                  r = in.readFloat();
40
41                  // update orientation
42                  muclient.updateOrientation(id, x, y, z, r);
43              }
44              System.out.println(id + ": " + x + " " + y + " " + z);
45          } catch (IOException e) {
46              e.printStackTrace();
47              return;
48          }
49       }
50     }
51   }
```

To run this example requires, as in the previous example, that you start the server and, after it has initialized, load the VRML file into the browser.

When the browser connects to the server, it is informed of its identifier. Subsequently, every time the user navigates through the scene, the browser sends position and rotation information to the server. When a second browser loads the same scene, it also connects to the server. At that point, movement from one browser is sent to the other browser, via the server. When movement for another browser is received, the receiving browser uses it to manipulate the avatar representing the other user.

In figure 5.9, you can see a screen capture showing three users who are sharing the same simple scene. The object in the background represents a house. The browser window in the top left is showing the viewpoint from one of the users, user A. User A is looking down onto the scene and can see the avatars representing user B and user C. The avatars are simple figures that consist of a cone for the body, a sphere for the head, and a cylinder for the arms.

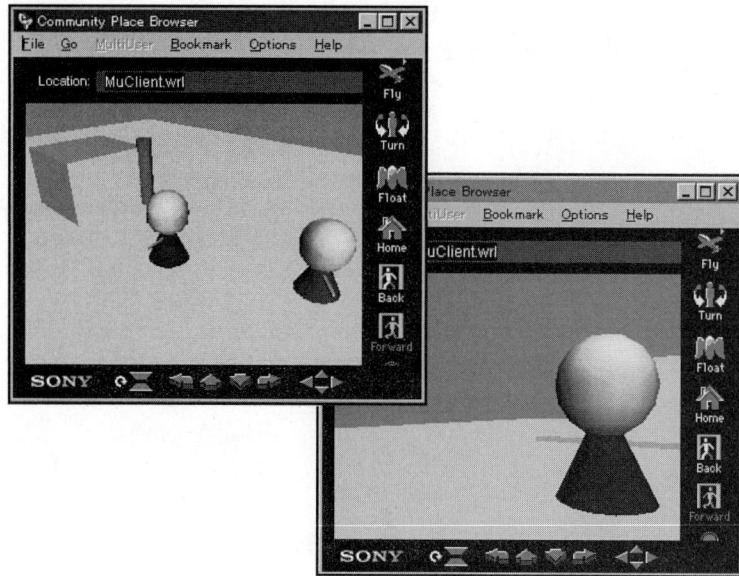

FIGURE 5.9

Multiple avatars in the shared VRML scene.

As you can see, the avatars for users A and B are standing in front of the house and looking at each other. In the other browser window, you can see the same scene, but this time it's from user B's point of view. User B is looking directly at user C's avatar and so you can see user C's avatar in their browser window.

EXTENDING THE EXAMPLE

This example shows the bare minimum needed to build a multiuser, shared VRML scene. As you can see, the process is quite simple and requires only a few hundred lines of Java code.

In addition this example also shows several VRML techniques that were discussed earlier in this book. These include

➤ Use of a **ProximitySensor** to trigger initialization code when a world is loaded

➤ Use of a **ProximitySensor** to track the user's movement throughout the entire scene

➤ Use of PROTOs to describe the avatar

➤ Use of node fields in the **Script** node that are manipulated directly by the Java program

This example begs for improvement, however. Some simple, yet interesting extensions would be making the avatar model more realistic by replacing the avatar definition in listing 5.16; relaxing the inbuilt limitation on three avatars, which has been used to simplify the example code; sending position updates only at regular intervals to reduce communication load rather than currently where position updates are sent as often as possible; and using interpolators to move between positions when the position updates are infrequent so that smooth movement is maintained, but requiring less communication traffic.

You should note that although the example uses a simple VRML scene, you can use this code to share any VRML 2.0 file. This means that you can create as complex a scene as you like and allow anybody to share it if they connect to your server. To do this, all you need to do is add more VRML to the MuClient.wrl file shown in listing 5.16.

ROUNDUP

This chapter has shown you how to connect a VRML scene to the real world. The ability to do this effectively takes a 3D scene description language and turns it into a window on the real world. Although VRML on its own can be put to many uses without a real-world connection, it will always be a simulation language. By harnessing Java's I/O facilities, and in particular its integration with the Internet, it is possible to build VRML scenes that represent and even control real-world data.

The examples shown provide only a taste of what is possible. You are limited only by your imagination and time. However, the basic mechanisms that have been discussed provide a solid basis for any number of systems. Examples include the following:

➤ Extending the multiuser system to support a chat feature

➤ Building a real-time stock display

➤ Controlling a real world device, such as a robot, via manipulations of the VRML version of the device

➤ Building a database access and manipulation tool

➤ Using the basic multiuser system as the basis for a shared CAD tool

At this stage, you should be fully familiar with the way Java and VRML work together and the possibilities they afford. The next chapter provides a set of tips for improving the performance of your VRML worlds.

## CHAPTER 6

HINTS AND TIPS FOR EFFECTIVE AND EFFICIENT VRML

VRML is a complicated scene description language.

When coupled with Java, there are many instances

where the most obvious solution to a problem may

not necessarily be the most efficient one. Although it

is not possible to provide examples for every appli-

cation that you will write, this chapter provides a

basic set of tips on features of VRML, Java, and the

two working in cooperation that will help you build

effective and efficient VRML scenes.

WHAT THIS CHAPTER COVERS

This chapter contains hints and tips on a wide range of issues relating to efficient or elegant VRML and Java. To help you assimilate, it has been organized into four sections:

➤ **Execution model.** Here you can find tips on ROUTE compatibility, timers, and the use of interpolators.

➤ **VRML.** This section comprises information on various aspects of VRML and provides tips on the best way to build efficient VRML scenes.

➤ **Java and VRML.** The interaction between VRML scenes and Java behaviors is complicated and has many performance implications. This section points out areas where performance can be improved based on coding style.

➤ **Sound.** The last section provides an overview of the sound capabilities of VRML and Community Place and offers some advice on which to use and when.

At the end of this chapter, you will have a better understanding of some of the more obscure facets of VRML and its interaction with Java. This will enable you to build more effective VRML scenes that have smoother animation, faster display speed, and more complicated features.

However, using VRML and Java will be, at least for the next few years, on the cutting edge of the Internet and the WWW. The tips offered in this chapter represent some of the wisdom gained during the development of VRML 2.0 and the Java binding. What you get from these tips will vary according to your applications, your goals, and probably most important, your browser. The best way to understand what works and what doesn't work is to try it, so the main message of this chapter is: experiment!

PERFORMANCE AND VRML 2.0

Building high-performance 3D worlds on standard PCs is neither a science nor an engineering discipline. There are no hard and fast rules. As 3D graphics cards become more prevalent in the next two years, the possibilities will grow. Currently, however, most VRML browsers are running on mid-range machines that use software packages for 3D graphics and are connected to the Internet via dial-up lines.

As a VRML scene designer, you are faced with two areas of concern: file size and scene complexity. As a Java programmer using VRML as your display vehicle, you have to deal with additional performance issues concerning Java as it interacts with the VRML scene. These are outlined as follows:

➤ **File size.** The size of the VRML file you create has a direct impact in two places—in the transfer time between server and browser machine and in the load time at the browser machine. Your goal as a scene designer is to balance the size of the file against its actual content. This is never an easy task, but you should be aware that no matter how exciting your scene, if it's a 5 MB file, few people will ever download it and see how exciting it is. Some of the most common techniques for reducing file size will be discussed later in the section on VRML tips. Others tips include the following:

   1. Use GZIP to reduce file size. Most VRML 2.0 browsers will uncompress GZIPed files.

   2. Use **Inline** nodes for complex models that will not be viewed when the scene is initially loaded. Using **Inline**s in combination with **LOD**s also enables you to reduce your main file size.

   3. Avoid excessive use of textures, movies, and sound files; all are large.

➤ **Scene complexity.** After the scene loads, the performance of your world is directly proportional to the scene complexity.

The more complex the scene, the more the browser will have to render and the lower the frame rate will be. This chapter touches on several techniques to help you reduce scene complexity. However, the final analysis is up to you. For a world to be compelling, it needs to have a certain degree of complexity. Unfortunately, users are notoriously fickle when it comes to the smoothness of animation. As usual, it is a trade-off.

➤ **Java and VRML.** Because VRML 2.0 has a built-in execution model, you can think of it as a simple programming language. Because it is simple, you have to make use of a more complex programming language, such as Java, for a lot of the more interesting effects. This means that you have two programming languages working with each other. Every time one of them needs to pass control to the other, it is forced to cross a language boundary. Thus, an event passing through a **Script** node on its way to a Java program is not simply making a method call; it is making a cross-domain call. Cross-domain calls are both computationally expensive and time-consuming, and their use has a direct impact on the performance of your VRML scene.

Because of the complexity of these three factors, and in particular their inter-relationship, there are no clear-cut rules when building VRML scenes. As a scene designer, your job is to weigh these factors when deciding on a particular strategy. Like most things, techniques that work for one scene may not be appropriate for another. At the risk of repetition, the best advice that can be offered is to experiment!

THE EXECUTION MODEL

Chapters 2, "Adding Action to 3D Worlds," and 3, "Letting Java Loose," explained the execution model that VRML supports and how it relates to Java. Throughout this book, you see examples that use similar sets of nodes to begin or sustain execution—the use of **TimeSensor**s with various interpolators, for example.

These pairs of nodes work well together because the output of a particular sensor is exactly the required input for a particular interpolator. One of the quickest ways to exploit the execution model is to more fully understand the possibilities that routing makes available.

ROUTING COMPATIBILITY

As discussed in Chapter 2, VRML 2.0 is designed to realize many simple behaviors without resorting to the use of Java. To use the full power of VRML 2.0, you need a good understanding of useful patterns of ROUTEs—in other words, useful combinations of eventOuts and eventIns. **Script** nodes should be used only when what you want is beyond the expressive power of the in-built nodes.

To return to a typical event cascade, the cascade always starts from a **Sensor** node, which autonomously generates an event. Table 6.1 shows all the eventOuts of sensors sorted according to their type.

Table 6.1   Sensor Nodes and Their eventOuts

Sensor Node	Event Class	Event Type	Field Name
ProximitySensor	eventOut	SFBool	isActive
PlaneSensor	eventOut	SFBool	isActive
VisibilitySensor	eventOut	SFBool	isActive
TouchSensor	eventOut	SFBool	isOver
CylinderSensor	eventOut	SFBool	isActive
TouchSensor	eventOut	SFBool	isActive
TimeSensor	eventOut	SFBool	isActive
SphereSensor	eventOut	SFBool	isActive
TimeSensor	eventOut	SFFloat	fraction_changed
CylinderSensor	eventOut	SFRotation	rotation_changed
SphereSensor	eventOut	SFRotation	rotation_changed
ProximitySensor	eventOut	SFRotation	orientation_changed

continues

Table 6.1, Continued.

Sensor Node	Event Class	Event Type	Field Name
TouchSensor	eventOut	SFTime	touchTime
TimeSensor	eventOut	SFTime	time
ProximitySensor	eventOut	SFTime	enterTime
ProximitySensor	eventOut	SFTime	exitTime
VisibilitySensor	eventOut	SFTime	exitTime
VisibilitySensor	eventOut	SFTime	enterTime
TimeSensor	eventOut	SFTime	cycleTime
TouchSensor	eventOut	SFVec2f	hitTexCoord_changed
CylinderSensor	eventOut	SFVec3f	trackPoint_changed
TouchSensor	eventOut	SFVec3f	hitPoint_changed
TouchSensor	eventOut	SFVec3f	hitNormal_changed
PlaneSensor	eventOut	SFVec3f	translation_changed
ProximitySensor	eventOut	SFVec3f	position_changed
SphereSensor	eventOut	SFVec3f	trackPoint_changed
PlaneSensor	eventOut	SFVec3f	trackPoint_changed

You can see from this table that many sensors have a common set of events. The first of these is the SFBool field type, isActive and isOver.

These Boolean events (TRUE or FALSE) are generated when a sensor's state changes. Unfortunately, there are few cases where direct routing of these events into any other node's eventIns makes much sense. The one exception to this is the **Script** node, which is used extensively throughout the book.

One possible scenario uses the fact that the isActive field of a **TouchSensor** becomes TRUE when the mouse button is pressed and FALSE when it is released. You can use this as a way of animating only when the mouse button is held down. For example, you can turn on the light when you hold down the mouse button with the mouse and turn it off when you release the button.

Listing 6.1   Using the isActive Field of a TouchSensor Node (LightDirectOnOff.wrl)

```
1    #VRML V2.0 utf8
2    #
3    # turn on/off the light by pressing / releasing the mouse
       ➥button.
4    #
5    Transform{
6      children[
7        DEF LIGHT PointLight{
8          on FALSE      # initially the light is turned off.
9        }
10       Transform{
11         translation 0 1 0
12         children[
13           # lamp shade
14           DEF LAMP_SHADE Shape{
15             geometry Cone{
16               height 2
17               bottomRadius 4
18               bottom FALSE
19             }
20           }
21         ]
22       }
23       # sensor to turn the light on / off
23       DEF LIGHT_ON_SWITCH TouchSensor{}
24     ]
25   }
26   # dummy object to reflect the light.
27   Transform{
28     translation 0 -5 0
29     children[
30       Shape{geometry Box{size 10 0.3 10}}
31     ]
32   }
33   ROUTE LIGHT_ON_SWITCH.isActive TO LIGHT.on
```

A more powerful type of event are time-related ones: the SFTime fields touchTime, time, enterTime, exitTime, and cycleTime.

Those events are also generated when a sensor's state changes. In contrast to the SFBool events, SFTime events are extremely useful when you want to realize simple behaviors without resorting to **Script** nodes.

Two patterns of routing utilize SFTime events. One pattern is to directly control time-dependent nodes such as the **TimeSensor** and **AudioClip**. The second is to use the SFTime events generated by the **TimeSensor** to directly control interpolators.

SFTIME AND TIME-DEPENDENT NODES

Table 6.2 shows all SFTime fields in VRML 2.0. You can see that each node generates a startTime and stopTime.

Table 6.2   Nodes That Use SFTime Events

Node Name	Field Class	Field Type	Field Name
AudioClip	exposedField	SFTime	startTime
TimeSensor	exposedField	SFTime	startTime
TimeSensor	exposedField	SFTime	stopTime
MovieTexture	exposedField	SFTime	startTime
MovieTexture	exposedField	SFTime	stopTime
AudioClip	exposedField	SFTime	stopTime
TimeSensor	exposedField	SFTime	cycleInterval

The startTime field specifies when the node becomes active, and the stopTime field specifies when the node goes inactive. The pseudo-code algorithm in listing 6.2 shows the states that any time-dependent node goes through. Remember from Chapter 2 that the key fields in the time-dependent nodes are the startTime and stopTime fields, which dictate the period during which these nodes are active. The algorithm for understanding the state of such nodes is based on these fields.

Listing 6.2   State Transitions for Time-Dependent Nodes (Pseudo-code).

```
1  if(stopTime <= startTime){
2     // stopTime is not applicable.
3     if(currentTime < startTime){
4        // the start time has not come.
5        // === case 1 ===
6        state = inactive;
7     }else{
8        // the current time has passed the start time.
9        // === case 2 ===
10       state = active.
11    }
12 }else{
13    // stop time is applicable.
14    if(currentTime < startTime){
15       // the start time has not come.
16       // === case 3 ===
17       state = inactive;
18 }else if(currentTime < stopTime){
19    // the current time has passed the start time.
20    // the current time has not reached the stop time.
21    // === case 4 ===
22    state = active;
23 }else{
24    // the current time has passed the stop time.
25    // === case 5 ===
26    state = inactive;
27 }
28 }
```

The logic of the pseudo-code shows five different cases to consider, each of which drives the node into one of two states, active or inactive. You can see from this pseudo-code that the only way to control a time-dependent node is to route a time event to the startTime or stopTime fields. As an example of this, imagine a room scene with a TV in it. The TV has play and stop buttons and will play a movie when the play button is clicked. To understand when the movie will play, you need to consider the startTime, stopTime, and loop fields of the **MovieTexture** node. See listing 6.3.

Listing 6.3   A Simple VRML TV Set (TV.wrl).

```
1    #VRML V2.0 utf8
2    #TV
3    #
4    # TV body
5    Transform{
6       children[
7       Shape{
8          geometry IndexedFaceSet{
9             coord DEF COORD Coordinate{
10               point[
11                  0 0 0,        #0
12                  15 0 0,       #1
13                  15 10 0,    #2
14                  0 10 0,       #3
15               ]
16            }
17            coordIndex [0, 1, 2, 3, -1]
18            solid FALSE
19         }
20         appearance Appearance{
21            texture DEF TV MovieTexture{
22               url "tv.jpg"
23               loop TRUE
24               startTime 0    # initially not playing
25               stopTime 1
26            }
27         }
28      }
29      ]
30   }
31   # play button
32   Transform{
33      translation 2 -1 0
34      children[
35      Shape{geometry Box{size 4 1 0.1}},
36      DEF PLAY_BUTTON TouchSensor{}
37      ]
38   }
39   Transform{
40      translation 1 -3 0
```

```
41      children[
42      Shape{
43        geometry Text{
44            string "Play"
45            fontStyle FontStyle{}
46        }
47      }
48      ]
49   }
50   # stop button
51   Transform{
52      translation 13 -1 0
53      children[
54      Shape{geometry Box{size 4 1 0.1}},
55      DEF STOP_BUTTON TouchSensor{}
56      ]
57   }
58   Transform{
59      translation 12 -3 0
60      children[
61      Shape{
62        geometry Text{
63            string "Stop"
64            fontStyle FontStyle{}
65        }
66      }
67      ]
68   }
69   ROUTE PLAY_BUTTON.touchTime TO TV.set_startTime
70   ROUTE STOP_BUTTON.touchTime TO TV.set_stopTime
```

Notice that lines 24 and 25 of listing 6.3 initialize the **Movie-Texture** node with a startTime of 0 and a stopTime of 1. According to the pseudo-code algorithm in listing 6.2, this is an example of case 5, and the **MovieTexture** node is in the inactive state. This is because the current time is much later than the stop time. As a result, the **MovieTexture** does not play when the world is loaded. The next step is to analyze what happens when you click the play button. The key is the ROUTE at line 69, which sets the startTime of the **MovieTexture** with a SFTime event holding the current time. Because the startTime is now greater than the stopTime and the currentTime is greater than the startTime, case 2 is applicable. This forces the **MovieTexture** node into the active state, and the movie begins to play. The process of clicking the stop button works in the same way. This is an example of case 5, which forces the **MovieTexture** node into the inactive state.

This example shows how to control time-dependent nodes with only the ROUTE mechanism and without using any **Script** nodes. The compatibility between eventOut fields of sensor nodes and exposed field of time-dependent nodes enables this efficient control flow.

TIME AND INTERPOLATOR

Another way to utilize SFTime events is to give them to **TimeSensor**s, which then drive interpolators. **TimeSensors**, in conjunction with interpolators, convert SFTime events into other types of events and help you to easily produce smooth animation. The detailed usage of interpolators has already been discussed in Chapters 2 and 3, so this chapter summarizes only the events generated by the six types of interpolators, as shown in table 6.3.

Table 6.3   Interpolators and Their eventOuts

Interpolator Node	Event Class	Event Type	Field Name
CoordinateInterpolator	eventOut	MFVec3f	value_changed
NormalInterpolator	eventOut	MFVec3f	value_changed
ColorInterpolator	eventOut	SFColor	value_changed
ScalarInterpolator	eventOut	SFFloat	value_changed
OrientationInterpolator	eventOut	SFRotation	value_changed
PositionInterpolator	eventOut	SFVec3f	value_changed

The actual result of an interpolator's generation of continuous events is browser dependent. Obviously it is not possible to continuously generate events for each interpolator in the system, so browser implementers will decide on the best rate. This decision is usually dependent on the system load at any point in time.

SMOOTH ANIMATION IS EXPENSIVE: USE TIMESENSORS WISELY

Using continuous events (time and fraction_changed) of **TimeSensor**s in conjunction with interpolators provides an easy and efficient way of producing smooth animation. Remember, however, that animation frames can be culled when the system becomes heavily loaded due to excessive numbers of entities animated by interpolators. If you overload the browser in this way, it is possible to reduce the scene animation to a series of jerky frames.

The obvious solution to this is to limit the number of **TimeSensor**s, especially when their time or fraction_changed eventOuts are routed to other nodes. Instead of attaching a **TimeSensor** to each moving object, share a **TimeSensor** among several moving objects as far as possible. Remember that an eventOut can be routed to an arbitrary number of eventIns. Although the cost of per-frame translation of entities still exists, the cost of **TimeSensor** invocation is reduced.

MODELING TECHNIQUES

This section gathers a number of tips related to the use of VRML. Also, this section revisits a few areas that are known to be areas of confusion (discussed in Chapter 4, "Advanced VRML") and offers techniques to help you produce interesting scenes that do not result in poor performance.

DOUBLE FACED POLYGONS

For performance reasons, the default value of the field, solid, of the nodes **IndexedFaceSet**, **ElevationGrid**, and **Extrusion** is TRUE. This means that the browser may assume polygons are single faced. The result is that the browser does not have to worry about the backfaces of the surfaces of the node and can reduce the amount of rendering it is forced to do.

Listing 6.4 contains two walls: the red one is single faced, and the green one is double faced.

Listing 6.4   Using Single and Double Faced Polygons (DoubleFace.wrl).

```
1   #VRML V2.0 utf8
2   # show the difference of single face and double face.
3   #
4   # single face wall
5   Transform{
6       translation 0 -5 0
7       children[
8       Shape{
9          geometry IndexedFaceSet{
10            coord DEF COORD Coordinate{
11               point[
12                 0 0 0,        #0
13                 10 0 0,       #1
14                 10 10 0,    #2
15                 0 10 0,        #3
16               ]
17            }
18            coordIndex [0, 1, 2, 3, -1]
19            solid TRUE
20          }
21          appearance Appearance{
22            material Material{
23               diffuseColor 1 0 0    # red
24            }
25          }
26       }
27       ]
28  }
29
30  # double face wall
31  Transform{
32      translation -10 -5 0
33      children[
34      Shape{
35         geometry IndexedFaceSet{
36            coord USE COORD
37            coordIndex [0, 1, 2, 3, -1]
38            solid FALSE
39         }
40         appearance Appearance{
```

```
41              material Material{
42                  diffuseColor 0 1 0    # green
43                  }
44              }
45          }
46      ]
47 }
```

Check the difference between the single and double faced walls by going around the back of both walls. You can see the green wall from the back, but you cannot see the red one, which is single faced.

The culling of backface is an option, and some browsers, including Community Place, do the culling to speed up rendering. You should always consider whether users will see the backfaces of your models. If so, you have to specify "solid FALSE" explicitly. As you browse the Internet for VRML models, you will come across many instances where designers have failed to remember this and have produced scenes in which objects disappear as you move around them!

NAVIGATION USING VIEWPOINTS

Chapter 4 introduced techniques for moving the user's viewpoint. This is quite a complicated and easy-to-misunderstand concept and has several pitfalls. To make the explanation clear, the following list defines two terms: camera and viewpoint.

➤ **Camera.** Specifies the position and orientation from where the scenery in a VRML scene is captured and rendered on the browser screen.

➤ **Viewpoint.** The position that is defined by a **Viewpoint** node in a VRML world. When the **Viewpoint** is bound (and if its "jump" field is TRUE), the camera adjusts its position and orientation to that of the **Viewpoint**.

The first point to recognize is that the **Viewpoint** node's position and orientation fields are write-only—that is, they do not reflect the current position and orientation of the camera. **Viewpoint**s work only as an entry point to set the current camera position when the **Viewpoint** is bound. After setting these fields, the user may move the camera by navigating, and the user's position will soon differ from the field values set by **Viewpoint**. To get the current camera position and orientation, you must use a **ProximitySensor**.

Next, remember that binding a **Viewpoint** determines in which coordinate system the camera is located. When the camera is bound to a **Viewpoint** that is included in a **Transform** node and the user navigates in this scene, the camera's position changes within this local coordinate space.

To make the situation more complicated, assume that the local coordinate system is moved continuously. Simultaneously, the user navigates by using the browser UI. As a result, the camera captures the scenery in much the same way as you would see the scenery from a moving bus. The local coordinate system (a **Transform** node containing the **Viewpoint** node) acts as the bus, whereas the user navigation corresponds to walking about on the bus.

In figure 6.1 you can see the effect of moving the **Transform** node, which contains the **Viewpoint** node. As the **Transform** node is moved in the X direction, the user's camera is moved by the same amount. Additionally, if the user navigates within the world, the navigation is relative to the local coordinate system within the **Transform** node. In figure 6.1, therefore, the total movement of the user in the world coordinate system is a combination of the buses movement, which is 5 meters (the **Transform** node), plus the user's navigation, which is 2 meters.

This difference between the camera position and the **Viewpoint** node is crucial. The **Viewpoint** does not define the current location of the user and cannot be used to find out the user's location in the scene.

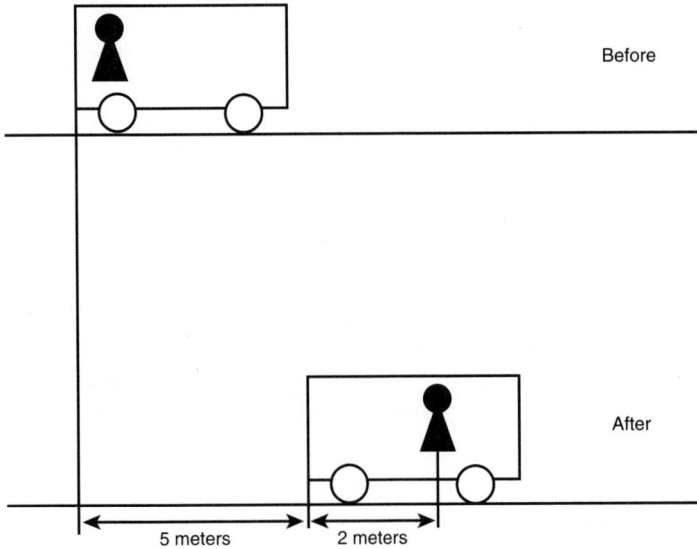

FIGURE 6.1

*Moving a **Transform** node that contains a **Viewpoint** node.*

ANIMATION: TRADING OFF SPEED AGAINST EXPRESSIVE POWER

In the previous section on animation, the use of interpolators as a way to achieve smooth animation was discussed. However, interpolators are a relatively expensive way to animate scene entities and, depending on your requirements, may not be sufficiently flexible. There are three other approaches to animation; these approaches offer different levels of flexibility and efficiency than interpolators.

TECHNIQUE 1: THE SWITCH NODE

The easiest but most efficient way to realize a simple animation is to use the **Switch** node. If you look back to listing 4.4 in Chapter 4, the intelligent agent used this technique to animate the greeting gesture. This example shows that the **Switch** node is quite useful if each posture of animation is predefined. There are many cases where a simple predefined animation based on this use of the **Switch** node is quite powerful and perfectly adequate to convey the impression of animation without having to resort to the use of interpolators.

TECHNIQUE 2: ANIMATION BASED ON ANOTHER MOVING ENTITY

This technique may be the most common way of realizing animation when each posture is decided at runtime. Again referring back to Chapter 4, the tracking behavior of the intelligent agent uses this technique. The agent position is calculated at runtime according to the user's position. The behavior is started by using a **ProximitySensor** that tracks the user's position and then controls the agent's position based on this information. By using two **Transforms**—the first providing the coordinate space for the agent and the second the actual agent—the user's position can be fed to the top level **Transform**, and the agent will remain a fixed offset from the user's coordinates.

TECHNIQUE 3: ADD AND REMOVE NODES DYNAMICALLY AT RUNTIME

The last technique is quite powerful because it enables you to create nodes at runtime according to the user's action. However, this technique is more expensive than the previous two and relies on a Browser class method call—that is, it requires an associated piece of Java code. Because the browser is calling across into the Java program, the execution cost is quite high. This issue will be discussed later in this chapter in the section "Java Performance." Listing 6.5 shows an example of adding nodes dynamically.

Listing 6.5 uses the createVrmlFromString() method of the Browser class to create a new **Sphere** node with a random color at runtime.

Listing 6.5   Adding a Sphere Node with createVrmlFromString
(DynamicJen.java).

```
1   //
2   // dynamic generation of geometry nodes
3   //
4   import java.util.*;
5   import vrml.*;
6   import vrml.node.*;
7   import vrml.field.*;
8
9   public class DynamicGen extends Script{
10      MFNode addSphere;
11      Random randomNumGenerator = new Random();
12      float posX = 0.0f;
13
14      public void initialize(){
15          // get the reference of the event-out 'addSphere'.
16          addSphere = (MFNode)getEventOut("addSphere");
17      }
18
19      public void processEvent(Event e){
20          if(e.getName().equals("touched") == true){
21              String sphereDesc1 =
22                  "Transform {" +
23                  "    translation ";
24              String sphereDesc2 =
25                  "        0.0 0.0 " +
26                  "    children[" +
27                  "    Shape{geometry Sphere{}" +
28                  "        appearance Appearance{" +
29                  "            material Material
                             ➥{diffuseColor ";
30              String sphereDesc3 =
31                  "            }" +
32                  "            }" +
33                  "    }" +
34                  "    ]" +
35                  "}";
36
37              float red = randomNumGenerator.nextFloat();
38              float green = randomNumGenerator.nextFloat();
```

continues

Listing 6.5, CONTINUED.

```
39              float blue = randomNumGenerator.nextFloat();
40
41              Browser browser = getBrowser();
42              BaseNode baseNodes[];
43
44              // next position.
45              posX += 3.0f;
46
47              try{
48                  baseNodes = browser.createVrmlFromString

                        (sphereDesc1 + posX +
49
                        sphereDesc2 + red + " " +
50
                        green + " " +
51
                        blue + sphereDesc3);
52                  if(null != baseNodes) {
53                      addSphere.setValue(baseNodes);
54                  }
55              } catch (Exception ex) {
56                  ex.printStackTrace() ;
57              }
58          }
59      }
60  }
```

Lines 21–35 actually create the VRML description as a string. This technique has already been used in Chapter 5, "Advanced Java," for the 3D directory browser. The VRML nodes are then created at line 48 and are inserted into the scene at line 53.

The advantage of this approach is that a large and complex piece of VRML code can be created and added to the scene dynamically. In contrast to the **Switch** node, it is not necessary that this VRML is added when the scene is created. Instead, nodes may be created according to the current state of the scene and added dynamically at runtime.

REALIZING GOOD PERFORMANCE AND GOOD LOOKS

The rendering cost of any scene is directly proportional to the number of polygons in a scene. To make a world more realistic and attractive, scene creators tend to use models with hundreds of polygons that are generated by modeling tools whose main target is non-real-time computer graphics.

Refer to the simple car model used by listing 4.7 in Chapter 4. This relatively simple model has 115 vertices and 318 polygons. It is very easy to quickly build scenes with thousands of polygons in the quest for the perfect look!

Sadly, given the current state of the art in software 3D graphics and the limited availability of 3D graphic accelerators for the PC, reducing the number of polygons is the most important technique for acceptable rendering speeds.

One efficient solution is to use the **Billboard** node, which shows 2D images instead of real 3D models. The great advantage of the **Billboard** node is that it tracks the user's position in the scene and always turns to face him. In many cases, elaborate 2D images look much better than poor 3D models and making a **Billboard** always turn to face the users achieves both good performance, an acceptable scene quality, and a sense of action.

Listing 6.6 shows the power of **Billboard**. Wherever you go, the **Billboard** always shows you a 2D image of a lion.

Listing 6.6   Using a Billboard (Lion.wrl).

```
1   #VRML V2.0 utf8
2   Billboard{
3      children[
4      Shape{
5         geometry IndexedFaceSet{
6            coord Coordinate{
7               point[   0 0 0,
```

continues

Listing 6.6, CONTINUED.

```
 8                    1 0 0,
 9                    1 1 0,
10                    0 1 0]
11            }
12           coordIndex[   0, 1, 2, 3]
13         }
14       appearance Appearance{
15          texture ImageTexture{
16             url "lion.gif"
17          }
18        }
19     }
20     ]
21 }
```

You may not be satisfied with this example because it has no animation feature and is, therefore, a little static—although the image is expressive. A solution to the static nature of the previous example is to use the **MovieTexture**. This is an efficient solution to compensate for the lack of animation of 2D images and yet realize good performance. Listing 6.7 uses the original lion example of listing 6.6 but replaces the **ImageTexture** with a **MovieTexture**. When the world is loaded, it looks just the same as before, but clicking the lion makes the lion roar and move toward you! Even when you move away, the lion continues to move toward you until you click it again.

Listing 6.7   Adding a MovieTexture to a Billboard (LionMovie.wrl).

```
 1   #VRML V2.0 utf8
 2   # lion is moving toward you.
 3   #
 4   DEF LION_TRANS Transform{
 5     children[
 6      Billboard{
 7         children[
 8         Shape{
 9            geometry IndexedFaceSet{
10               coord Coordinate{
```

```
11                      point[   0 0 0,
12                          1 0 0,
13                          1 1 0,
14                          0 1 0]
15                    }
16                  coordIndex[   0, 1, 2, 3]
17                }
18              appearance Appearance{
19                texture DEF LION_MOVIE MovieTexture{
20                  loop TRUE
21                  url "lion_movie.gif"
22                  startTime 0
23                  stopTime 1   # initially not playing
24                }
25              }
26            },
27            DEF LION_TOUCH TouchSensor{}
28          ]
29        }
30        ]
31    }
32    DEF LION_PROX ProximitySensor{
33       size 200 200 200      # big enough
34    }
35    DEF LION_TIME TimeSensor{
36       loop TRUE
37       cycleInterval 0.2
38       startTime 0
39       stopTime 1          # initially deactivated
40    }
41    DEF LION_SCRIPT Script{
42       url "LionMovie.class"
43       # when you click the lion...
44       eventIn SFTime touched
45       eventOut SFTime startLion
46       eventOut SFTime stopLion
47       # when the lion is moving toward you...
48       eventIn SFTime interval
49       eventOut SFVec3f setLionPosition
```

continues

Listing 6.7, CONTINUED.

```
50        # watch your current position.
51        eventIn SFVec3f getUserPosition
52    }
53    # when you click the lion...
54    ROUTE LION_TOUCH.touchTime TO LION_SCRIPT.touched
55    ROUTE LION_SCRIPT.startLion TO LION_MOVIE.startTime
56    ROUTE LION_SCRIPT.startLion TO LION_TIME.startTime
57    ROUTE LION_SCRIPT.stopLion TO LION_MOVIE.stopTime
58    ROUTE LION_SCRIPT.stopLion TO LION_TIME.stopTime
59    # when the lion is moving toward you...
60    ROUTE LION_TIME.cycleTime TO LION_SCRIPT.interval
61    ROUTE LION_SCRIPT.setLionPosition TO
      ➥LION_TRANS.set_translation
62    # watch your current position
63    ROUTE LION_PROX.position_changed TO
      ➥LION_SCRIPT.getUserPosition
```

The **ProximitySensor** for the lion entity is defined at line 32. Its position_changed field is routed through to the **Script** node via the ROUTE at line 63.

The **TouchSensor** is used to inform the Java program that the user has clicked on the lion, causing the animation sequence to begin. In listing 6.8, you can see that at line 48 the touched event is used to start the movie playing by setting the start time of the **MovieTexture** via the **Script** node.

After the **MovieTexture** begins to play, it cycles every 0.2 seconds (listing 6.7, line 37). At the end of each cycle, a new cycleTime event is generated, routed through to the event handler class, and handled at line 54 in listing 6.8. This method calculates a new position for the lion entity by looking at the current position of the user as reported by the **ProximitySensor**. This new position is written back to the VRML scene at line 75 in listing 6.8.

Listing 6.8   Controlling the Billboard Position Using Java (LionMovie.java).

```
1    //
2    // lion is moving toward you.
3    //
4    import vrml.*;
5    import vrml.node.*;
6    import vrml.field.*;
7
8    public class LionMovie extends Script{
9        SFTime startLion;
10       SFTime stopLion;
11       SFVec3f setLionPosition;
12
13       // lion is moving or stopped.
14       boolean moving = false;
15
16       // your position and lion position.
17       float userPosition[] = new float[3];
18       float lionPosition[] = new float[3];
19
20       public void initialize(){
21           // get the reference of the event out 'startLion'.
22           startLion = (SFTime)getEventOut("startLion");
23           // get the reference of the event out 'stopLion'.
24           stopLion = (SFTime)getEventOut("stopLion");
25           // get the reference of the event out 'startLion'.
26           setLionPosition = (SFVec3f)getEventOut
             ➥("setLionPosition");
27           // initialize lion position
28           lionPosition[0] = 0.0f;
29           lionPosition[1] = 0.0f;
30           lionPosition[2] = 0.0f;
31       }
32       public void processEvent(Event e){
33           if(e.getName().equals("touched") == true){
34               touched(e);
35           }else if(e.getName().equals("interval") == true){
36               interval();
```

continues

```
37          }else if(e.getName().equals("getUserPosition") ==
         ➥true){
38             getUserPosition(e);
39          }
40       }
41       // when you click the lion...
42       void touched(Event e){
43          double currentTime = ((ConstSFTime)
         ➥e.getValue()).getValue();
44          // toggle the lion state.
45          moving = !moving;
46          // start or stop the lion.
47          if(true == moving){
48             startLion.setValue(currentTime);
49          }else{
50             stopLion.setValue(currentTime);
51          }
52       }
53       // when the lion is moving toward you...
54       void interval(){
55          if(true == moving){
56             // move the lion toward you.
57             float dx = userPosition[0] - lionPosition[0];
58             float dy = userPosition[1] - lionPosition[1];
59             float dz = userPosition[2] - lionPosition[2];
60             float distance = (float)Math.sqrt((double)
            ➥(dx * dx +
61                                              dy * dy +
62                                              dz *
                                           ➥dz));
63             if(distance < 3.0){
64                // if the lion is near to you enough, do not
                  ➥move it anymore.
65                return;
66             }
67             // relative movement distance is 1m.
68             dx = dx / distance;
69             dy = dy / distance;
```

```
70              dz = dz / distance;
71              // update lion position.
72              lionPosition[0] += dx;
73              lionPosition[1] += dy;
74              lionPosition[2] += dz;
75              setLionPosition.setValue(lionPosition);
76          }
77      }
78      // watch your current position.
79      void getUserPosition(Event e){
80          ((ConstSFVec3f)e.getValue()).
              ➥getValue(userPosition);
81      }
82  }
```

If you attempted to realize the same behavior with a pure 3D model, the content would be extremely expensive in terms of computational requirements. The naive approach of making a lion model with polygons and using translation and rotation of its parts at run-time would require sophisticated modeling tools and quite a number of interpolators or Java programs. An alternative approach, based on the techniques discussed previously, would be to prepare all postures of the lion and put all of them in a **Switch** node. However, to achieve any degree of realism would require a lot of postures and would greatly increase the file size of the VRML scene.

Reviewing listing 6.7, you can see that the solution results in both good performance at run-time and smaller file size. Moreover, the 2D image lion is much more realistic than a 3D model with a restricted number of polygons. The combination of the **Billboard** and **ImageTexture**, or **MovieTexture** nodes is quite powerful and can produce impressive effects without resorting to complex animation of 3D objects.

USE LOD FOR LARGE, COMPLICATED SCENES

Another solution for reducing the number of polygons to be rendered is to use a **LOD** (Level of Detail) node. As described in Chapter 4, this node is powerful when your world is quite large and many objects are out of sight or too far away to see and, therefore, unnecessary to render. By using **LOD**s, you are able to give the rendering engine a hint about which objects to render in detail and which not to render.

However, remember to build your scenes in such a way that **LOD**s are not all forced to fire simultaneously when the user navigates into a new part of the scene. This causes a marked slowdown in most browsers.

REUSING MODELS WITH INLINES

In many examples throughout this book, the **Inline** node is used to reduce file size. Generally this has allowed the examples to be complete without having to show all the associated VRML. However, by reusing VRML nodes in various places in a scene, the **Inline** node enables you to reduce the overall size of the VRML file.

Another advantage of the use of **Inline**s is that it makes it easy to maintain common parts of the code. If you modify a common model of a car, all contents using the model are automatically updated. This is especially true if the **Inline** code is not just VRML, but contains **Script** nodes and the associated Java classes.

USE PROTO

As described in Chapter 4, PROTO is useful when you have to make many similar entities but wish to individualize them. Listing 4.21 in Chapter 4 showed how to build a set of autonomously walking men. Each of them had a different walking cycle and direction, but shared the underlying walking mechanism. Used in this way, PROTO has the same merits as **Inline**, by making the file size smaller and easier to maintain.

USE EXTERNPROTO TO BUILD COMMON LIBRARIES

The EXTERNPROTO is extremely powerful and can be seen as the combination of the **Inline** and PROTO mechanisms. It inherits from **Inline** the capability to share a common set of models among many contents, and from PROTO it inherits the capability to parameterize those common sets of models according to each specific content.

These features enable you to build up a set of common VRML libraries that can be reused in many scenes. Each library would be one or more VRML nodes defined as PROTOs. When you are creating a new scene, you reference these library nodes by using an EXTERNPROTO in your new scene and supply the parameters that you need for this particular instance of the PROTO node. The browser then locates the actual definition of the VRML held in your library file and adds it to the current scene with whatever parameters you have specified.

This technique was discussed in more detail in Chapter 4 in the EXTERNPROTO version of the walking man example.

EXPLOITING FEATURES OF COMMUNITY PLACE

The Community Place browser exploits the format of your VRML file for two key features: incremental loading and collision detection. In both cases, the browser looks for separate VRML hierarchies in your VRML file, and if there is more than one, treats them as independent units for the purposes of loading and collision detection. If you construct your VRML scene as a single hierarchy—that is, a single group node with all other nodes defined as children—Community Place is forced to treat your entire VRML scene as one entity.

However, if you build your scene as a set of separate hierarchies—that is, several top level group nodes—the browser can exploit this. The first benefit is when loading the file. Community

Place offers a form of incremental loading that enables the user to begin navigating through the scene before it is fully loaded. While loading, the browser checks for user input and enables you to navigate. However, it checks only after it has finished loading a top level grouping object and all its children. If your file consists of a single top level grouping object, the browser essentially loads everything and then lets you move. If you construct your file as a series of top level objects, the browser checks for user movement between each top level object. If you have large scenes that take time to load, this technique is useful to enable users to begin navigation before the scene is fully loaded.

In a similar manner, the Community Place browser uses the top level node to define the extent of any collision detection it has to perform. The bounding box used in collision detection is dictated by the size of the VRML entities within a hierarchy. If you define your entire scene as a single top level grouping node, Community Place is forced to check all objects that are sub-objects of the initial node you collide with. In some cases, this may result in the browser checking to see whether you have collided with an object that is spatially very far away, but because you have defined it as a single hierarchy, is treated by the browser as close together. Again, the message is simple: try to use scene hierarchies that represent the spatial nature of your scene; don't group everything in one scene hierarchy.

JAVA PERFORMANCE

The interaction between Java and VRML is complicated and subtle. Additionally, different browser implementations have different characteristics. This section provides a few basic tips that will be common to any browser that supports Java. Where necessary, aspects of Community Place's characteristics that may not always be true of other browsers are identified.

Note, however, that the intention is not to discuss the performance of Java in isolation. Any good Java programming book will address those issues. Check the resources in Appendix C.

KEEP VALUES INSIDE SCRIPT NODES

The Java API provides a Java program with methods to get the current value of a field of another node. This is useful, for example, when you want to move an object relative to its current position. However, you need to be aware of the communication overhead between the Java interpreter and the VRML scene.

Community Place is written mostly in C, with some small parts written in Java. When a Java program is running as a result of an event, the program is managed by the Java interpreter. Whenever that Java program uses the Java VRML API, the program is calling across to the C code in the browser. This call is much more costly than a normal method call.

Getting the current value of a field results in invoking this expensive communication, thus reducing performance. Therefore, a good programming technique is to read any field values you need when the Java program is initially called and store those values locally. This means that you are not forced to use the Java VRML API each time you wish to use a field value, and you do not incur the overhead of communicating with the browser.

LIMIT THE NUMBER OF SCRIPT INVOCATIONS

Because crossing the VRML-Java boundary is expensive, you should limit the number of Script invocations your scene makes.

Obviously, the ability to use Java programs to manipulate VRML scenes is essential if you wish to build interesting 3D scenes. However, with some forethought you can build scenes that use Java programs efficiently. For example, when you want to realize an object moving randomly, the naive way is to invoke a Java program again and again to calculate the next position of the object. But you can mimic the same behavior by making a random sequence of location data beforehand and sending that data to a **PositionInterpolator**. The program is then invoked once in a while to reshuffle the position data. This technique diminishes the number of invocations dramatically.

The same technique has already been used in Chapter 4 (listing 4.6). In that case, the program was invoked just once when the user clicked the CD to initialize the rotation axis randomly. After the rotation axis was specified, the program started the time sensor, which drove an **OrientationInterpolator** to rotate the CD smoothly.

The use of programs versus interpolators is dependent on the individual circumstance. Both have advantages and disadvantages.

Table 6.4   Advantages and Disadvantages of Scripts and Interpolators

Technique	Advantage	Disadvantage
Script	Allows complex algorithms. Can use Java Features— for example, AWT or networking.	Expensive invocation.
Interpolator	Supports smooth animation. Cheap invocation costs.	Animation is simple and pre-defined.

LIMIT THE USE OF RUNTIME OBJECT CREATION

The Java-VRML binding uses arrays to get and set MFFields in VRML nodes. For example, to set the translation field of a **Transform** node, a float array is necessary. There are two positions in your code to put this array declaration. One is in the method that actually uses the array; the other is directly in the Script body— that is, making the array an instance variable. Listing 6.9 shows the former; listing 6.10 shows the latter.

With respect to code readability, listing 6.9 is preferable because the array parameter is used only in the method setTranslation(). Unfortunately, this results in allocating and freeing (automatically) float arrays whenever this method is invoked, which is not efficient. On the other hand, listing 6.10 is less easy to read, but more efficient from a memory usage viewpoint.

If your program is not complicated, the style in listing 6.10 is recommended because it is memory efficient. After your program becomes complicated, the style in listing 6.9 is better because it improves overall code readability.

Listing 6.9   Creating an Array Where It Is Used.

```
public class ExampleScript extends Script{
   SFVec3f translation;

   public void initialize(){
      translation = (SFVec3f)getEventOut("translation");
   }
   .....
   setTranslation(){
      float parameter[] = new float[3];
      // set parameter
      ....
      translation.setValue(parameter);
    }
}
```

The following code places the creation of the array, parameter, in the constructor part of the event handler class rather than in the method that uses the array. Although less easy to read, this approach leads to better performance because the array is created only once rather than each time the setTranslation( ) method is called.

Listing 6.10   Creating an Array in the Constructor.

```
public class ExampleScript extends Script{
   SFVec3f translation;
   float parameter[] = new float[3];

   public void initialize(){
      translation = (SFVec3f)getEventOut("translation");
   }
   .....
   setTranslation(){
      // set parameter
      .....
    translation.setValue(parameter);
   }
}
```

MISCELLANEOUS DEBUGGING TIPS

Although an important part of the development process, Java debugging is too large an area to be discussed in this book. Again, you can refer to Appendix C for more information. However, the following sections describe two useful tips for working with Java and VRML.

PUT PARAMETERS IN SCRIPT NODE'S FIELDS

When you create a scene, you tend to continue adjusting parameters, such as the cycle interval of a **TimeSensor**, set by a program using routes. In such a case, a straightforward program implementation tends to incorporate parameters inside the Java class code. If you want to modify the parameters, you must recompile the Java source code, which is often time-consuming.

One solution is to place the parameters in the VRML file as part of the **Script** node and to read the parameters into the Java program. You can then modify the parameters in the file and check the result just by reloading the content, without recompiling the Java code.

This usage of fields of the **Script** node is quite useful while debugging your contents, especially when your Java compiler is slow. However, remember that when you finally ship your scene, you should move all parameters back to the Java program because accessing these values from the VRML scene is expensive.

USE "TRY AND CATCH"

Based on Java's recommended programming style, the VRML 2.0 Java binding notifies users of most errors by using the exception mechanism. Looking back at listing 6.5, you can see that the exception mechanism is used to catch any error from the use of createVrmlFromString(). If an error occurs, it stops operation immediately and throws an exception to its caller, in this case the method, DynamicGen.processEvent(). This exception is displayed in the Java console.

The use of "try and catch" within your Java programs is strongly recommended when manipulating any of the VRML Java classes. Failure to do so will cause a considerable amount of frustration when you are trying to locate the source of errors.

SOUND, COMMUNITY PLACE, AND VRML 2.0

The use of sound is a crucial aspect of any interesting 3D scene. However, the current status of sound support on PCs and for Community Place and the sound mechanisms in VRML 2.0 conspire to make sound a complicated area.

As sound formats, MIDI and WAV are popular with PC users and are the ones required in the VRML 2.0 specifications. However, Community Place supports MOD in place of MIDI, due to the former's widespread use. The following sections provide an indication of the relative strengths and weaknesses of the three sound formats.

MIDI

MIDI is a compact sound format because it holds only score data. MIDI is also the de facto standard in the field of electronic musical instruments, so there is a vast quantity of material available.

However, MIDI has a limited sound source type. Because MIDI was originally designed for musical instruments, it cannot introduce new sound sources, making it difficult to realize totally new sounds (for example, sound effects for games).

Furthermore, there is poor support on PCs and only a limited number of sound cards for the PC support MIDI. Although there are several software emulation drivers for the MIDI format, they use the sound card's FM sound device, not the PCM device. MIDI sound on the PC tends to be of poor quality, although it is potentially an excellent sound format.

Last, because MIDI specifies only the score data and the sound type, different vendor equipment produces different sounds.

WAV

The WAV format provides natural sounds because it holds raw PCM sound data. If the sampling rate is high, it is possible to produce CD-quality natural sound. In addition, WAV is the de facto standard for PCs running Windows.

The downside of the WAV format is that the file size is in proportion to the length of the sound. Moreover, because it holds only raw data, there is no means to specify how to modify the data when playing sound. This is inconvenient when you want to reuse a WAV file holding a crash sound in different situations— one is to play the sound with high pitch and the other is with low pitch.

MOD

The MOD format has the merits of both MIDI and WAV. It can hold sound source data in PCM format so that you can specify, for example, a realistic crashing sound recorded in PCM. It can also hold score data and yet use new sound sources.

MOD specifies how to generate the actual sound output: modifying the sound source data according to attached scores, mixing several sound sources, and generating PCM data. With this specification, software drivers can generate PCM sound data that all sound boards accept. As a result, content creators can rely on the fact that MOD realizes the same sound effects on all machines, something that is impossible with MIDI.

However, there are some drawbacks to using MOD. MOD is not yet as popular as MIDI or WAV, and therefore, fewer tools to manipulate MOD data are available.

Community Place chose to implement MOD sound rather than MIDI because MOD is extremely flexible and well-suited to most computer-related 3D scenes.

DIRECTSOUND

The PC supports two types of sound devices: wave devices and DirectSound. Wave devices have been used as the standard sound device in Windows but are quite raw; they do not support sound mixing. On the other hand, DirectSound is a brand-new, much more powerful sound device. The important point is that DirectSound provides APIs to manipulate sound data, such as mixing, uses hardware support if available, and emulates the process if not. This means that application software does not have to worry about what kind of sound processing is supported by the PC it runs on. It uses DirectSound APIs, and DirectSound does the work.

Community Place checks your PC's configuration and if DirectSound is available, uses its power. Currently, two mechanisms are used: sound mixing and sound spatialization.

SOUND MIXING

When several sound areas overlap in a VRML world, the browser has to mix the sound sources to realize a realistic soundscape. When DirectSound is available, Community Place browser uses its mixing mechanism for both WAV format and MOD format sound data. If you are lucky enough to have a sound board with a hardware mixing feature, you will enjoy high-quality, high-speed sound mixing. Even if your sound board does not support sound mixing, DirectSound takes care of the mixing via software emulation. Obviously, that happens at the expense of performance and quality.

When DirectSound is not available, Community Place uses its own mixing routine for WAV sound data, but does not support MOD format sound, let alone the mixing of MOD sounds. If you want to make your contents available to most PC users— including users with PCs that do not yet support DirectSound— we recommend that you use WAV format sound. If you want to create high-quality worlds that utilize sound mixing and you know your users will have DirectSound, you may want to use MOD format sound.

SOUND SPATIALIZATION

Another useful mechanism that DirectSound provides is sound spatialization. Imagine a scene in which a car making an engine sound is moving toward you from the right and then passes you, driving away to the left. If you have stereo speakers, you would expect the sound at the right speaker to becomes louder while the car is coming toward you. Subsequently, the sound of the left speaker should decrease while the car is moving away. This is what is meant by sound spatialization. You can specify the sound spatialization by setting the **Sound** node's spatialize field to TRUE (which is the default value).

With the spatialize field set to TRUE, you can realize the above sound effect by moving the **Sound** node in your VRML scene. There is, however, a slight difference between the specification of sound spatialization in VRML 2.0 and the actual internal process in DirectSound. VRML 2.0 specifies that stereo sound data is first converted into monaural sound and then fed to the spatialization process to calculate the actual sound for each speaker. This is the ideal approach for a realistic sound, but the overhead of converting is too high. Moreover, DirectSound does not support this conversion. Instead, DirectSound's spatialization of stereo sound is simplistic. When the sound source is located virtually at your right side, the right part of the sound is played louder on the right speaker; when the source is located on your left side, the left-hand sound becomes louder. From the viewpoint of ideal sound spatialization, this implementation is obviously not correct.

As a general rule, if you want to utilize sound spatialization, use monaural sound data. If you want to use music, such as background music for a certain area, turn off the sound spatialization and use stereo sound.

ROUNDUP

Those of you who begin to create complex interactive scenes with Java and VRML are really sailing into uncharted waters. There is not enough experience yet with VRML 2.0—let alone Java combined with VRML—to be able to provide neat answers to most questions.

This chapter brought together a set of hints, tips, and pieces of advice from some of the people who have been working with VRML and Java for the longest time. However, you will inevitably use VRML and Java in ways that haven't been tried before. The tips provided will give you some guidelines on areas that are difficult or prone to performance problems.

At this stage you should know all you need to know about Java and VRML; all that is left is to experiment. The final chapter rounds up this book with a few thoughts on the future of VRML and some discussions on the original motivation for this book—CyberSpace.

CHAPTER

7

THE FUTURE OF VRML

Since 1994, VRML has evolved rapidly, moving from

a little-known 3D language to an integral part of

the booming WWW. Its evolution has been steered

by a dedicated band of enthusiasts based on their

vision for its use. During that time, VRML has gone

from being a simple static scene description lan-

guage to an interactive 3D language with its own

built in execution model. With its gradual accep-

tance into the Internet community and its increas-

ing use by a diverse set of users, the guiding hand of

its original developers will become less relevant.

Instead, the future evolution of VRML will be

dictated by the people who use it to create 3D scenes.

WHAT THIS CHAPTER COVERS

Although it is often dangerous to try to predict the future, this chapter takes a modest look at the factors that will influence VRML's development over the coming years. This chapter is divided into three sections:

➤ What is currently happening in the VRML community, which is likely to surface within the next few months

➤ How the computerization of the consumer electronics industry may provide a platform for VRML that will catapult it into the nation's living rooms

➤ How the first steps in the quest for multiuser shared 3D spaces, CyberSpace, are already being taken and how Community Place enables you to join in that exploration

Although these issues are certainly not the only issues that affect VRML, they offer an interesting, and perhaps alternative, insight into how VRML may be used in the next few years.

This last chapter provides a summary of some of the factors that will affect the possible evolutionary paths that VRML may take. After you read this chapter, you will have one viewpoint on what factors are important. However, this represents only one viewpoint, and you are encouraged to explore further to synthesize your own vision for VRML.

WHERE NEXT FOR VRML?

It is fair to say that VRML is reaching a crossroads in its development. To date, the driving force behind its evolution has been the technologists. The people who shaped it have been predominately those who built the tools to deliver VRML to the community. Although they were influenced greatly by the VRML community, until recently that community was dominated by technologists with the content creators a small, although vocal minority.

That situation is rapidly changing—3D content creators are picking up and beginning to use VRML in earnest. Their requirements, desires, and goals often differ from those of the original technologists. They will dictate how VRML evolves by demanding the functionality that they perceive is important in the quest to deliver interesting content. This, although a difficult fact for the technologists to accept, is the correct way for VRML to evolve. Technologically driven developments that are not firmly grounded in user requirements always fail. Rather than being developed, VRML is now beginning to be used.

CURRENT WORK

The VRML community is large and diverse. What's more, it is growing daily. There are many areas where groups of people are currently discussing evolution to VRML. However, the following three issues are currently widely debated and are likely to cause changes to VRML very soon:

➤   Binary file format

➤   External interfaces

➤   Internal scripting languages

BINARY FILE FORMAT

One of the main performance issues raised in Chapter 6, "Hints and Tips for Effective and Efficient VRML," was the question of file size and the related problem of load time. Because VRML 2.0 is an ASCII format, VRML files tend to be large. In many cases, especially when the files are created automatically using authoring tools, VRML files contain significant amounts of wasted space and redundant information.

A simple solution to this waste is to write small programs that remove white space and redundant information. A more acceptable solution is to use a compression utility such as GZIP.

However, the correct solution is to define a binary format for VRML that enables scene authors to create the most efficient version of their scene by converting the final VRML file to a binary format suitable for transmission on the Internet. The advantages of this binary format are threefold:

➤ **Reduced file size.** Clever compression routines are able to reduce the size of a VRML file by up to 40 percent.

➤ **Reduced load time.** The VRML file, when first loaded into the browser, must be parsed to enable the browser to build up an internal scene structure. A binary file format is far better suited for efficient parsing because it contains the minimum data needed by the browser to build internal structures.

➤ **Some degree of security.** For some people, the amount of time and effort that they put into the development of their VRML scene represents a significant investment. Making this file available as an ASCII file enables anyone to view the contents. When only binary versions of the file are available, casual snoopers will be deterred from trying to borrow parts of the VRML scene without permission.

A binary format for VRML is currently under discussion and will be added to the VRML 2.0 specification in early or mid 1997, after which the main browser developers will start to support this format as well as the existing ASCII format.

EXTERNAL INTERFACES

The Java API that you have been using in this book is referred to as an *internal interface*. This means that the Java program is running internally to the browser.

In some circumstances you may want to use a simple internal language and an external program to manipulate the VRML scene. A good example of this is the use of the VRML browser as a display device for an external authoring tool. The user can create VRML inside the authoring tool, which may already exist. Then, rather than saving the scene data and loading it into VRML browser, the authoring tool would make an on-the-fly conversion to VRML and dynamically add the new VRML to the existing VRML scene via the browser's external interface.

With a sophisticated internal language such as Java, you can achieve the same effect by using Java's capabilities. However, you may prefer to use a simple internal language and the external interface to connect the VRML browser to other applications.

The VRML community is currently debating the precise definition of the external interface. It is likely that the results of this debate will be incorporated as an appendix to the VRML 2.0 specification. Again, by early or mid 1997, implementations of the external interface will become available. Following this, tools that manipulate browsers and the VRML scene via this external interface will begin to appear later in 1997.

INTERNAL SCRIPTING LANGUAGES

As implied previously and discussed in Chapter 2, "Adding Action to 3D Worlds," Java is not the only language that can be used with VRML. Some people feel that authoring content with a simpler language, such as JavaScript or VBScript, is a better choice.

Obviously, no one language answers everyone's needs. The proposal for VRML 2.0 made by Microsoft was based on its own functional language, and as was pointed out in Chapter 1, "Fulfilling the CyberSpace Dream," functional languages have a role for specific applications. In much the same way, a good case can be made for any programming language.

The VRML 2.0 specification allows for the use of any language—it simply states that if a browser implements Java or JavaScript, the implementation should conform to a well-defined interface. It is likely that in the future, other language interfaces will be added to the specification in the same way.

TECHNOLOGIES OF INTEREST

The WWW is a rapidly evolving system, and new technology appears almost every week. Although it does not make sense to try to guess how new technology will affect the evolution of VRML, there are several areas where existing technology is improving so rapidly that it is not hard to predict its impending marriage with VRML. These include continuous media, consumer electronics, and support for multiuser and shared scenes.

CONTINUOUS MEDIA

Continuous media is obviously one of these technological areas. In terms of playing back audio and video from local storage, VRML 2.0 browsers already have simple capabilities. As these browsers improve, their capability to handle continuous media and to mix various media sources will also improve.

The more interesting area is continuous media delivered to the browser via the Internet. Currently, technologies for streaming audio and video into 3D VRML scenes do exist, but they are rudimentary and poorly integrated with VRML.

It is likely that during 1997 we will see dramatic improvements in this area, both in the capability to deliver audio and video across the Internet, and more important, in the capability of the VRML browser to receive these media streams and to integrate them into the VRML scene.

CONSUMER ELECTRONICS VERSUS HOME PCs

The Internet and the WWW are currently characterized by three features: high-speed, high-bandwidth backbones connected using high performance server machines; low-speed connections to the home using dial-up technology; and PCs as the Internet access device of choice.

Two technological developments in the area of consumer electronics that may affect these characteristics are Web TVs and Set Top Boxes.

WEB TVS

Although many people have heard of the Network Computer (NC), the low-cost access device designed to act as a dumb Internet terminal, few people view TVs as examples of these.

Consumer electronics companies all over the world are currently eyeing the Internet market and deciding how best to attack it. These companies view computers differently from traditional computer manufacturers. For them, computers should be dedicated, easy-to-use devices that permeate the home and business environment.

These companies are now in the process of readying their first type of home computers: Internet or Web TVs. These are standard TVs with built-in computers that support Internet access. At the time of writing, Sony, along with Phillips, had launched low-cost Internet TVs in the USA. More sophisticated versions, with better graphics support and better software, are under development. It is very likely that in the future, most Web surfing will be carried out using these devices, simply because most consumers feel happy with TVs and know how to operate them.

Once these devices proliferate, they will offer excellent vehicles for VRML. Not only will VRML be able to provide the in-home graphics interface that the TV user will expect, but it will also provide a 3D window onto the WWW that is currently dominated by textual interfaces.

SET TOP BOXES

Although Web TVs will probably always be simple Network Computers, the next generation of Set Top Boxes (STB) promise to be much more. Most people have already come across some form of STB, either in hotels or as part of a cable system into the home. To date, these devices have concentrated almost exclusively on getting TV programs into the home, although a few trials have offered e-mail facilities and so on.

As digital set top boxes become more prevalent and devices such as cable modems or high-bandwidth Internet links to the STB become commonplace, the STB is set to become the home computer.

This goes hand in hand with another trend that consumer electronics companies are pushing forward: the home network. Within a few years, most home devices will be networked with simple but high-speed links. These devices will use the STB as the master control device and the gateway to the outside world.

Once this technology is in place, the STB becomes the perfect platform for a VRML browser. Not only will it provide the user interface to the WWW that the Web TV will offer, but it will become the interface to the home network and control of the home devices.

Furthermore, because the STB will access a high-bandwidth network, the limitations of the traditional dial-up line will disappear. At this point, integrating high-quality audio and video into the VRML scene running on the STB will become a reality.

Support for Multiuser and Shared Scenes

This book started with a discussion of CyberSpace and the potential of VRML 2.0 to help realize the CyberSpace vision. It seems fitting that it should finish by discussing the first tentative steps in that direction.

Several companies and research groups have been experimenting with VRML and multiuser systems. Some of these are already discussing the evolution of VRML to support multiuser scenes, sometimes referred to as VRML 3.0.

There are two significant issues to consider when thinking about shared VRML scenes. The first is the low-level mechanics of how to make shared scenes work, and the second is the actual semantics of the shared entities in those scenes.

In both of these areas, work is underway to reach some sort of consensus on what VRML should support and what should be left to the scene builders themselves.

LIVING WORLDS

The Living Worlds group, which consists of Sony and two small VRML companies, ParaGraph International and Blacksun Interactive, has made an initial proposal for a multiuser standard for VRML 2.0. The proposal is designed to work with existing VRML 2.0 and enables anyone to implement multiuser functionality as an extension to any existing VRML 2.0 browser.

More important, Living Worlds enables content authors to create multiuser VRML 2.0 content that will work in any browser. Currently, multiuser extensions are proprietary and work only in the browser they were written for.

Initial implementations of the proposed Living Worlds standard will likely begin to appear in early 1997.

UNIVERSAL AVATARS

The Universal Avatars group is attacking the second of these problems, that of the semantics of interaction. Its goal is to define a standard avatar definition that enables a user to create an avatar and then use that avatar in a wide range of multiuser systems, not just VRML-based.

Unlike the Living Worlds group, which concentrates on the mechanisms needed to allow sharing to take place, the Universal Avatars group is trying to define some of the semantics of interactions between avatars so that actions such as greetings are correctly interpreted and displayed in any world that an avatar is used in. Because the remit of the Universal Avatars group is large, it is not yet clear when elements of its work will be available in VRML 2.0 browsers and scenes.

SHARED BEHAVIORS

The general consensus is that shared VRML scenes will support a notion of presence, a representation of the user in the shared scene. This representation is usually referred to as an *avatar*, a 3D version of the user that is sent out to act on behalf of the user. Building a multiuser VRML system that enables many users to see each other in a shared scene is not difficult. The last example in Chapter 5, "Advanced Java," did just that. However, an issue not raised in Chapter 5 is the notion of shared behaviors.

Sharing a scene is about sharing all that happens to the scene. Because changes to the scene are caused by behaviors, being able to share the results of behaviors is the basis for shared scenes. In turn, sharing behaviors implies consistency. Changes that one browser initiates to its local copy of the shared scene have to be seen by others in the shared scene or else they soon become inconsistent—that is, what one person sees is no longer the same as what others see. When this happens, the notion of a shared scene breaks down. The example in Chapter 5 did not address this issue of shared behaviors; the only information that was shared was position information.

Many technical issues are involved in achieving this shared consistency, and for each issue there are many possible solutions. No one solution is correct. The following section briefly discusses how Community Place supports shared behaviors.

THE SEMANTICS OF SHARED SCENES

After the mechanisms for supporting shared scenes are in place, there are many problematic issues relating to how users work and are perceived in those scenes.

Even simple issues such as the size of an avatar can cause problems. A user may choose to build his avatar 15 meters high because his own scenes are large scale. If he uses his avatar in someone else's scene, in which houses are only 1 meter high, he will break the illusion of reality. At a more complex level, if one scene provides money objects that can be picked up and used in shops in the scene, what happens to that money when it is taken to another scene? If this isn't complex enough, what happens if a scene built by somebody from a real society that allows people to carry and use guns and allows avatars to use guns? Taking those guns into more civilized scenes would cause chaos.

It is unlikely that issues as complicated as these will ever be dealt with by VRML. To do so would require VRML to become a far more complex language than it currently is. However, these are issues that need to be addressed before CyberSpace can become more than a dream.

The Internet has now reached the stage where the basic technological infrastructure is in place to enable people to begin to experiment with these issues and to try and resolve them. The next section discusses one such infrastructure—Community Place.

MULTIUSER ASPECTS OF COMMUNITY PLACE

If you have been using Community Place as your default browser, you are probably aware of its multiuser capabilities. If not, take some time to load the multiuser world Circus Park, which is part of the Community Place installation package. This scene automatically connects to a multiuser server where you can explore a little and meet other people sharing that scene.

Built into the Community Place VRML 2.0 browser is support for multiuser scenes, avatars, and, most important, shared behaviors.

In addition, Community Place has a set of mechanisms that enable you to interact with other users: the gesture panel, with which you can express emotion by using smiles, waves, and so on, and the chat feature, which enables you to chat with other users, either in groups or one to one.

To support these features, Community Place is more than just a VRML 2.0 browser. It is a complete distributed application environment. The VRML 2.0 browser can be seen as the viewer component of a multiuser system. The multiuser system consists of the multiuser server, Community Place Bureau, and application objects. Figure 7.1 shows the overall system design.

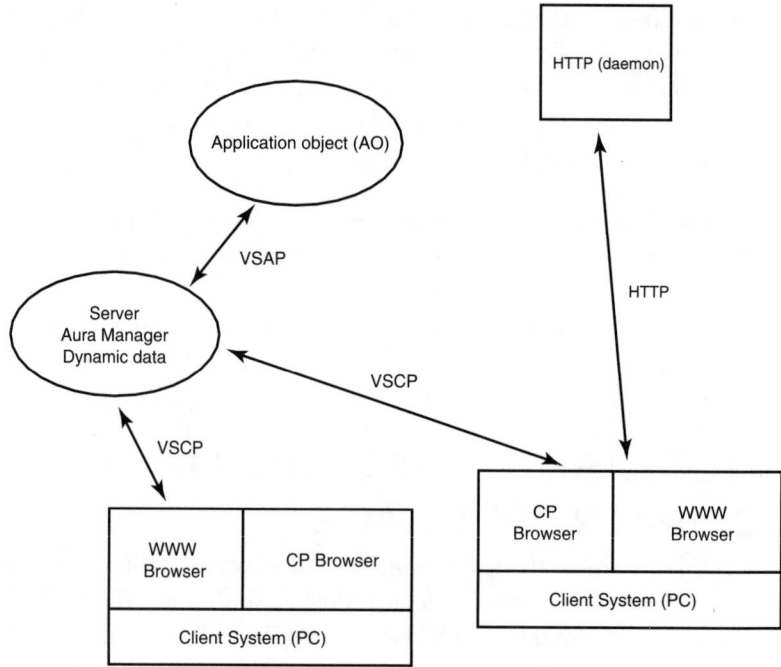

FIGURE 7.1

The Community Place architecture.

BROWSER-SERVER COMMUNICATIONS

The browser communicates with other browsers via the multiuser server (Community Place bureau) by using a protocol called Virtual Society Communications Protocol (VSCP). VSCP has two goals: efficient communication of 3D scene transformations and open-ended support for script-specific messages.

The first goal is achieved by ensuring that VSCP has a compact representation of both 3D transformations and multiuser control messages. The typical size for such a message is 70 bytes. This efficiency is crucial considering our target of dial-up connections.

For the second goal, VSCP has an object-oriented packet definition that enables applications to extend the basic packet format with application-specific messages.

This mechanism enables the browser to send and receive script-level messages that enable the browsers to share events and so support shared interaction within the 3D scene. For example, a local user event causes a local script to run, which in turn uses the message sending facility of the CP system to deliver the event to a remote browser sharing the scene. At the remote browser, this network event is transformed into a local event, which in turn causes execution of the local script.

SERVER

The server, known as the Bureau, acts as a position tracker and message forwarder. Each user's browser, as it navigates through the shared scene, sends position information to the server. The server then uses AOI (area of interest) algorithms to decide which other browsers need to be aware of these position changes. The server sends out the position to the chosen browsers, which use the information to update the position of the local representative (the avatar) of the remote user. The role of the server is limited to managing state on behalf of connected users. The server is generally unaware of the original scene loaded by the browser.

The second role of the server is to carry out a similar function for any script level messages that are generated by a browser as a result of user interaction. Again, in a typical scenario, a user event, such as a mouse click, causes a local script to run. This script updates the local scene graph and then posts the event (or the resulting change) to the server. The server then redistributes this message to other users in the scene so that the scene update is replicated and shared by all users.

APPLICATION PROGRAMMING MODELS

The CP system provides two models for application building. The first is known as the Simple Shared Script (SSS) model, and the second is known as the Application Object (AO) model. The two share some elements but are targeted at different applications and different scene types.

SIMPLE SHARED SCRIPTS

The SSS model is a simple mechanism designed for small shared applications in the 3D world. The model is a replicated script model with each browser downloading the same script and executing it locally. Typically these scripts will be associated with objects that are downloaded in the initial VRML file.

As discussed previously, the VSCP protocol supports script message sending, enabling a local script to send a message to all other browsers sharing the scene. By using this mechanism, it is possible for scene authors to develop small-scale applications that share events by sending those events to other browsers via the server.

Figure 7.2 shows message flows as a result of a user selection in the SSS model (left side). A user selection (1) causes a local script to run (2). This, in turn, converts the event into a message and sends it to the server (3). The server sends the message to all other browsers (4), which then convert the message to an event that causes execution of the local script (5).

The drawbacks of the SSS model are related to ownership and persistence. Because all scripts are equal, they need to communicate among themselves to ensure that any issues such as ownership and locking are resolved. Second, when all users leave the scene, unless one of the scripts takes responsibility for writing out a new initial VRML file, all changes are lost.

Community Place provides a simple set of script objects to help solve these problems, but the burden still rests on the scene authors. As such, this model is generally used for simple shared applications that do not have sophisticated synchronization or persistency requirements.

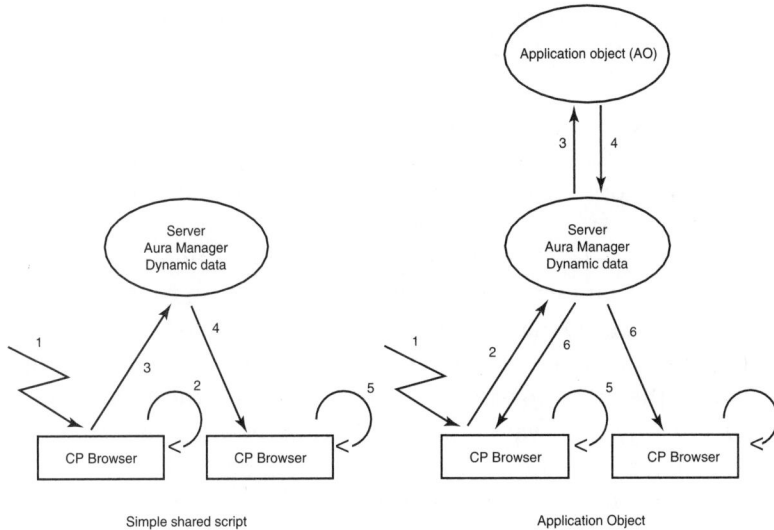

FIGURE 7.2

SSS versus AO scripting.

APPLICATION OBJECTS

Whereas the SSS approach is suitable for a number of simple shared scene updates, more complicated applications require a more sophisticated mechanism. To support this, CP has a notion of an application object that exists externally to the browser and the server. The application object is an application runtime that enables application builders to create 3D objects and to inject them into existing shared scenes. It enables users, via local scripts, to interact with these applications. The applications use the Virtual Society Application Protocol (VSAP) to register their application objects with the server. Registration informs the server about the 3D visual representation, written in VRML, and the spatial positions of the objects. The server then informs the relevant browsers about the existence of these application objects and the VRML file to be downloaded to display them. Last, the server forwards application-specific messages between the AO and the browsers. Therefore, an AO consists of three parts: the 3D data description, written in VRML, that represents the application in the shared scene; the associated scripts that accept user input and communicate back to the AO; and the AO side code that implements the application logic.

The application model presented by the AO is subtly different from the SSS model described previously. In particular, the AO defines a master or controller for the application, whereas in the SSS model, the scripts are essentially peer-to-peer. In addition, the AO mechanism, because it registers objects via the server, benefits from the server's use of AOI to reduce communications.

Returning to the AO model in figure 7.2 (right side), the user event (1) causes a message to be sent to the server (2), which sends the event to the AO managing the selected object (3). The AO carries out internal processing and then typically sends back a message (4) via the server to each browser (5) that runs the local script (6). Obviously, many variations exist within these models. However, the major difference is that the AO model has a designated owner for an object that has sole control over its update.

A key aspect of the AO model is that it allows dynamic addition of VRML data and associated scripts to an existing scene. The feature enables you to build shared scenes that evolve over time. The basic scene description is set up in a base VRML file and downloaded by browsers. Subsequently, new scene elements can be added by creating AOs that manage the new elements and by using the server and the VSAP protocol to add the new scene element to the basic model already loaded by browsers. In a commercial environment, this enables service providers to dynamically inject an application into an existing shared scene. For example, a 3D shopping mall would consist of a basic 3D scene that is downloaded initially by the user. Subsequently, service providers can add shops into the scene by creating AOs and connecting to the server. This model allows a decoupling between server managers and service providers, thus providing an open and extensible mechanism for application provision.

In conjunction with the flexibility of Java and VRML, the use of flexible application scripting mechanisms provides a powerful tool for networked 3D scenes.

USES OF MULTIUSER TECHNOLOGY

Although it is beyond the scope of this book to discuss in detail the development of multiuser applications using Community Place, this chapter finishes with a few screen shots to show some of the features that have been built with CP.

Users who want to explore further the use of CP in building multiuser scenes should check out the CP information on the accompanying CD as well as Sony's Virtual Society home page at http://vs.sony.co.jp.

Figure 7.3 shows a screen shot with two browsers and three users sharing a VRML 2.0 scene. Within the browser window, you can see the avatars representing the two other users who are sharing the scene. One user has chosen a female avatar; another has chosen a male avatar. Community Place enables a scene author to provide as many avatars as he wants and also enables users to customize avatars.

FIGURE 7.3

The multiuser interface of Community Place.

On the right side of the browser window is the multiuser window. This window is used for group chat and avatar gestures, and provides information on the users in the scene. The gesture buttons at the top of the multiuser window provide a means to animate your avatar in the shared scene by using a set of simple gestures. Looking back at the browser window, you can see that the female avatar is using the "hello" gesture.

Text typed into the text chat field of the multiuser window is displayed both in the multiuser window and as a balloon above the user's head. You can follow the conversation in the multiuser window as a series of remarks, each associated with an avatar name.

Last, you can see at the bottom of the multiuser window an indication of the number of users in the shared scene and a facility that enables you to automatically teleport to any one of those users. This feature is helpful when you want to quickly locate another user.

Figure 7.4 shows a shared behavior in action. The behavior is caused by clicking on the ball near the seal. The seal picks up the ball and juggles it. In the figure you can see two browser windows, each representing a user and both viewing the seal from different angles. When one of the users clicks on the ball, the animation begins in his local browser. This animation event is then sent to the other browser, and the animation begins in the second browser.

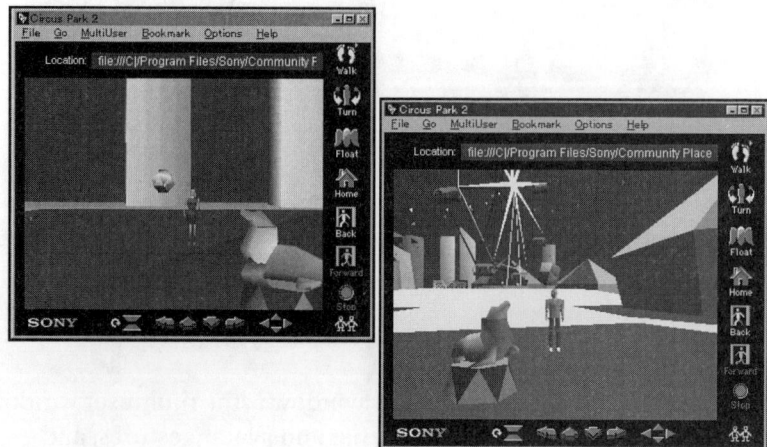

FIGURE 7.4
A simple shared object.

At the point where the screen capture is taken, the animation is happening simultaneously in both browsers. The implementation for this uses Java and a **PositionInterpolator** and relies on the SSS model.

ROUNDUP

This chapter has given you an idea of where VRML will go next, both in terms of the technology and in terms of the use of the technology. Predicting the future is a difficult business and one best left to soothsayers and fools. The intention here was to identify several important trends and show some possibilities that may lay the foundation for CyberSpace.

However, the future really rests in your hands. Our job has been to build this technology and to tell you how it works. You, the people who create the contents, are the ones who will decide how to use the tools we have provided to build your version of CyberSpace. We wish you luck.

Appendix A

VRML and 3D Principles

Janet McAndless, John D. DeCuir, Christopher Janney, Joseph Munkeby, Jai Natarajan, Nick Bali, and Karen Eppinger.

The Virtual Reality Modeling Language (VRML) provides a specification for the description of three-dimensional space, a scene corresponding to reality or completely imaginary and conceptual. A VRML browser program acts as an interpreter of ASCII text files written according to the VRML specification; the browser renders in real time a visual form of the textual scene description. As the 3D rendered space is traversed by a user of the VRML browser interface, the browser software must regenerate the visual scene contents in real time from the user's viewpoint.

This appendix is designed as an introduction to computer graphics principles using the VRML 2.0 scene description and is not intended to rigorously describe the VRML 2.0 specification or its implementation by VRML world authors. The complete VRML 2.0 specification document can be found on the Web at http://vag.vrml.org/VRML2.0/FINAL/.

A basic familiarity with programming principles—and especially object-oriented paradigms—is assumed. The information contained on the following pages will help prepare you to build three-dimensional worlds by using the VRML 2.0 file format, a graphical special case extension of the programming methodology pioneered with Smalltalk, C++, and Java.

Getting Started

To make identification of VRML 2.0 standard ASCII files, known as *.wrl* files, straightforward for browser and other interpreter software, each VRML 2.0 file listing must begin with the following first line, known as a *file header*:

```
#VRML V2.0 utf8
```

The reference "utf8" refers to a unicode international standard for displaying language characters inside VRML **Text** nodes.

Any other text line within your VRML file that begins with a pound or hash symbol (#) is considered a comment, up to the next carriage return, and is ignored by VRML interpreter software. Example comment lines are as follows:

```
#VRML V2.0 utf8
#This is a comment line which the VRML browser will
➥ignore.
#Use comments liberally to describe what your VRML code
#is intended to do.
```

This first VRML identification line constitutes a completely valid VRML 2.0 file (although your browser may inform you that there's no meaningful data included in this file). However, you will want to add further information in order to define something other than a dark, empty space. Following this required VRML 2.0 header, a .wrl file can contain any number of geometry, light, grouping, or other *nodes* (descriptions of discrete scene elements)—as well as event routing statements to create behaviors and interaction—within 3D space.

Listing A.1 constructs an evenly lit red sphere with a 10-unit radius. The code used in this example will be examined closely in later sections of this appendix; for now, notice the field values for emmisiveColor and radius. By passing the arguments 1 0 0 to the emmisiveColor field, you are defining the **Shape**'s surface material to reflect 100 percent red light and 0 percent green and blue light respectively.

Listing A.1   sphere.wrl.

```
#VRML V2.0 utf8
Shape {
  appearance Appearance {
    material Material {
      emissiveColor 1 0 0
    }
  }
  geometry Sphere {
    radius 10
  }
}
```

VRML is an object-based language that provides a file format definition for describing objects in 3D space, called nodes. A node would correspond to an "object" in C++ or Java. You can consider node to be a base class with derived types of **Box**, **Sphere**, **Sound**, **SpotLight**, and so on. Each object node has common properties such as a type name, default field values, and the capability to send and receive messages (events in VRML 2.0) that set field values. When you instantiate a derived class, you can overide the default field values in much the same way you can specify paramters to a C++ class instance. A benefit of VRML is that when you instantiate a node, you generally obtain a visually tangible result.

VRML offers many predefined nodes, such as a library of objects from which your scene elements may inherit characteristics, and also enables you to derive and use your own nodes by prototyping.

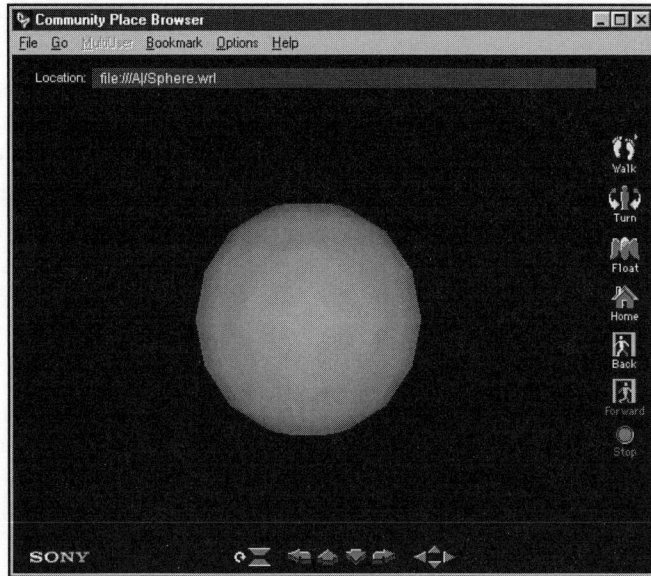

FIGURE A.1

The rendered sphere.wrl.

You can group these nodes in the VRML scene to organize your virtual world's layout and functionality by creating a *scene graph*. The scene graph resembles the roots of a tree where the trunk is the highest hierarchical level with *children* grouped into branch, or *grouping*, nodes beneath it. Your child node inherits characteristics such as position and orientation from each of its parent nodes in an object-to-world (scene graph) hierarchical order.

To illustrate, listing A.2 has been graphed in figure A.2 to show the hierarchical order of nodes in the VRML scene graph. In the example, DEF is the keyword to add the name to the node.

Listing A.2   scene.wrl.

```
#VRML V2.0 utf8
DEF TRUNK Transform {        #parent node in the scene graph
  translation 0.0 1.0 0.0  #all children will be moved 1 meter
  ➥in Y
  rotation 0.0 1.0 0.0 0.39  #all will be rotated 22.5 degrees
  ➥about Y
```

```
children [
   DEF BALL Transform {    #child of TRUNK Transform node
      translation 3.0 0.0 0.0  # the sphere will be moved 3 units
      ➥on X
      children [
         Shape {                  #child of
            appearance Appearance {
               material Material {
                  emissiveColor 1 0 0
               }
            }
            geometry Sphere {   radius 1   }
         }
      ]
   }
   DEF CUBE Anchor {
      url [ "http://spiw.com/" ]
      children [
         Shape {
            geometry Box { size 1 2 2 }
         }
      ]
   }
]
}
```

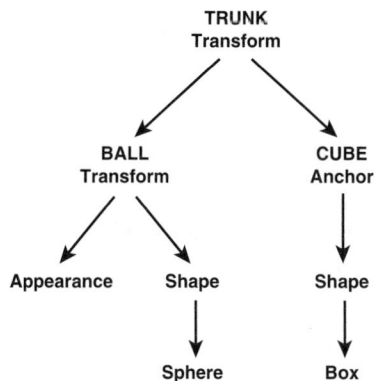

FIGURE A.2
The scene.wrl scene graph hierarchy.

Node's fields are parameters or keywords whose values describe the properties of the node object. Fields can be divided into two categories: attribute fields, which enable you to set properties for nodes you instantiate such as the ambientIntensity of a **Spotlight** or the radius of a **Sphere**, and "glue" fields, which enable you to pass another node description as a property value. The VRML **Shape** node includes two examples of glue fields: the geometry field, which accepts a geometry node argument such as **Sphere**, **Box**, or **Cone**, and the appearance field, which accepts the **Appearance** node description.

Many of the fields—including glue fields—within a given node are *exposed* so that you can alter their values at runtime by using event triggers such as sensors and scripts (see Chapter 3, "Letting Java Loose"). Other fields are private: values can be set only at startup.

VRML STANDARD UNITS

VRML units have been standardized to represent meters for linear distance and radians for rotational angles. If you create a shape such as a box defined as 1 unit in length, 1 unit wide, and 1 unit high, you have defined a virtual cube that corresponds to a real-world cube that is 1 meter on a side. If the cube is resting on the floor and you rotate it 45 degrees so that you are now viewing the cube from a corner position, you are rotating it around the Y axis Pi/4, or 3.14/4, or 0.785 radians.

WARNING

> The VRML export facilities for many 3D modeling packages perform a one-to-one conversion into meters of whatever units you are currently using to model. For example, if you modeled an 80-inch tall human avatar, the exported VRML model would be 80 meters high! To avoid this problem, make a habit of shifting to meter units before you begin modeling.

To position an object in a VRML world, use the rotation field within the **Transform** group node to define its orientation and then use the translation field to define the number of units along each axis you want the object to lie. Transformations are discussed in more detail in the following sections.

COORDINATE SYSTEM, LIGHTING MODEL, AND RENDERING

VRML organizes a two-dimensional display representation of three-dimensional space by using a right-handed Cartesian coordinate system. That is, if you hold your right hand up to your monitor with your palm facing you, fingers pointed upward, and thumb pointed to your right, your thumb is pointing in the direction of the positive X axis and your index finger is pointing in the direction of the positive Y axis. Bend your other fingers toward you to locate the direction of the positive Z axis, which points outward from your computer display monitor.

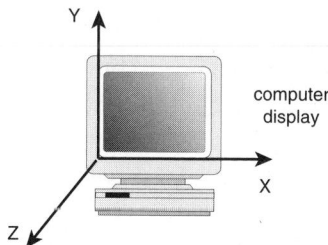

FIGURE A.3

The VRML coordinate system.

VRML geometry node objects are described with reference to this coordinate system by constructing points in space using three-dimensional coordinates. These points are then connected by lines to form a *mesh,* which describes the surface area of the geometry, often referred to as a *model.* Figure A.4 shows a sphere rendered in *wireframe mode* to display the points and lines which describe the model[1].

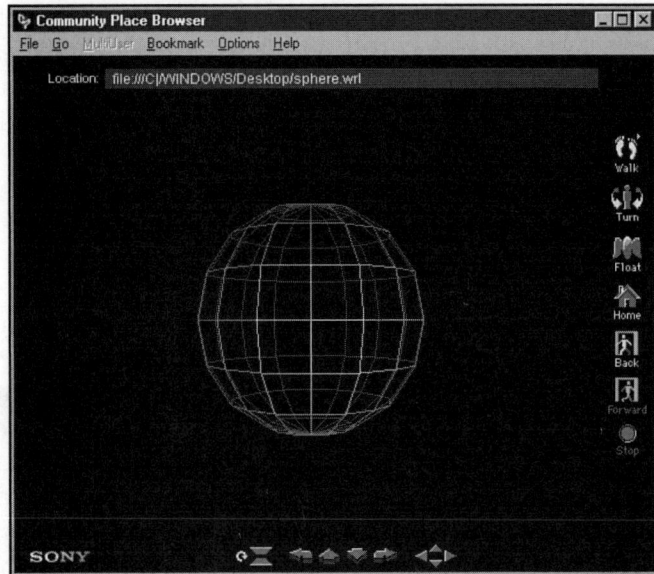

FIGURE A.4
The sphere.wrl shown in wireframe.

Without any specified transformation, your VRML geometry nodes—unless **Text**—are centered by default at world coordinates 0,0,0 on the X, Y, and Z axes respectively with height values extending in the positive Y (up) direction. (**Text** nodes begin a text string by default with its left side aligned to world coordinates 0,0,0, placing each successive text character in the direction of the positive X axis, as shown in figure A.5.)

VRML offers many base node objects, known as *primitives*, including **Box**, **Sphere**, **Cone**, and **Cylinder**, from which you can construct your 3D scene. However, if you build and export a mesh from a 3D modeling package, the object will appear in your .wrl file as an **IndexedFaceSet** node, or a set of polygons.

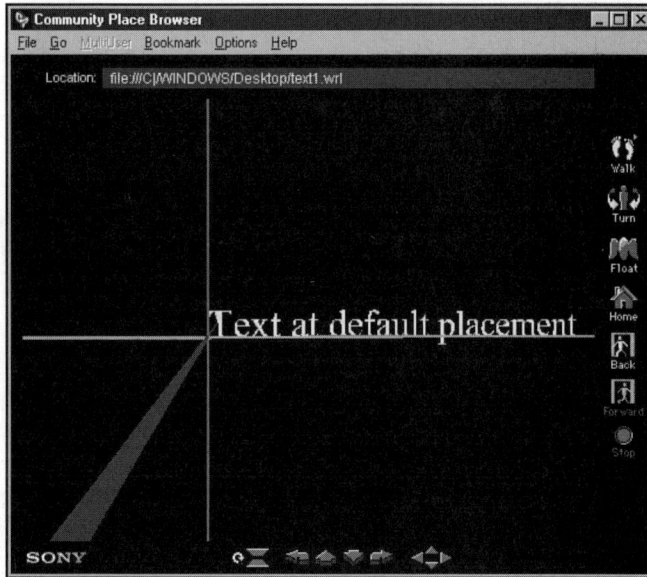

FIGURE A.5

*Tubes have been rendered along the X (green), Y (red), and Z (blue) world coordinate axes to show the default placement of a **Text** node character string. When the scene is rendered by a VRML browser program, the mesh surface is shaded according to the color, material, and texture properties you assigned as well as the lighting configuration you described for the scene. This creates the perception of dimension, or depth, along the Z axis.*

Each vertex contained in an **IndexedFaceSet** mesh is described by a three-dimensional point in its child **Coordinate** node listing. The **IndexedFaceSet** node's coordIndex listing then defines the grouping and order of point set vertices to define face (a *normal* is a vector that extends from the surface of a polygon outward). The side of a polygon from which the normal projects is the face that VRML browser programs render; the opposite side of this face does not exist.

To determine the direction of a polygon's normal, check whether points listed in the **Coordinate** point set appear in counterclockwise order when taken in the order listed in the coordIndex set. If you curl your right-hand fingers around these points in the order they are listed in the coordIndex, your thumb points in the direction of the face normal, the direction in which light is reflected by the polygon.

If you encounter a face whose normal is directed away from you, that polygon will not be rendered by the browser. To correct the problem, simply "flip" the normals by reversing the coordIndex values for each affected face. If *all* the polygon's face normals are directed inside the mesh so that outward faces are not being rendered, you can flip all normals in a single step by setting the **IndexedFaceSet**'s ccw (counterclockwise) field to FALSE in place of its default TRUE value.

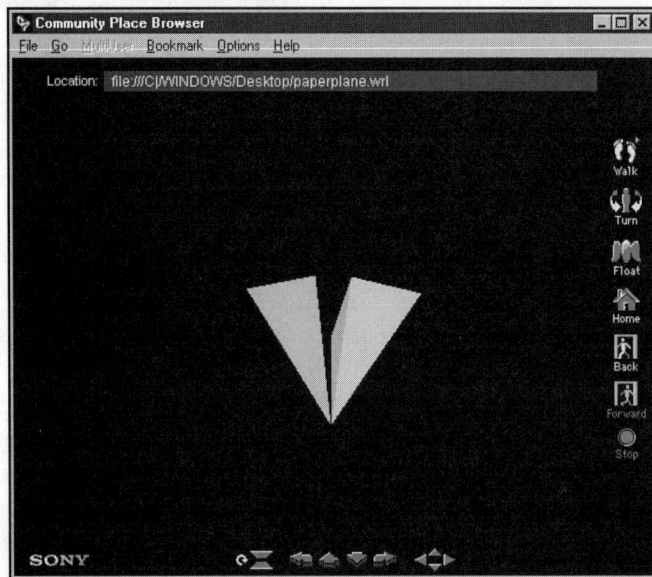

FIGURE A.6

Figure A.6 shows the rendered result of the VRML file listing given in listing A.3. As you can see, the inside left face is missing in the rendered image.

FIGURE A.7

A quick wireframe check shows that the missing face does indeed exist. After the VRML file listing has been corrected by flipping the face normal as noted in the comment on the second line of the coordIndex listing (see listing A.3), all faces are correctly rendered.

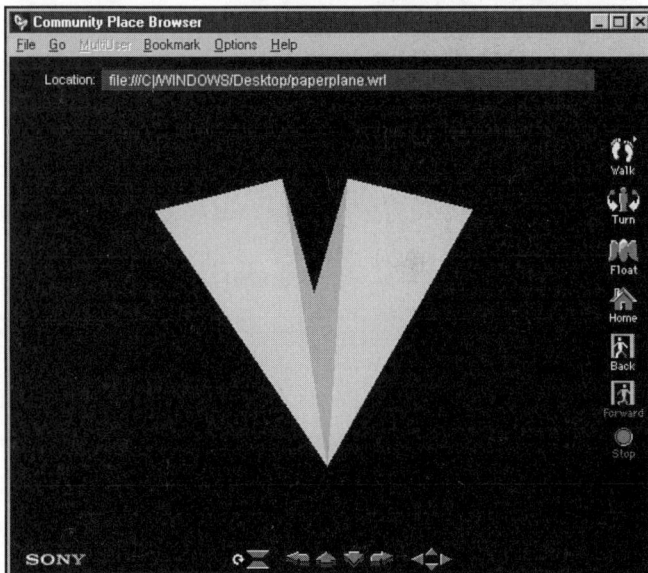

FIGURE A.8

The rendered result of the corrected VRML file listing.

Listing A.3   Paperplane.wrl.

```
#VRML V2.0 utf8
Shape {
  appearance Appearance {
    material Material {
      diffuseColor   1.0 1.0 1.0
      emissiveColor   0.5 0.5 0.5
      shininess     5
    }
  }
  geometry IndexedFaceSet {
    coord Coordinate {
      point [ 0.0  0.0  0.5,
             -0.5  0.0 -0.5,
             -0.1  0.1 -0.5,
              0.0 -0.3 -0.5,
              0.1  0.1 -0.5,
              0.5  0.0 -0.5 ]
    }
    coordIndex [ 0, 1, 2, -1,
                 3, 2, 0, -1,  # This face must be flipped to 0,
                ➥2, 3
                 3, 4, 0, -1,  # -1 means a delimiter.
                 4, 5, 0, -1 ]

    normalPerVertex FALSE  #renders sharp angles at creases
    ➥between faces
    ccw     FALSE          #coordIndex points are listed in
    ➥clockwise order
    #solid   FALSE  #faces are defined to be 2-sided when this is
    ➥uncommented
  }
}
```

LINEAR TRANSLATION IN THREE DIMENSIONS AND OTHER TRANSFORMS

A **Transform** is a basic construct in VRML, a general grouping node that can serve as a container for many objects. However, **Transform** offers a greater functionality. In computer graphics, a *transformation* is a generic term for a "movement"—whether scaling, rotation, or translation. A **Transform** node in VRML 2.0 can apply a generic transformation to a group of objects simultaneously to help you arrange your 3D world space. The **Transform** node fields we're interested in are defined with their default values as follows:

```
Transform{
  center 0 0 0
  translation 0 0 0
  rotation 0 0 1 0
  scale 1 1 1
  scaleOrientation 0 0 1 0
  children [ ]
}
```

Group is an equivalent grouping node that offers the same "container" functionality as the **Transform** node, but it has no capability to operate on its children. Because you can achieve the **Group** node's hierarchy containment in using **Transform** *and* you retain the ability to quickly add a transformation later, you should habitually group your scene hierarchies under **Transform** in place of the **Group** node.

A VRML scene graph can contain any number of group nodes to define a convenient hierarchy for manipulating your world scene. In addition, you can group **Transform** and other group nodes *within* group nodes (as you'll want to do, for example, to place an event triggering sensor at some level inside an object hierarchy while retaining the ability to manipulate the group as a whole).

The values of the **Transform** fields, such as translation or rotation, are inherited by any **Shape** node or other child of the **Transform**'s children field. The children field keyword signals that the following nodes are subsidiary to the parent group node. In listing A.4, we are about to tell the browser about the **Box** named CUBE in the scene and how it looks. We can then use the **Transform** parent group node to translate, scale, and rotate the **Box**.

Listing A.4   cube.wrl.

```
#VRML V2.0 utf8
# move the Box
DEF transformCUBE Transform {
  translation -3.0 2.0 1.0   # 3 units to the left on x
  children [
    DEF CUBE Shape {
      appearance Appearance {
        material Material {
          diffuseColor 1 0 0
          specularColor 0.9 0.9 0.9
        }
      }
      geometry Box {}
    }
  ]
}
```

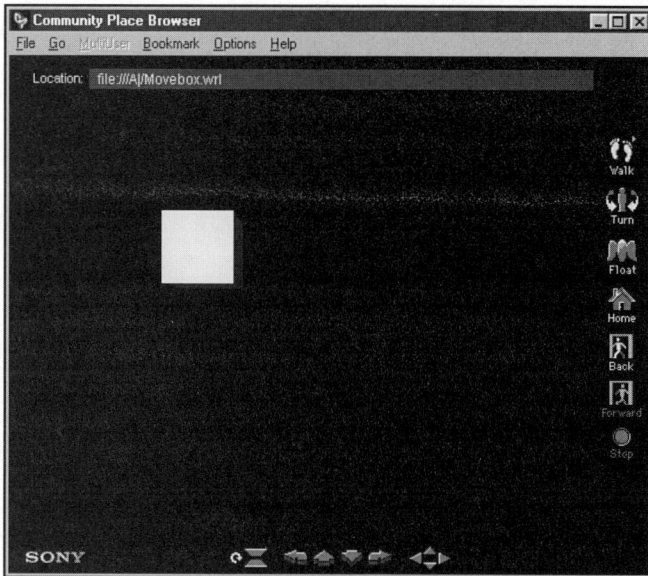

FIGURE A.9

The rendered cube.wrl, translated on the X, Y, and Z axes.

This example moves, or translates, the **Box** node geometry from the origin 3 meters to the left along the negative Z axis, 2 meters up on the positive Y axis, and 1 meter toward you on the positive Z axis. Note that an **Appearance** node has been added to this example to make it more visually appealing. You can ignore the **Appearance** node for the purposes of this discussion.

To reiterate, whenever you use a group node of any type to organize your VRML scene graph elements, you must specify the group node contents between children field brackets. These children nodes inherit the transforms of the parent group node that defines the local coordinate space for the hierarchy. The parent group node, in turn, also inherits any transforms from its parent group nodes so that local translation, scaling, or rotation transforms are always relative to the last transform performed on the higher grouping. That is, transforms for group nodes are cumulative within the hierarchy.

To demonstrate this transformation hierarchy, we can add new geometry objects to the scene both inside and outside the transformCUBE **Transform** group node.

Listing A.5   vrmllogo.wrl.

```
#VRML V2.0 utf8
# move the Box
DEF transformCUBE Transform {
  translation -3.0 2.0 1.0  # 3 units to the left on x
  children [
    DEF CUBE Shape {
      appearance Appearance {
        material Material {
          diffuseColor 1 0 0
          specularColor 0.9 0.9 0.9
        }
      }
      geometry Box {}
    }
    DEF transformBALL Transform {
      translation 3.0 -2.0 -1.0 # reverses trCUBE translation
      children [
        DEF BALL Shape {
          appearance Appearance {
            material Material {
              diffuseColor 0 1 0
              specularColor 0.9 0.9 0.9
            }
          }
          geometry Sphere {}
        }
      ]
    }
  ]
}
DEF transformCONE Transform {
  translation 3 0 0
  # 3 meters to the right on x from the origin to avoid
  # overlaying the sphere. This Cone is not affected
  # by the transformCUBE translation above.
  children [
```

```
DEF CONE Shape {
  appearance Appearance {
    material Material {
      diffuseColor 0 0 1
      specularColor 0.9 0.9 0.9
    }
  }
  geometry Cone {}
}
]
}
DirectionalLight {
  direction -1 -1 -5
  intensity 0.8
}
```

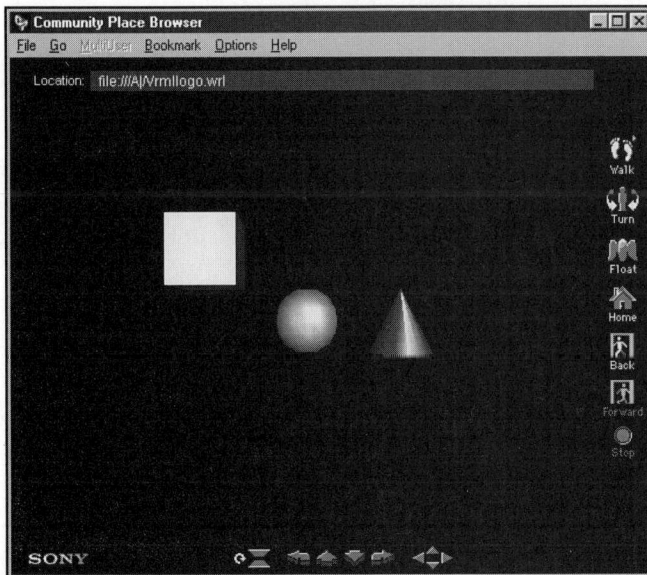

FIGURE A.10

Vrmllogo.wrl.

The CONE has been defined outside the transformCUBE **Transform** hierarchy to provide a reference point for the translations of the CUBE and BALL. The CONE is not affected by transforms performed on the CUBE and BALL. However, because the BALL's **Transform** parent has been defined as a child of the CUBE's **Transform** parent, BALL inherits the same CUBE translation. BALL's precise opposite translation accomplished by its local **Transform** node returns the BALL center to the world origin.

As you can see in this example, one group node can be contained by another group node (of the same or differing type) and inherits its parent's **Transform**s including translation. If the CONE object were also contained within this hierarchy, the entire scene could be moved within 3D space by using a single translation at the highest **Transform** level. This capability can be quite useful as your scene graph becomes more complex.

OBJECT ROTATION

Several elements now exist within the VRML world, but the scene could use some dramatic effect. In the VRML logo, which consists of these same elements, the cube and cone are shown at angles to provide some perspective and a clear visual cue that the scene is being presented in 3D. Let's rotate those elements and take a fresh look. As you saw previously in the **Transform** node's partial definition, you can set values in the rotation field to be inherited by all the **Transform**'s children.

The rotation field accepts three values from –1.0 to 1.0 that describe a vector in terms of the X, Y, and Z axes respectively, followed by a rotation amount expressed in radians.

Think of the first three rotation field values as defining a new point (X, Y, Z) in 3D space. If you connect this point to the origin (either the world origin or the geometry's local origin if you have defined a translation for this node or its parent), you define your rotation vector—the axis about which the object rotates. If you type rotation 1 0 0, for example, you define the X axis as your rotation vector for the object.

The radian angle value then describes, in terms of Pi (approximately 3.14, which is equivalent to 180 degrees rotation), the degree of rotation that is applied to the object on this rotation axis. To determine whether your rotation angle should be positive or negative, point your right-hand thumb away from the origin in the direction of your rotation vector and curl your fingers around the vector. Your curled fingers point in the direction of positive rotation. To rotate in the opposite direction, use a negative radian value.

Listing A.6   vrmllogo2.wrl.

```
#VRML V2.0 utf8
#let's move the sphere outside the box transform hierarchy
#and give the logo a little twist
DEF transformCUBE Transform {
  translation  -3.0 2.0 1.0  # 3 meters left(X), 2 up(y) and 1
  ➥back(Z)
  rotation -1 1 0.8 0.785   # rotate about 45[dg] around an
  # axis whose origin is <-3,2,1> and vector <-1,1,0.8>
  children [
    DEF CUBE Shape {
      appearance Appearance {
        material Material {
          diffuseColor 1 0 0
          specularColor 0.9 0.9 0.9
        }
      }
      geometry Box {}
    }
  ]
}
# The ball is now outside the cube hierarchy
DEF transformBALL Transform {
  translation 0.0 2.0 1.0
  children [
    DEF BALL Shape {
      appearance Appearance {
        material Material {
          diffuseColor 0 1 0
          specularColor 0.9 0.9 0.9
```

continues

Listing A.6, CONTINUED

```
          }
        }
        geometry Sphere {}
      }
    ]
  }
DEF transformCONE Transform {
  translation 3 2 1
  # 3 meters to the right on x to avoid overlaying the sphere
  rotation 0.5 0.1 0.75 0.785   # rotate about 45 degrees around
  # an axis whose origin is <-3,2,1> with vector <0.5,0.1,0.75>
  children [
    DEF CONE Shape {
      appearance Appearance {
        material Material {
          diffuseColor 0 0 1
          specularColor 0.9 0.9 0.9
        }
      }
      geometry Cone {}
    }
  ]
}
DirectionalLight {
  direction -2 1 -5
  #adjust the light for new geometry placement
  intensity 0.8
}
```

SCALING

The scene is starting to come together better now, but the cube
appears slightly bigger than the sphere and cone—nothing a little
scaling won't fix. You may find you often need to use the **Transform** node's scale field to perform a uniform scale operation
(scale applied equally to all axes) depending on the modeling
tools you use and the scale used by another VRML author whose
work you integrate into your own scene graph.

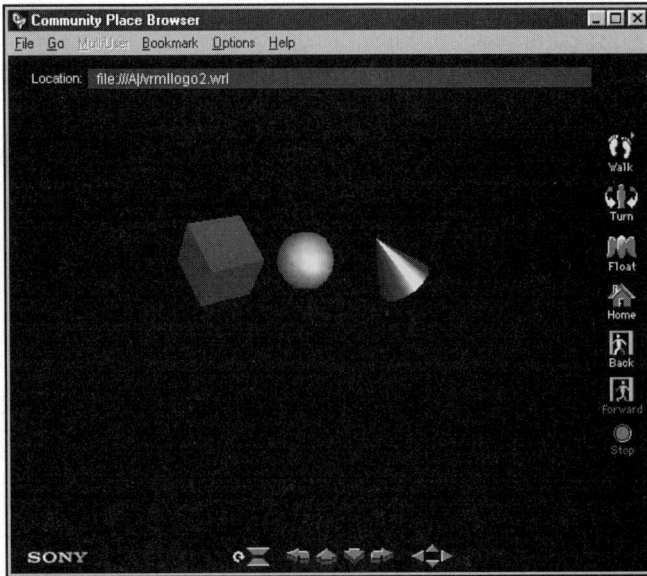

FIGURE A.11
Rotated objects in logo.wrl.

Add the following line to your wrl file after the CUBE's **Transform** line and before its children line:

```
scale 0.75 0.75 0.75
```

You can rescale geometry in a **Transform** node by any factor from 0 through infinity on each axis individually. By animating (via a **TimeSensor** or **TouchSensor** event route) a scale on one or two axes, you can achieve interesting geometric distortion effects.

Note that when you use nested **Transform** nodes, the order of your translation, scale, and rotation operations becomes important. This would be most obvious, for example, if you do not scale by the same amount on all axes because a rotation affects the orientation of your object with respect to the axes along which it will then be scaled. To demonstrate, a cylinder scaled 50 percent along the X axis and then rotated –90 degrees around the Z axis appears very different from a cylinder that is first rotated –90 degrees around the Z axis and then scaled 50 percent on X (see figures A.13 and A.14).

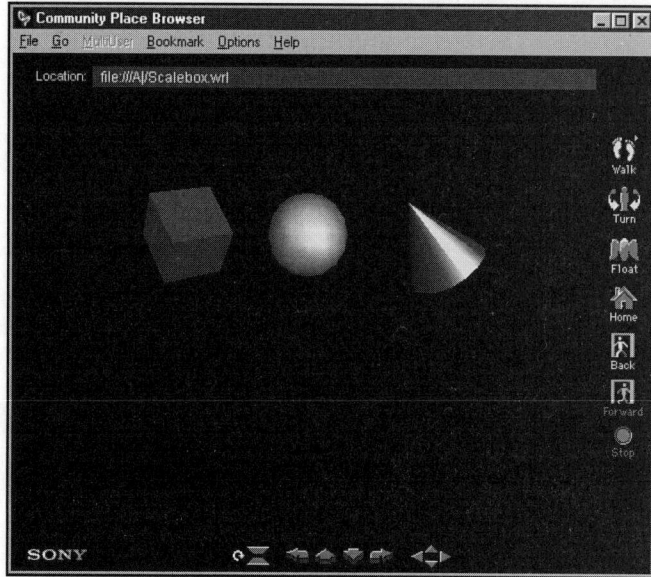

FIGURE A.12

Scaled down box in logo.wrl.

Listing A.7   l1.wrl.

```
#VRML V2.0 utf8
#c1.wrl file listing
Transform {
  rotation 0 0 1 -1.57
  children[
    Transform {
      scale 0.5 0.0 0.0
      children [
        Shape { geometry Cylinder{} }
      ]
    }
  ]
}
```

FIGURE A.13
C1.wrl.

Listing A.8   cyl2.wrl.

```
#VRML V2.0 utf8
#c2.wrl file listing
Transform {
  scale 0.5 0.0 0.0
  children[
    Transform {
      rotation 0 0 1 -1.57
      children [
        Shape { geometry Cylinder{} }
      ]
    }
  ]
}
```

FIGURE A.14
C2.wrl.

Likewise, if you translate a child node's local coordinate system 100 meters on the positive X axis and then perform a rotation in a parent **Transform** node around the Z axis, rather than the child spinning around its object center, you produce a revolution of the child node around the parent's center, or origin.

CENTER AND SCALEORIENTATION TRANSFORM NODE FIELDS

When performing a **Transform** on a scene or object, you can supply an offset by using the center field to define an arbitrary point from which translation, rotation, or scale is calculated for the children of the **Transform** hierarchy. The scale operation further enables you to set a vector value for the **Transform**'s scaleOrientation field to rotate the local coordinate system prior to scaling.

VRML Nodes

VRML 2.0 nodes can be divided into two basic categories: graphical and nongraphical. The graphical nodes include geometry types such as **Box** and **Sphere**, attribute nodes such as **Appearance** and **Material**, and parent nodes, including **Shape** and **Transform**. These are the nodes that together build your rendered scene. The VRML 2.0 graphical nodes are arranged in the following table.

Grouping Nodes	Geometry Nodes	Attribute Nodes
Shape	Box	Appearance
Anchor	Cone	Color
Billboard	Cylinder	Coordinate
Collision	ElevationGrid	FontStyle
Group	Extrusion	ImageTexture
Transform	IndexedFaceSet	Material
Inline	IndexedLineSet	MovieTexture
LOD	PointSet	Normal
Switch	Sphere	PixelTexture
	Text	TextureCoordinate
		TextureTransform

Nongraphical nodes augment your 3D world by providing the means in VRML 2.0 to add dynamic effects through sound, event triggering, and animation data. These nodes are listed in the following table.

Sound	Event Triggers	Animation Data
AudioClip	CylinderSensor	ColorInterpolator
Sound	PlaneSensor	CoordinateInterpolator
	ProximitySensor	NormalInterpolator

continues

Sound	Event Triggers	Animation Data
	SphereSensor	OrientationInterpolator
	TimeSensor	PositionInterpolator
	TouchSensor	ScalarInterpolator
	VisibilitySensor	
	Script	

Other useful nodes, including lights, group nodes other than **Transform**, and bindable nodes, are discussed later in this appendix in the section titled "Useful Node Descriptions."

NODE FIELDS

As previously mentioned, VRML 2.0 node fields enable you to assign attributes to distinguish one node from another of the same type.

The most general types of node fields are those that accept a single value (prefixed by SF) and those that accept multiple parameter values (prefixed by MF). For MF fields, you must enter parameter values within square brackets [] separated by commas, spaces, or other white space.

For example, the children field of a grouping node such as **Transform** or **Anchor** acts as a container for one or more node objects—the members of the group node's hierarchy. Likewise, the **ImageTexture** node's url field accepts multiple URL location listings for material texture maps. This enables the VRML browser to load any locally found textures before attempting to do so from a network server. That is, if you list first a local drive path name to an image map or .wrl file, the browser attempts to load this local copy, stopping if the file is found, and proceeding to the next URL location—which may be pointed to a network server—only if the file is not located at the initial URL pointer.

All nodes contain fields of one or more of the following types:

Field Type	Argument Accepted
SFNode/MFNode	VRML node
SFBool	TRUE or FALSE
SFColor/MFColor	A set of three floating point values from 0.0–1.0 corresponding to red, green, and blue
SFFloat/MFFloat	Single-precision floating point number(s)
SFImage	Pixel description of an image map
SFInt32/MFInt32	32-bit integer
SFRotation/MFRotation	Four values: first three describe a rotation vector and the last is radian rotation amount
SFString/MFString	String(utf8)
SFTime/MFTime	Number of seconds since a set time of origin (in double-precision floating point)
SFVec2f/MFVec2f	Two-dimensional vector of SFFloat
SFVec3f/MFVec3f	Three-dimensional vector of SFFloat

At the highest level of abstraction, fields may be classified as either describing node attributes or as node "glue." A glue field defines which other VRML 2.0 nodes may be passed as an argument to this node type.

The diagram shown in figure A.15, which corresponds to the following VRML text file, illustrates this distinction between glue fields and attribute fields.

Listing A.9   Glue fields vs. attribute fields

```
Shape {
  geometry Cone {
    height 1.0
  }
  appearance Appearance {
    material Material {
      diffuseColor 1.0 1.0 1.0
    }
  }
}
```

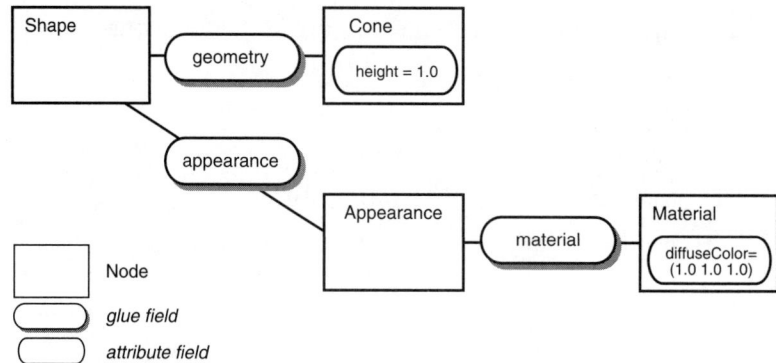

FIGURE A.15

"Glue" fields connect nodes whereas attribute fields describe node instances.

The only glue type of node field that has been predefined for VRML 2.0 is the SFNode/MFNode field type. Each SFNode/MFNode field has rules about which type of node can be connected to it depending on the node object to which the field belongs. We have examined some of the instances of SFNode glue fields in previous examples, including the **Shape** node's appearance field, which accepts an **Appearance** node argument, and the **Appearance** node's material field, which accepts a **Material** node argument. Examples of MFNode fields include the children field of the group nodes such as **Transform**, the level field of the **LOD** node, and the choice field of the **Switch** node.

RENDERING COLOR SYSTEM

In example A.1 we created an evenly lit red sphere by using the emissiveColor field of the **Material** node. The **Material** node was then passed as an argument to the **Appearance** node's material field. The **Appearance** node enables you to define the visually rendered appearance of VRML geometry by defining its reflective (Material) properties or a texture map. This is how we told the browser to render the sphere red.

When you are not texture mapping VRML geometry, you will normally want to define its material properties in this way. However, by using a combination of the available **Material** node options including shininess and sometimes transparency, you will achieve a much more realistic and appealing effect than does our red sphere. The emissiveColor material produces an effect similar to self-illumination and is thus more appropriately used for objects such as light bulbs or 3D text titles.

The surface of a solid colored object in the real world is not evenly lit but generally reflects light to a lesser or greater degree depending on the angle of incidence when light strikes the object surface. By passing RGB values in the range 0.0–1.0 to the **Material** node's diffuseColor field, you can define the amount and color of light that is reflected from an object surface directly facing the light source. The VRML 2.0 browser will then shade the object based on the angle of incidence for each point of the object surface.

In a similar manner, you can use the **Material** node's specularColor field to define a (usually brighter) RGB value for specular highlights on the object surface. The specular property of a surface is closely related to the object's shininess, another **Material** node field you can set from 0.0–1.0, whose value is inversely proportional to the size and sharpness of specular highlights. That is, a greater shininess value produces small, sharp highlights, and a lesser shininess value results in larger and softer specular highlights.

The browser will combine your defined color values with those you set for lights placed in the VRML scene to shade the object surface, thereby creating the illusion of three dimensions by using a two-dimensional display.

LIGHTING A VIRTUAL SCENE

In listing A.4 we created a cube object in VRML that was defined with a red surface material. However, when rendered in the browser window, the cube appeared bright white. This is because the browser "headlight" is turned on by default and is flooding the scene with white light, washing out any diffuse color defined for the **Box** geometry. The browser's interface enables you to turn off the headlight (or you can turn it off in the VRML file **NavigationInfo** node, which we'll get to later), by using "Options:Headlight" in the menu bar. However, if you have not placed lights in your scene, there will be no light at all for the cube to reflect, and you'll find yourself in utter darkness!

VRML offers three types of light sources to help illuminate your world: **PointLight** (called an omnidirectional light in some 3D systems), which represents a light source as a single point in space emitting light equally in all directions similar to a light bulb; **SpotLight**, which originates at a point and creates a cone of light in a given direction you specify; and **DirectionalLight**, which seems to come from a given direction but has parallel light rays rather than the conically diffuse rays of a **SpotLight**.

A directional light is generally used to simulate a distant light source such as the sun. Unlike point and spotLights, directional lights do not support attenuation—that is, falloff after a given distance radius.

In the following example, we've defined a DirectionalLight aligned along the <–1, –1, –5> vector in Cartesian space. The intensity of illumination for all lights can be set on a scale from 0.0 to their default greatest intensity 1.0.

Listing A.10   box.wrl.

```
#VRML V2.0 utf8
# build a Box
DEF CUBE Shape {
  appearance Appearance {
    material Material {
      diffuseColor 1 0 0
        specularColor 0.9 0.9 0.9
        shininess 1.0
    }
  }
  geometry Box {}
}
DirectionalLight {
  direction -1 -1 -5
  intensity 0.8
  }
```

To demonstrate the effect of lighting versus the browser head-light, copy the contents of listing A.9 excluding **DirectionalLight** and the lines following into a text file named box.wrl. Load this file into your Community Place browser and compare it with a reloaded .wrl file that includes the light source description. In the latter case, you'll be able to turn off the headlight and see the front side of a bright red cube.

USEFUL NODE DESCRIPTIONS

The following sections provide node descriptions.

GROUPING NODES

VRML 2.0 offers several useful group nodes in addition to the **Transform** node covered in detail earlier in this appendix. Recall that group nodes enable you to set properties for any number of child nodes, including child group nodes. The group nodes available to you for special purposes other than transforms are described in this section.

ANCHOR{}

Anchor is a grouping node that enables you to link your VRML world with other Internet resources, whether it's a 2D Web page to be displayed in an HTML browser window/frame or a 3D VRML world that when loaded via the **Anchor** link replaces your own world inside the VRML browser window.

Listing A.11   link.wrl.

```
#VRML V2.0 utf8
# link from room to room in a house
Transform {
  children [
    Anchor {
      description "Open Bedroom Door"
      url [ "bedroom.wrl" ]
      children [
        DEF Doorknob Shape { geometry Sphere{} }
      ]
    }
  ]
}
```

Assuming this code segment example describes a doorknob, when the user clicks on the sphere named "Doorknob," the **Anchor** node causes the browser to fetch and load its url field file name, replacing the currently loaded world contents.

BILLBOARD{}

The **Billboard** grouping node is a special purpose node that enables you to create "sprites" in your VRML world. A VRML 2.0 browser orients the local Z axis of a **Billboard** node to always point directly toward the user's viewpoint. This enables you, for example, to create the illusion of complex 3D geometry by using a single faced polygon that is mapped with a 3D rendered texture image. This not only produces special effects and better quality special purpose images but is also much easier for the browser to render. Use it often.

You can select an axisOfRotation for the **Billboard** node by defining the X, Y, and Z coordinates of a point in space that forms the rotation axis when connected to the group node's local origin. This point is often defined as axisOfRotation 0 1 0 to rotate around the Y axis a single faced object reproducing, for example, street lamps lining an avenue and rooted in a ground plane. To create a billboard that faces your user regardless of whether he pitches or rolls his viewpoint, define an axisOfRotation 0 0 0. This latter type of **Billboard** node is known as a *sprite*.

INLINE{}

The **Inline** node enables you to "import" an external VRML .wrl file, such as an avatar or other geometry, into your current scene by providing an URL reference to its location. By using **Inline** nodes (and maintaining a consistent modeling scale), you can build a library of reusable objects from which you can assemble many different VRML applications.

```
DEF earthORB Inline {
    url ["orbits/earthorbit.wrl"]
}
```

Multiple URL locations can be listed in the **Inline** node's url field enabling the browser to, for example, first check a user's local directory for an avatar geometry file and next locate the file on the World Wide Web if a local copy is not found.

ENVIRONMENTAL NUANCES

VRML 2.0 offers a number of bindable nodes, including **Viewpoint**, **NavigationInfo**, **Background**, and **Fog**, that enable you to enhance the aesthetic experience of your VRML world. A unique property in VRML 2.0 for bindable nodes is that only one of each type can be active at any given time.

VIEWPOINT{ }

The **Viewpoint** node is like a camera—it is the author-defined point-of-view position from which the VRML world file user sees the rendered scene when he enters your world via his VRML 2.0 browser. By adjusting the fieldOfView parameter (expressed in radians) to a higher value, you can produce frame distortion at the edges of the browser window to simulate a wide-angle lens. To view the effect in an extreme example, add the following **Viewpoint** node description to your growing VRML logo world file (listing A.12).

Listing A.12   Viewpoint node.

```
Viewpoint {
  fieldOfView 2.0
  position 1.75 2 3
  orientation 0 0.5 1 0.785
  description "HangOver"
}
```

If you do not define a viewpoint in your .wrl file, most browsers will "dolly" outward along the positive Z axis to a distance from which the entire VRML scene can be viewed inside the window. Although this constitutes perfectly functional behavior, forcing all objects to fit within the frame breaks the rules of good composition. Defining **Viewpoint**s within your VRML worlds helps your user to more fully appreciate your vision.

Note that your defined **Viewpoint** must be contained within the original .wrl file that is loaded into the browser and cannot be obtained from an inlined, or URL referenced, .wrl file.

NAVIGATIONINFO{}

The **NavigationInfo** node enables you to define the size of the user's presence or avatar in your VRML scene. Navigation information is used by the browser to perform collision detection with your scene elements, determine whether or not the user's "headlight" should be rendered, set the user's visibility distance for render clipping, and set the speed of his traversal through your world space.

The following are the **NavigationInfo** default values assumed by VRML browsers unless otherwise specified by the world author.

```
NavigationInfo {
  avatarSize [ 0.25, 1.6, 0.75 ]
  headlight TRUE
  speed 1.0
  type "WALK"
  visibilityLimit 0.0
}
```

The avatarSize field defines three values for the avatar. The first numerical value in the avatarSize field relates the distance from the user to an object in the world at which time collision should be detected; the second value sets the height of the user's viewpoint above the "ground" plane; the third value is designed to enable avatars to mount a staircase, curb, or other small obstacle in the world by denoting the acceptable height of such an obstacle. The default value given for this last field is the VRML Architecture Group's (VAG) recommendation for the height of individual stairs and curbs you build into your VRML worlds in order to ensure that any VRML 2.0 browser can enable its users to easily ascend these obstacles.

The speed field is expressed in meters/second to determine how quickly a user traverses VRML space. If the user is stationary, this field denotes his scene panning speed.

You can use the type field with proximity or other sensors to trigger an EXAMINE navigation mode wherein the user can pick up and spin an object depending on the functionality of the browser in use. At a minimum, all browsers support the WALK navigation type, and most also support some sort of FLY navigation option that does not enforce a notion of gravity upon the user.

The visibilityLimit field may be used in conjunction with the **Fog** node's visibilityRange field to ensure that objects at a given distance from the user fade smoothly into the background.

Note that any scale transformation that occurs in a world to affect a user will also automatically scale the avatarSize, speed, and visibilityLimit values of the **NavigationInfo** node.

BACKGROUND{}

The **Background** node enables you to specify a background color, gradient, or texture as a backdrop for your world in place of the default black. You can even use the **Background** node's backUrl, frontUrl, bottomUrl, leftUrl, rightUrl, and topUrl fields to set different background textures for each of six "walls" as though your world were contained inside a cube. The **Background** node is not affected by the **Fog** node, which enables you to fade objects into your specified fog color with distance from the user to provide the illusion of distance cueing.

```
Background {
    frontUrl   "textures/bg.jpg"
    backUrl    "textures/bg.jpg"
    bottomUrl  "textures/bg.jpg"
    leftUrl    "textures/bg.jpg"
    rightUrl   "textures/bg.jpg"
    topUrl     "textures/bg.jpg"
}
```

FOG{}

The **Fog** node offers distance cueing and atmospheric effect by fading objects into the fog color according to distance from the user's viewpoint. The default Fog field values are as follows:

```
Fog {
  color 1 1 1
  fogType "LINEAR"
  visibilityRange  0
}
```

The Fog color field enables you set a color value with which distant objects will be blended to achieve the illusion of atmospheric fog.

The fogType field accepts the arguments LINEAR or EXPONENTIAL, depending on whether you want to simulate distance cueing or fogginess respectively.

The visibilityRange field denotes the distance in meters from the **Fog** node's origin at which objects become completely engulfed in fog and are no longer visible. You must enter a value greater than zero for the visibilityRange field in order to produce **Fog** effects within your VRML scene.

WORLDINFO{}

Following your VRML file comments, you will normally add a **WorldInfo** node to record the world name (title) and any copyright information (info) you want the VRML file to retain when served over the Web. Although this documentation is normally accomplished in the source code for most programming languages by using one or more comment lines, many Web servers strip comments and other white space from an ASCII VRML file before servicing a client request. The **WorldInfo** node enables you to ensure that your copyright information will be retained regardless of its route to a viewer.

```
#VRML V2.0 utf8
WorldInfo {
    info [ "This world was created by Sony." ]

    title "My World"
}
```

Publishing Your VRML Files on the Internet

To successfully publish your VRML worlds on the Web, you need to keep the total download size small (less than 1 MB including textures and sound) or package your compressed world for predownloading so that users can load the files from a local disk. Although the former option is preferred, if you are creating multiuser worlds in which you expect several return visits, offering a predownload version will save the user much time on his return visits.

In either case, before you begin preparing your VRML world file(s) for publishing on your Web server, ensure that your world loads and operates correctly when loaded from a local drive. Debugging remotely is painful.

When you are ready to upload your files to your Web server, be sure to maintain any directory structure that is referenced in your .wrl files. For example, if your texture url fields point to a directory named IMAGES, be sure to create that directory on your server drive and copy your texture maps into it if you're planning to serve VRML worlds in real time.

Next, if you're operating a Unix-based Web server, remember that Unix is case-sensitive so that a file named world.wrl can coexist with files named WORLD.WRL, world.WRL, and WORLD.wrl in the same directory and that each of these files are different entities. If you discover that the case is changed in your file names when you transfer your VRML world to your Web server, you'll need to rename each file under Unix to the proper case, edit your .wrl file references, or find a compression solution, such as TAR, that will compress your local disk VRML files into a single archive and then decompress the archive on your Web server retaining original file names.

After your VRML world files, including all referenced external files such as inlined .wrl files and avatar geometry, texture map image files, and sound files, have been copied to your Web server and are arranged in the proper directory hierarchy, start the Community Place VRML 2.0 browser and then load your main .wrl file via a Web browser such as Netscape Navigator. If the Web browser attempts to display the wrl and/or any Java class file contents in its HTML browser window, you need to set your Web server MIME type file to include the following MIME definitions for each file extension:

```
x-world/x-vrml          wrl
application/x-java       class
```

The location of the MIME type file varies depending on the Web server software in use. Usually this information is stored in a file named mime.types found in your server install or configuration directory. If you are unsure of this procedure, consult your local system administrator.

CALL FOR PARTICIPATION

This introduction to object-oriented graphics principles and VRML 2.0 has provided a sufficient framework to start you on your way to building CyberSpace. But there is no substitute for personal experience and imagination applied. Here we have barely scratched the surface of possibilities for the graphical effects and vision that can be achieved. We encourage you to experiment with all the field options available with any node object you use in your VRML worlds. Explore and learn. Make your own contribution to the Internet community that has worked to develop the open, portable architecture of the Virtual Reality Modeling Language, rendered in real time.

[1] To display 3D scene in wireframe mode with Community Place browser, select [Options]...[Detail level]...[Wire Frame].

APPENDIX B

JAVA CLASSES FOR VRML 2.0

Within the text of the book there have been descriptions of several of the base classes that make up the Java packages for VRML. This appendix gives a full listing of those Java classes. For each class it specifies the methods the class supports and the parameters each method takes. This appendix is based on Appendix C of the VRML 2.0 specification.

The appendix is ordered as follows:

- ➤ B1 discusses the basic methods supported by the Node and Field classes.

- ➤ B2 and B3 state policy on standard and user-defined Java packages.

- ➤ B4 discusses exceptions that can be thrown by the VRML package classes.

- ➤ B5 gives an overview of the class hierarchy and lists all supported classes.

- ➤ B6, B7, and B8 discuss the three VRML-related packages—vrml, vrml.node, and vrml.field—and for each package define each class, listing methods, and parameters.

- ➤ B9 gives examples of the exception class.

B1: Exposed Classes and Methods for Nodes and Fields

The Field class extends Java's Object class by default; thus, Field has the full functionality of the Object class, including the getClass() method. The rest of the package defines a "Const" read-only class for each VRML field type, with a getValue() method for each class and another read/write class for each VRML field type, with both getValue() and setValue() methods for each class. A getValue() method converts a VRML-type value into a Java-type value. A setValue() method converts a Java-type value into a VRML-type value and sets it to the VRML field.

Most of the setValue() methods and set1Value() methods are listed as "throws exception," meaning that errors are possible. You may need to write exception handlers (using Java's catch() method) when you use those methods.

Any method not listed as "throws exception" is guaranteed to generate no exceptions. Each method that throws an exception includes a prototype showing which exception(s) can be thrown.

Field Class and ConstField Class

All VRML data types have equivalent classes in Java.

```
class Field {
    }
```

Field class is the root of each field type. This class has two sub-classes: read-only class and writable class.

Read-Only Class

The read-only class supports the getValue() method. In addition, some of the classes support convenient methods to get values from the object itself. The following read-only classes are supported:

ConstSFBool, ConstSFRotation, ConstSFColor,
ConstMFRotation, ConstMFColor, ConstSFString,
ConstSFFloat, ConstMFString, ConstMFFloat,
ConstSFVec2f, ConstSFImage, ConstMFVec2f,
ConstSFInt32, ConstSFVec3f, ConstMFInt32,
ConstMFVec3f, ConstSFNode, ConstSFTime,
ConstMFNode, ConstMFTime

WRITABLE CLASS

The writable version of the classes support both getValue() and
setValue() methods. If the class name is prefixed with MF it
means that it is a multiple valued field class and also supports the
set1Value(), addValue(), and insertValue() methods.

In addition, some classes support some convenient methods to
get and set the value of the object:

SFBool, SFColor, MFColor,SFFloat, MFFloat, SFImage,
SFInt32, MFInt32, SFNode, MFNode, SFRotation,
MFRotation, SFString, MFString, SFVec2f, MFVec2f,
SFVec3f, MFVec3f, SFTime, MFTime

FIELD CLASS METHODS

The Java Field class and its subclasses have several methods to
get and set values.

➤ **getSize()** Returns the number of elements of each multiple
value field class(MF class).

➤ **getValue()** Converts a VRML-type value into a Java-type
value and returns it.

➤ **get1Value(int index)** Converts a VRML-type value (index-th
element) into a Java-type value and returns it. The index of
the first element is 0. Getting the element beyond the
existing elements throws an exception.

➤ **setValue(value)** Converts a Java-type value into a VRML-
type value and sets it to the VRML field.

> **set1Value(int index, value)** Converts from a Java-type value to a VRML-type value and sets it to the index-th element.

> **addValue(value)** Converts from a Java-type value to a VRML-type value and adds it to the last element.

> **insertValue(int index, value)** Converts from a Java-type value to a VRML-type value and inserts it into the index-th element. The index of the first element is 0. Setting the element beyond the existing elements throws an exception.

In these methods, getSize(), get1Value(), set1Value(), addValue(), and insertValue() are available only for multiple value field classes (MF classes). See the section "B6: vrml Package" for each classes' methods definition.

NODE CLASS

Node class has several methods:

> **getType()** Returns the type of the node.

> **getEventOut(String eventName)** Gets the reference to the node's eventOut field whose name is eventName. The return value can be converted to an appropriate Java Field Class.

> **getEventIn(String eventName)** Gets the reference to the node's eventIn field whose name is eventName. The return value can be converted to an appropriate Java Field Class. When you call getValue() method on a field object obtained by getEventIn() method, the return value is unspecified. Therefore, you can not rely on it. EventIn is a write-only field.

> **getExposedField(String eventName)** Gets the reference to the node's exposedField whose name is eventName. The return value can be converted to an appropriate Java Field Class.

> **getBrowser()** Gets the browser that this node is managed by. See the following section, "Browser Class," for more information.

When you call a setValue(), set1Value(), addValue(), or insertValue() method on a field object obtained by getEventIn() method, the value specified as an argument generates an event to the node.

When you call a setValue(), set1Value(), addValue(), or insertValue() method on a field object obtained by getExposedField() method, the value specified as an argument generates an event in VRML scene. The effect of this event is specified by the associated ROUTE in the VRML scene.

BROWSER CLASS

This section lists the public Java interfaces to the Browser class, which enables scripts to get and set browser information.

Return Value	Method Name
String	getName()
String	getVersion()
float	getCurrentSpeed()
float	getCurrentFrameRate()
String	getWorldURL()
void	replaceWorld(BaseNode[] nodes)
Node[]	createVrmlFromString(String vrmlSyntax)
void	createVrmlFromURL(String[] url, BaseNode node, String event)
void	addRoute(Node fromNode, String fromEventOut, BaseNode toNode, String toEventIn)
void	deleteRoute(BaseNode fromNode, String fromEventOut,BaseNode toNode, String toEventIn)
void	loadURL(String[] url, String[] parameter)
void	setDescription(String description)

See the section "B6: vrml Package" for more details of each method's definition.

The following is a conversion table from the types used in the Browser class to their equivalent Java types.

VRML Type	Java Type
SFString	String
SFFloat	float
MFString	String[]
MFNode	BaseNode[]

B2: USER-DEFINED CLASSES AND PACKAGES

Any Java classes defined by a user can be used in the Java program. The search path is rooted in the directory where the original Java program is located.

If the Java class is in a package, this package is searched for, again from the directory where the Java program is located.

B3: STANDARD JAVA PACKAGES

Java programs have access to the full set of classes available in java.*. The handling of these classes—especially AWT and the security model of networking—will be browser-specific. Threads are required to work as normal for Java.

B4: EXCEPTIONS

Java methods may throw the following exceptions:

➤ **InvalidFieldException** Thrown at the time getField() is executed and the field name is invalid.

➤ **InvalidEventInException** Thrown at the time getEventIn() is executed and the eventIn name is invalid.

➤ **InvalidEventOutException** Thrown at the time getEventOut() or getEventOut() is executed and the eventOut name is invalid.

➤ **InvalidExposedFieldException** Thrown at the time getExposedField() is executed and the exposedField name is invalid.

➤ **InvalidVRMLSyntaxException** Thrown at the time createVrmlFromString(), createVrmlFromURL(), or loadURL() is executed and the VRML string is invalid.

➤ **InvalidRouteException** Thrown at the time addRoute() or deleteRoute() is executed and one or more of the arguments is invalid.

➤ **InvalidFieldChangeException** May be thrown as a result of all sorts of illegal field changes, for example:

  ➤ Adding a node from one World as the child of a node in another World

  ➤ Creating a circularity in a scene graph

  ➤ Setting an invalid string on enumerated fields, such as the fogType field of the Fog node

  There is no guarantee that such exceptions will be thrown, but a browser should do the best job it can.

➤ **ArrayIndexOutOfBoundsException** Generated at the time setValue(), set1Value(), addValue(), or insertValue() is executed and the index is out of bound. This is the standard exception defined in the Java Array class.

If exceptions are not redefined by authors, a browser's behavior is unspecified. See the section "B9: Example of Exception Class," later in this appendix.

B5: Class Hierarchy

The classes are divided into three packages: vrml, vrml.field, and vrml.node.

```
ava.lang.Object
    |
    +- vrml.Event
    +- vrml.Browser
    +- vrml.Field
    |         +- vrml.field.SFBool
    |         +- vrml.field.SFColor
    |         +- vrml.field.SFFloat
    |         +- vrml.field.SFImage
    |         +- vrml.field.SFInt32
    |         +- vrml.field.SFNode
    |         +- vrml.field.SFRotation
    |         +- vrml.field.SFString
    |         +- vrml.field.SFTime
    |         +- vrml.field.SFVec2f
    |         +- vrml.field.SFVec3f
    |         |
    |         +- vrml.MField
    |         |       +- vrml.field.MFColor
    |         |       +- vrml.field.MFFloat
    |         |       +- vrml.field.MFInt32
    |         |       +- vrml.field.MFNode
    |         |       +- vrml.field.MFRotation
    |         |       +- vrml.field.MFString
    |         |       +- vrml.field.MFTime
    |         |       +- vrml.field.MFVec2f
    |         |       +- vrml.field.MFVec3f
    |         |
    |         +- vrml.ConstField
    |                 +- vrml.field.ConstSFBool
    |                 +- vrml.field.ConstSFColor
    |                 +- vrml.field.ConstSFFloat
    |                 +- vrml.field.ConstSFImage
    |                 +- vrml.field.ConstSFInt32
    |                 +- vrml.field.ConstSFNode
    |                 +- vrml.field.ConstSFRotation
    |                 +- vrml.field.ConstSFString
    |                 +- vrml.field.ConstSFTime
    |                 +- vrml.field.ConstSFVec2f
    |                 +- vrml.field.ConstSFVec3f
    |                 |
```

```
        |                      +- vrml.ConstMField
        |                              +- vrml.field.ConstMFColor
        |                              +- vrml.field.ConstMFFloat
        |                              +- vrml.field.ConstMFInt32
        |                              +- vrml.field.ConstMFNode
        |                              +- vrml.field.ConstMFRotation
        |                              +- vrml.field.ConstMFString
        |                              +- vrml.field.ConstMFTime
        |                              +- vrml.field.ConstMFVec2f
        |                              +- vrml.field.ConstMFVec3f
        |
       +- vrml.BaseNode
               +- vrml.node.Node
               +- vrml.node.Script


java.lang.Exception
        |
       +- java.lang.RuntimeException
        |       +- vrml.InvalidRouteException
        |       +- vrml.InvalidFieldException
        |       +- vrml.InvalidEventInException
        |       +- vrml.InvalidEventOutException
        |       +- vrml.InvalidExposedFieldException
        |
        |       +- vrml.InvalidFieldChangeException
       +- vrml.InvalidVRMLSyntaxException
```

B6: VRML PACKAGE

```
package vrml;
public abstract class Field implements Cloneable
{
   public Object clone();
}

public abstract class ConstField extends Field
{
}
```

```java
public abstract class ConstMField extends ConstField
{
   public abstract int getSize();
}

public abstract class MField extends Field
{
   public abstract int getSize();
   public abstract void clear();
   public abstract void delete(int index);
}

public class Event implements Cloneable {
  public String getName();
  public double getTimeStamp();
  public ConstField getValue();
  public Object clone();
}

public class Browser {
  // Browser interface
  public String getName();
  public String getVersion();

  public float getCurrentSpeed();

  public float getCurrentFrameRate();

  public String getWorldURL();
  public void replaceWorld(Node[] nodes);

  public BaseNode[] createVrmlFromString(String
  ➥vrmlSyntax)
    throws InvalidVRMLSyntaxException;

  public void createVrmlFromURL(String[] url, BaseNode
  ➥node, String event)

  public void addRoute(BaseNode fromNode, String
  ➥fromEventOut,
    BaseNode toNode, String toEventIn);
```

```
   public void deleteRoute(BaseNode fromNode, String
  ➥fromEventOut,
    BaseNode toNode, String toEventIn);

  public void loadURL(String[] url, String[] parameter)

  public void setDescription(String description);
}


//
// This is the general BaseNode class
//
public abstract class BaseNode
{
  // Returns the type of the node.  If the node is a
    ➥prototype
  //   it returns the name of the prototype.
  public String getType();

  // Get the Browser that this node is contained in.
  public Browser getBrowser();
}
```

B7: VRML.FIELD PACKAGE

```
package vrml.field;
public class ConstSFBool extends ConstField
{
   public boolean getValue();
}

public class ConstSFColor extends ConstField
{
   public void getValue(float color[]);
   public float getRed();
   public float getGreen();
   public float getBlue();
}
```

```java
public class ConstSFFloat extends ConstField
{
    public float getValue();
}

public class ConstSFImage extends ConstField
{
    public int getWidth();
    public int getHeight();
    public int getComponents();
    public void getPixels(byte pixels[]);
}

public class ConstSFInt32 extends ConstField
{
    public int getValue();
}

public class ConstSFNode extends ConstField
{
  /* ****************************************
   * Return value of getValue() must extend BaseNode
   ➥class.
   * The concrete class is implementation dependent
   * and up to browser implementation.
   **************************************** */
    public BaseNode getValue();
}

public class ConstSFRotation extends ConstField
{
    public void getValue(float[] rotation);
}

public class ConstSFString extends ConstField
{
    public String getValue();
}

public class ConstSFTime extends ConstField
```

```
{
   public double getValue();
}

public class ConstSFVec2f extends ConstField
{
   public void getValue(float vec2[]);
   public float getX();
   public float getY();
}

public class ConstSFVec3f extends ConstField
{
   public void getValue(float vec3[]);
   public float getX();
   public float getY();
   public float getZ();
}

public class ConstMFColor extends ConstMField
{
   public void getValue(float colors[][]);
   public void getValue(float colors[]);
   public void get1Value(int index, float color[]);
   public void get1Value(int index, SFColor color);
}

public class ConstMFFloat extends ConstMField
{
   public void getValue(float values[]);
   public float get1Value(int index);
}

public class ConstMFInt32 extends ConstMField
{
   public void getValue(int values[]);
   public int get1Value(int index);
}

public class ConstMFNode extends ConstMField
```

```
   {
     /*********************************************
      * Return value of getValue() must extend BaseNode
      ➥class.
      * The concrete class is implementation dependent
      * and up to browser implementation.
      *********************************************/
     public void getValue(BaseNode values[]);
     public BaseNode get1Value(int index);
   }

public class ConstMFRotation extends ConstMField
{
   public void getValue(float rotations[][]);
   public void getValue(float rotations[]);
   public void get1Value(int index, float rotation[]);
   public void get1Value(int index, SFRotation rotation);
}

public class ConstMFString extends ConstMField
{
   public void getValue(String values[]);
   public String get1Value(int index);
}

public class ConstMFTime extends ConstMField
{
   public void getValue(double times[]);
   public double get1Value(int index);
}

public class ConstMFVec2f extends ConstMField
{
   public void getValue(float vecs[][]);
   public void getValue(float vecs[]);
   public void get1Value(int index, float vec[]);
   public void get1Value(int index, SFVec2f vec);
}

public class ConstMFVec3f extends ConstMField
```

```
{
   public void getValue(float vecs[][]);
   public void getValue(float vecs[]);
   public void get1Value(int index, float vec[]);
   public void get1Value(int index, SFVec3f vec);
}

public class SFBool extends Field
{
   public SFBool(boolean value);
   public boolean getValue();
   public void setValue(boolean b);
   public void setValue(ConstSFBool b);
   public void setValue(SFBool b);
}

public class SFColor extends Field
{
   public SFColor(float red, float green, float blue);
   public void getValue(float color[]);
   public float getRed();
   public float getGreen();
   public float getBlue();
   public void setValue(float color[]);
   public void setValue(float red, float green, float
   ➥blue);
   public void setValue(ConstSFColor color);
   public void setValue(SFColor color);
}

public class SFFloat extends Field
{
   public SFFloat(float f);
   public float getValue();
   public void setValue(float f);
   public void setValue(ConstSFFloat f);
   public void setValue(SFFloat f);
}

public class SFImage extends Field
```

```
{
    public SFImage(int width, int height, int components,
    ➥byte pixels[]);
    public int getWidth();
    public int getHeight();
    public int getComponents();
    public void getPixels(byte pixels[]);
    public void setValue(int width, int height, int
    ➥components,
                        byte pixels[]);
    public void setValue(ConstSFImage image);
    public void setValue(SFImage image);
}

public class SFInt32 extends Field
{
    public SFInt32(int value);
    public int getValue();
    public void setValue(int i);
    public void setValue(ConstSFInt32 i);
    public void setValue(SFInt32 i);
}

public class SFNode extends Field
{
    public SFNode(BaseNode node);

    /*******************************************
    * Return value of getValue() must extend BaseNode
    ➥class.
    * The concrete class is implementation dependent
    * and up to browser implementation.
    *******************************************/
    public Node getValue();
    public void setValue(BaseNode node);
    public void setValue(ConstSFNode node);
    public void setValue(SFNode node);
}

public class SFRotation extends Field
```

```
{
   public SFRotation(float axisX, float axisY, float
   ➥axisZ, float rotation);
   public void getValue(float[] rotation);
   public void setValue(float[] rotation);
   public void setValue(float axisX, float axisY, float
   ➥axisZ, float rotation);
   public void setValue(ConstSFRotation rotation);
   public void setValue(SFRotation rotation);
}

public class SFString extends Field
{
   public SFString(String s);
   public String getValue();
   public void setValue(String s);
   public void setValue(ConstSFString s);
   public void setValue(SFString s);
}

public class SFTime extends Field
{
   public SFTime(double time);
   public double getValue();
   public void setValue(double time);
   public void setValue(ConstSFTime time);
   public void setValue(SFTime time);
}

public class SFVec2f extends Field
{
   public SFVec2f(float x, float y);
   public void getValue(float vec[]);
   public float getX();
   public float getY();
   public void setValue(float vec[]);
   public void setValue(float x, float y);
   public void setValue(ConstSFVec2f vec);
   public void setValue(SFVec2f vec);
}
```

```
public class SFVec3f extends Field
{
   public SFVec3f(float x, float y, float z);
   public void getValue(float vec[]);
   public float getX();
   public float getY();
   public float getZ();
   public void setValue(float vec[]);
   public void setValue(float x, float y, float z);
   public void setValue(ConstSFVec3f vec);
   public void setValue(SFVec3f vec);
}

public class MFColor extends MField
{
   public MFColor(float value[][]);
   public MFColor(float value[]);
   public MFColor(int size, float value[]);

   public void getValue(float colors[][]);
   public void getValue(float colors[]);

   public void setValue(float colors[][]);
   public void setValue(int size, float colors[]);
   /*****************************************************
    color[0] ... color[size - 1] are used as color data
    in the way that color[0], color[1], and color[2]
    represent the first color. The number of colors
    is defined as "size / 3".
    *****************************************************/

   public void setValue(ConstMFColor colors);

   public void get1Value(int index, float color[]);
   public void get1Value(int index, SFColor color);

   public void set1Value(int index, ConstSFColor color);
   public void set1Value(int index, SFColor color);
   public void set1Value(int index, float red, float
```

```
    ↦green, float blue);

    public void addValue(ConstSFColor color);
    public void addValue(SFColor color);
    public void addValue(float red, float green, float
    ↦blue);

    public void insertValue(int index, ConstSFColor for
    ↦color);
    public void insertValue(int index, SFColor color);
    public void insertValue(int index, float red, float
    ↦green, float blue);
}

public class MFFloat extends MField
{
    public MFFloat(float values[]);

    public void getValue(float values[]);

    public void setValue(float values[]);
    public void setValue(int size, float values[]);
    public void setValue(ConstMFFloat value);

    public float get1Value(int index);

    public void set1Value(int index, float f);
    public void set1Value(int index, ConstSFFloat f);
    public void set1Value(int index, SFFloat f);

    public void addValue(float f);
    public void addValue(ConstSFFloat f);
    public void addValue(SFFloat f);

    public void insertValue(int index, float f);
    public void insertValue(int index, ConstSFFloat f);
    public void insertValue(int index, SFFloat f);
}

public class MFInt32 extends MField
{
```

```
        public MFInt32(int values[]);

        public void getValue(int values[]);

        public void setValue(int values[]);
        public void setValue(int size, int values[]);
        public void setValue(ConstMFInt32 value);

        public int get1Value(int index);

        public void set1Value(int index, int i);
        public void set1Value(int index, ConstSFInt32 i);
        public void set1Value(int index, SFInt32 i);

        public void addValue(int i);
        public void addValue(ConstSFInt32 i);
        public void addValue(SFInt32 i);

        public void insertValue(int index, int i);
        public void insertValue(int index, ConstSFInt32 i);
        public void insertValue(int index, SFInt32 i);
    }

    public class MFNode extends MField
    {
        public MFNode(BaseNode node[]);

      /*********************************************
        * Return value of getValue() must extend BaseNode
          ↦class.
        * The concrete class is implementation dependent
        * and up to browser implementation.
        *********************************************/
        public void getValue(BaseNode node[]);

        public void setValue(BaseNode node[]);
        public void setValue(int size, BaseNode node[]);
        public void setValue(ConstMFNode node);

        public Node get1Value(int index);

        public void set1Value(int index, BaseNode node);
        public void set1Value(int index, ConstSFNode node);
```

```java
    public void set1Value(int index, SFNode node);

    public void addValue(BaseNode node);
    public void addValue(ConstSFNode node);
    public void addValue(SFNode node);

    public void insertValue(int index, BaseNode node);
    public void insertValue(int index, ConstSFNode node);
    public void insertValue(int index, SFNode node);
}

public class MFRotation extends MField
{
    public MFRotation(float rotations[][]);
    public MFRotation(float rotations[]);
    public MFRotation(int size, float rotations[]);

    public void getValue(float rotations[][]);
    public void getValue(float rotations[]);

    public void setValue(float rotations[][])
    public void setValue(int size, float rotations[]);
    public void setValue(ConstMFRotation rotations);

    public void get1Value(int index, float rotation[]);
    public void get1Value(int index, SFRotation rotation);

    public void set1Value(int index, ConstSFRotation
    ➥rotation);
    public void set1Value(int index, SFRotation rotation);
    public void set1Value(int index, float ax, float ay,
    ➥float az, float angle);

    public void addValue(ConstSFRotation rotation);
    public void addValue(SFRotation rotation);
    public void addValue(float ax, float ay, float az,
    ➥float angle);

    public void insertValue(int index, ConstSFRotation
    ➥rotation);
    public void insertValue(int index, SFRotation
    ➥rotation);
```

```
        public void insertValue(int index, float ax, float ay,
        ➥float az, float angle);
}

public class MFString extends MField
{
    public MFString(String s[]);
    public void getValue(String s[]);
    public void setValue(String s[]);
    public void setValue(int size, String s[]);
    public void setValue(ConstMFString s);
    public String get1Value(int index);
    public void set1Value(int index, String s);
    public void set1Value(int index, ConstSFString s);
    public void set1Value(int index, SFString s);
    public void addValue(String s);
    public void addValue(ConstSFString s);
    public void addValue(SFString s);
    public void insertValue(int index, String s);
    public void insertValue(int index, ConstSFString s);
    public void insertValue(int index, SFString s);
}

public class MFTime extends MField
{
    public MFTime(double times[]);
    public void getValue(double times[]);
    public void setValue(double times[]);
    public void setValue(int size, double times[]);
    public void setValue(ConstMFTime times);
    public double get1Value(int index);
    public void set1Value(int index, double time);
    public void set1Value(int index, ConstSFTime time);
    public void set1Value(int index, SFTime time);
    public void addValue(double time);
    public void addValue(ConstSFTime time);
    public void addValue(SFTime time);
    public void insertValue(int index, double time);
    public void insertValue(int index, ConstSFTime time);
    public void insertValue(int index, SFTime time);
```

```
}

public class MFVec2f extends MField
{
   public MFVec2f(float vecs[][]);
   public MFVec2f(float vecs[]);
   public MFVec2f(int size, float vecs[]);
   public void getValue(float vecs[][]);
   public void getValue(float vecs[]);
   public void setValue(float vecs[][]);
   public void setValue(int size, vecs[]);
   public void setValue(ConstMFVec2f vecs);
   public void get1Value(int index, float vec[]);
   public void get1Value(int index, SFVec2f vec);
   public void set1Value(int index, float x, float y);
   public void set1Value(int index, ConstSFVec2f vec);
   public void set1Value(int index, SFVec2f vec);
   public void addValue(float x, float y);
   public void addValue(ConstSFVec2f vec);
   public void addValue(SFVec2f vec);
   public void insertValue(int index, float x, float y);
   public void insertValue(int index, ConstSFVec2f vec);
   public void insertValue(int index, SFVec2f vec);
}

public class MFVec3f extends MField
{
   public MFVec3f(float vecs[][]);
   public MFVec3f(float vecs[]);
   public MFVec3f(int size, float vecs[]);
   public void getValue(float vecs[][]);
   public void getValue(float vecs[]);
   public void setValue(float vecs[][]);
   public void setValue(int size, float vecs[]);
   public void setValue(ConstMFVec3f vecs);
   public void get1Value(int index, float vec[]);
   public void get1Value(int index, SFVec3f vec);
   public void set1Value(int index, float x, float y,
   ➥float z);
   public void set1Value(int index, ConstSFVec3f vec);
   public void set1Value(int index, SFVec3f vec);
   public void addValue(float x, float y, float z);
```

```
public void addValue(ConstSFVec3f vec);
public void addValue(SFVec3f vec);
public void insertValue(int index, float x, float y,
➥float z);
public void insertValue(int index, ConstSFVec3f vec);
public void insertValue(int index, SFVec3f vec);
}
```

B8: VRML.NODE PACKAGE

This is the general Node class.

```
package vrml.node;
public abstract class Node extends BaseNode {
    /* Get an EventIn by name. Return value is write-only.
    Throws an InvalidEventInException if eventInName isn't
    a valid event in name for a node of this type.*/
    public final Field getEventIn(StringfieldName);
    /* Get an EventOut by name. Return value is read-only.
    Throws an InvalidEventOutException if eventOutName
    isn't a valid event out name for a node of this
    type.*/
    public final ConstField getEventOut(String fieldName);
    /* Get an exposed field by name. Throws an
    InvalidExposedFieldException if fieldName isn't a
    valid exposed field name for a node of this type. */
    public final Field getExposedField(String fieldName);
}
```

This is the general Script class, to be subclassed by all scripts.
Note that the provided methods enable the script author to
explicitly throw tailored exceptions in case something goes wrong
in the script.

```
public abstract class Script extends BaseNode {
    // This method is called before any event is generated
    public void initialize();
    /* Get a Field by name. Throws an
    InvalidFieldException if fieldName isn't a
    valid event in name for a node of this type.*/
    protected final Field getField(String fieldName);
    /* Get an EventOut by name. Throws an
    InvalidEventOutException if eventOutName isn't a
    valid event out name for a node of this type.
    protected final Field getEventOut(String fieldName);
    /* Get an EventIn by name. Throws an
    InvalidEventInException if eventInName isn't a
    valid event out name for a node of this type.
    protected final Field getEventIn(String fieldName);
    /* processEvents() is called automatically when the
    script receives some set of events. It should not be
    called directly except by its subclass. count indi
    cates the number of events delivered.*/
    public void processEvents(int count, Event events[]);
    /* processEvent() is called automatically when the
    script receives an event. */
    public void processEvent(Event event);
    /* eventsProcessed() is called after every invocation
    of processEvents().*/
    public void eventsProcessed()
    // shutdown() is called when this Script node is
    deleted.
    public void shutdown();
}
```

B9: EXAMPLE OF EXCEPTION CLASS

```
public class InvalidEventInException extends
IllegalArgumentException
{
```

```
                            /* Constructs an InvalidEventInException with no
                            ➥detail message.*/
                            public InvalidEventInException(){
                                super();
                            }
                            /* Constructs an InvalidEventInException with the
                            ➥specified detail message.
                            A detail message is a String that describes this
                            ➥particular exception.
                            @param s the detail message */
                            public InvalidEventInException(String s){
                                super(s);
                            }
                        }


                        public class InvalidEventOutException extends
                        IllegalArgumentException
                        {
                            public InvalidEventOutException(){
                                super();
                            }
                            public InvalidEventOutException(String s){
                                super(s);
                            }
                        }


                        public class InvalidFieldException extends
                        IllegalArgumentException
                        {
                            public InvalidFieldException(){
                                super();
                            }
                            public InvalidFieldException(String s){
                                super(s);
                            }
                        }


                        public class InvalidExposedFieldException extends
                        IllegalArgumentException
                        {
```

```
   public InvalidExposedFieldException(){
      super();
   }
   public InvalidExposedFieldException(String s){
      super(s);
   }
}

public class InvalidVRMLSyntaxException extends Exception
{
   public InvalidVRMLSyntaxException(){
      super();
   }
   public InvalidVRMLSyntaxException(String s){
      super(s);
   }
}

public class InvalidRouteException extends
IllegalArgumentException
{
   public InvalidRouteException(){
      super();
   }
   public InvalidRouteException(String s){
      super(s);
   }
}

public class InvalidFieldChangeException extends
IllegalArgumentException
{
   public InvalidFieldChangeException(){
      super();
   }
   public InvalidFieldChangeException(String s){
      super(s);
   }
}
```

Appendix C

Resources

The following sections provide a list of references that we have found useful or feel that you will enjoy exploring. The books section provides some background reading and some essential Java references. The other resources are Web pages that are generally kept current and offer links to a wide variety of other information sources.

Books

Cyberspace: First Steps
Michael Benedikt, ed
1991, MIT Press
Cambridge MA
USA
ISBN 0-262-02327-X

Computer Graphics: Principles and Practice
Foley, van Dam, Feiner, and Hughes
1990, Addison-Wesley Publishing Company
Reading, MA
USA
ISBN 0-201-84840-6

Virtual Reality
Howard Rheingold
1991, Summit Books
New York, NY
USA
ISBN 0-671-69363-8

Core Java
Gary Cornell and Cay S. Horstmann
The Sunsoft Press
Prentice Hall
Upper Saddle River, NJ
USA
ISBN 0-13-565755-5

Java by Example
Jerry R. Jackson and Alan L. McClellan
The Sunsoft Press
Prentice Hall
Upper Saddle River, NJ
USA
ISBN 0-13-565763-6

Just Java
Peter van der Linden
The Sunsoft Press
Prentice Hall
Upper Saddle River, NJ
USA
ISBN 0-13-5658-39-X

Presenting Java
John December
Sams.net
Indianapolis, IN
USA
ISBN 1-57521-039-8

Programming with Java!
Tim Ritchey
New Riders Publishing
Indianapolis, IN
USA
ISBN 1-56205-533-X

The VRML 2.0 Sourcebook
Andrea L. Ames, David R. Nadeau, and John L. Moreland
John Wiley & Sons

VRML-RELATED WEB SITES

Sony Virtual Society Home Page
http://sonypic.com/vs
http://vs.sony.co.jp

Sony Pictures Entertainment Imagework's VRML 2.0 Tutorial
http://sonypic.com/vs/tutorials

An excellent VRML 2.0 tutorial including info on Java and shared behaviors.

The Official VAG Web Site
http://vag.vrml.org

VRML Architecture Group's home page.

The VRML FAQ
http://vag.vrml.org/VRML_FAQ.html

The official FAQ, good background but not gospel.

VRML Mailing List Archive
http://vag.vrml.org/VRML_FAQ.html

A complete Hypermail archive of the VRML mailing list.

The VRML Repository
http://www.sdsc.edu/vrml

The place to look for VRML resources.

The Terra Vista Virtual Community
http://www.teravista.org

A community of VRML addicts expanding VRML's horizons.

Len Bullard's Web Page
http://fly.hiwaay.net/~cbullard

A man with a mission, and some nice VRML, too!

VRML 2.0 Worlds
http://vrml.sgi.com/worlds/vrml2.html

Our friends at SGI have links to other VRML worlds.

***VRMLSite* Magazine**
http://www.vrmlsite.com

Monthly magazine full of tips for VRML authors.

The VRML Forum
http://vag.vrml.org/www-vrml

How to join the www-vrml ML.

***Wired* Magazine's VRML Site**
http://vrml.wired.com

Wired's very own VRML resource.

VRML 2.0 PROPOSALS

Active VRML—Microsoft
http://www.microsoft.com/intdev/avr

Dynamic Worlds—GMD and Others
http://wintermute.gmd.de:8000/vrml/dynamicWorlds.html

HoloWeb—Sun
http://www.sunlabs.com/research/tcm/holoweb/holoweb.html

Moving Worlds—SGI and Others
http://webspace.sgi.com/moving-worlds

Out of this World—Apple
http://product.info.apple.com/qd3d/VRML20/
Out_Of_This_World.HTML

Reactive Virtual Environment—IBM Japan
http://www.ibm.co.jp/trl/projects/rve/vrml2top.html

JAVA-RELATED WEB SITES

Sun's Java Site
http://java.sun.com/

The latest version of JDK is available on this site.

Java Programming FAQ
http://sunsite.unc.edu/javafaq/javafaq.html

Java Tutorial
http://sunsite.unc.edu/javafaq/javatutorial.html

Java Mailing List
http://www.javasoft.com/Mail/external_lists.html

Visual J++
http://www.microsoft.com/visualj/

Microsoft's Visual J++ developers information.

Appendix D

Installing

Community Place

This appendix contains information on the following:

- ➤ Installing and running Community Place
- ➤ Installing and running the Java Development Kit (JDK)
- ➤ Setting up Netscape Navigator to use Community Place
- ➤ Hardware requirements for Community Place

How to Install Community Place (Version 1.1 Evaluation)

To install the Community Place Browser from the accompanying CD onto your PC running Windows 95, complete the following steps. Before installing the Community Place Browser, check the hardware requirements detailed at the end of this appendix.

Copy

The Community Place Browser, manual, and some contents are packed into a self-extracting archive. You can find it in the

Vs\browser directory on the CD-ROM. Copy it to your local hard disk and then execute it by double-clicking.

Note that the Vs\browser directory contains four versions of this self-extracting archive. Two of the versions are for a stand-alone implementation of the browser. This runs as a helper application for Netscape Navigator. The other two versions are for a plug-in version of the browser that runs as a plug-in to Netscape Navigator. For the stand-alone implementation, the file cpb10ebx.exe contains the Community Place browser plus all support software for DirectX. If you already have DirectX installed or don't want to use DirectX sound capabilities, install the file cpb10eb.exe instead. Similarly, there are two archives for the plug-in version: cpn11b1x.exe contains DirectX, cpn11b1.exe does not.

You can choose to install the helper application or the plug-in version. Functionally, they are equivalent. Throughout this book, all examples have been demonstrated with the helper version.

WARNING

These files differ in one area, and that is in their security models. The helper version uses the security model described in Chapter 5, "Advanced Java." However, the plug-in version must use the security model imposed by the HTML browser that hosts it—in this case, Netscape Navigator. Because Navigator has a less flexible security policy than that implemented in the helper version, the examples in Chapter 5 that use network access will not work with the plug-in version.

If you want to use the latest version of Community Place Browser, you can download it from either http://sonypic.com/vs/ in Europe and USA or http://vs.sony.co.jp in Asia.

In the following instructions, we assume you are using cpb10ebx.exe.

UNZIP

When you double-click the self-extracting archive, Winzip executes and prompts you to specify the destination directory.

Usually the default directory is fine. If necessary, you can change the directory. After you make your choice, click Unzip. Unzipping all the files takes about one minute.

After unzipping, the message "24 files unzipped successfully" is displayed. You should now click OK. This automatically executes the Community Place installer that displays a Welcome dialog box.

INSTALLATION

After clicking Next in the Welcome dialog box, check the install directory (default directory is \Program Files\Sony\Community Place Browser). If you want to change it, click the Browse button to specify your favorite directory. Again, unless you have a specific reason, the default directory is fine. Click Next. You are now prompted for a series of replies; in all cases the default reply is recommended. Note that one of these prompts is for acceptance of a software license for Community Place. Read this carefully.

Another prompt concerns DirectX and MOD. Click OK to display the dialog box to install DirectX. If you already have DirectX, you don't need to install it.

After specifying how to install DirectX, click Next, and the installation process begins. Installation takes about one minute and displays a graphical representation of its status.

The final dialog box tells you that installation is complete. Click OK, and the installer will exit.

STARTING COMMUNITY PLACE BROWSER

After installation, you can start the Community Place Browser by double-clicking the Community Place Browser icon (see fig. D.1).

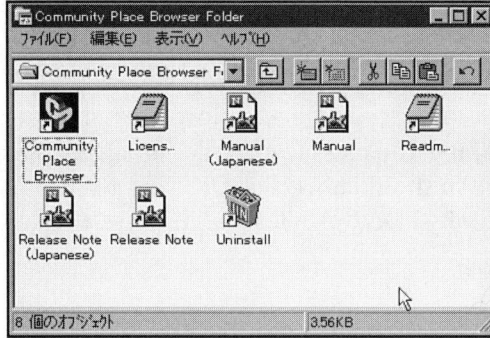

Figure D.1

The Community Place Browser icon.

If the Community Place Browser displays the window shown in figure D.2, the installation was successful. This figure is the default start-up scene for Community Place and is dynamically created from the contents on your hard disk.

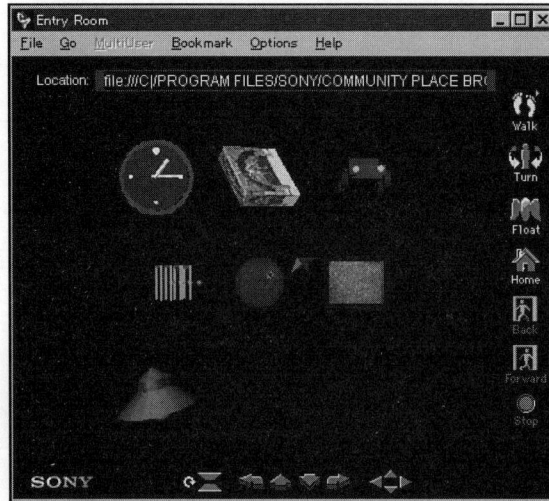

Figure D.2

The Community Place default start-up window.

UNINSTALLING COMMUNITY PLACE BROWSER

To uninstall Community Place, follow these steps:

1. Click the Start button.

2. Select the Community Place Browser folder from the Program menu.

3. Select Uninstall from the menu.

Notice that uninstall command uninstalls only the files installed at the installation time. (Bookmark files and some files created after installation are not deleted.) These files are under \Program Files\Sony\Community Place Browser. Delete them manually, by using the delete command as follows:

```
> cd "\Program files"
> deltree /Y Sony
```

COMMUNITY PLACE DIRECTORY STRUCTURE

After installation, the following directories and files are created on your hard disk. If you choose the default installation directory, all these directories will be underneath the following directory: \Program Files\Sony\Community Place Browser.

Directory	Contents
bin\	Binary and DLL files
doc\	Manual and release note
lib\	Java and some run-time libraries
snapshot\	Bookmarks
tmp\	Working directory
world\	Sample VRML worlds
*.isu	Information to uninstall Community Place Browser

If you remove *.isu, you will be unable to automatically uninstall Community Place and will have to do it manually. Do not remove these files.

How to Install the JDK from the CD (1.0.2)

The following steps detail how to install the Java JDK (Java Development Kit) from the accompanying CD-ROM onto your PC. In this book we have assumed that you will be developing Java code on your PC; however, as you know, Java's byte code is platform independent. If you want, you can use any platform's JDK to compile Java source code created for Community Place Browser.

If you want to use the latest version of the JDK, visit http://java.sun.com/.

Remove Previous Versions of JDK

Before installing the JDK, check to see whether you have a previous version of the JDK. If so, delete the entire Java directory by using the following command:

```
> deltree /Y C:\java
```

Copy

Copy the JDK from the CD-ROM to your hard disk:

```
> copy  D:\java\jdk-1-0-2-win32-x86.exe
```

We assume you will be using the directory c:\java for the JDK. You may need to create this directory on your hard disk.

Unpack

After removing the previous version of the JDK, execute the new self-extracting archive to unpack the JDK files. You should unpack the file in the root directory of C drive to create C:\java. If you want the JDK in another directory, unpack the archive file in that directory.

Notice that unpacking the archive also creates the files src.zip and lib\classes.zip. The file src.zip contains source for some of the Java classes and can be unzipped and viewed; classes.zip contains the executable class files.

WARNING

Do not unzip the classes.zip file. This file is specified in the CLASSPATH variable and managed by the Java compiler itself.

UPDATE PATH ENVIRONMENT VARIABLE

After unpacking, add the java\bin directory to your path. The easiest way to do this is to edit the autoexec.bat file and make the change to the path statement there, for example:

```
SET PATH=C:\java\bin;"%PATH%"
```

UPDATE CLASSPATH ENVIRONMENT VARIABLE

You also need to add the java\lib\classes.zip to your CLASSPATH environment variable. Again, the easiest way to do this is to edit the autoexec.bat file and make the change to the CLASSPATH environment variable as follows:

```
SET CLASSPATH=C:\java\lib\classes.zip
```

After completing these changes to autoexec.bat, save the file and then reboot your machine so that the changes take effect.

START USING THE JDK

Your computer system should now be configured and ready to use the Java Development Kit. To check that things are okay, you can use the Applet Viewer to view a Java applet.

Start the Applet Viewer by doing the following:

1. Change to a directory containing a demo applet HTML file:

   ```
   > cd java\demo\TicTacToe
   ```

2. Run the Applet Viewer by using the html file:

   ```
   > appletviewer example1.html
   ```

If everything works okay, you have successfully installed the Java Development Kit. If you are not able to successfully start the Applet Viewer and view the example applet, return to step 1 of this section and begin again. If after trying again you still run into problems, visit Sun's Java Web page where detailed instructions and help is available (http://java.sun.com).

SETTING UP THE JAVA DEVELOPMENT ENVIRONMENT FOR COMMUNITY PLACE BROWSER

To compile Java programs for Community Place, you need to install the JDK and VRML-related Java packages. The following sections show how to install the VRML-related Java packages.

UNPACK

The VRML-related Java packages are included in the Community Place self-extracting archive and are extracted to a file called vsclass.zip, which you can find in C:\Program Files\Sony\Community Place Browser\lib\java\vsclass.zip. (If you did not extract Community Place to the default directory, you will need to search for this file in the directory you specified at installation time.) Use Winzip to unzip the file in the directory under C:\java\vsclass (Winzip is available at http://www.winzip.com). If you want the packages in another directory, unzip the file in that directory.

If you don't have Winzip or don't want to unzip these yourself, copy Vs\vsclass from the CD-ROM to your chosen directory (we recommend C:\java\vsclass).

UPDATE CLASSPATH ENVIRONMENT VARIABLE

Next you need to tell Java about these VRML-related packages. Add the java\vsclass directory to your CLASSPATH environment variable. The easiest way to do this is to edit the autoexec.bat file and make the change to the path statement there, for example:

```
SET CLASSPATH=C:\java\vsclass;C:\java\lib\classes.zip
```

After completing these changes to autoexec.bat, save the file and reboot so that the changes take effect.

START COMPILING JAVA PROGRAM FOR COMMUNITY PLACE BROWSER

Your computer system should now be configured and ready to compile Java programs for the Community Place Browser. To check this, copy a sample program from the CD-ROM and compile it.

```
> copy D:\examples\chap03\ChangeColor.java c:\tmp
> copy D:\examples\chap03\changecolor.wrl c:\tmp
> cd c:\tmp
> javac ChangeColor.java
```

After you have successfully compiled the Java program and produced the class file, load changecolor.wrl by dragging and dropping it onto the Community Place Browser, or if you are using the plug-in version of the browser, double-click the file.

You can see one sphere in the scene. If you click it, its color changes from red to blue.

If this works successfully, you have correctly installed the Java JDK and the Community Place VRML-related Java packages. Congratulations!

If you have any problems with the installation of the Java JDK, check Sun's Java Web page at http://java.sun.com/. This page contains extensive details on installation and common problems.

NETSCAPE SETUP FOR THE HELPER VERSION OF COMMUNITY PLACE

If you are using the helper version of the Community Place Browser and not the plug-in version, these notes are relevant. By default, the Community Place Browser installer automatically sets up Netscape Navigator to use Community Place as the helper application when it encounters a VRML file (.wrl) If, however, you suspect that Navigator isn't correctly configured to use Community Place as a helper application, you should manually perform the following steps. You will know that Netscape Navigator is not correctly configured if, when you download a VRML file, it starts another browser or tells you it can't handle this type of file.

1. Select the General Preference item from the Netscape Navigator Options menu. The Preference dialog box appears.

2. Select the Helper tag.

3. Select x-world/x-vrml.

4. Select Launch the Application.

5. Specify Community Place Browser in the text field at the bottom. The Browse button on the side of the field will facilitate the job. (Community Place Browser is located, by default, in C:\Program Files\Sony\Community Place Browser\bin.)

6. Click OK.

WARNING

Netscape versions 3.0 and later bundle the Live3D plug-in as a VRML 1.0 browser. With a VRML browser plug-in installed in Netscape, even if you specify Community Place Browser as a helper application for VRML files, the setting becomes inactive after you restart Netscape. To ensure that the Community Place Browser is invoked when you open a VRML file, deactivate plug-in browsers, or more precisely, deactivate plug-in DLLs.

Usually plug-in DLLs for Netscape are stored in `c:\Program Files\Netscape\Navigator\Program\plugins\npXXX.dll`.

XXX is a plug-in's name. For example, the plug-in DLL for Live3D is npl3d32.dll. By moving a DLL away from the directory, the DLL becomes inactive, and Community Place Browser is invoked as a primary helper application for VRML files. Be careful to move the DLL into a directory that is not under the aforementioned Plugins directory. Netscape searches all directories under Plugins for plug-in DLLs.

Npchooser (Netscape Plugin Chooser) is a small program that is available on the CD-ROM (vs\npc10.zip) to help you choose which plug-in DLLs are active. You can find the latest version of this program at http://vs.sony.co.jp.

Hardware Requirements

Before installing the Community Place Browser, check whether your system meets the following requirements. The minimum required environment and the recommended environment for the Community Place Browser are shown in the following table.

	Minimum Required Environment	Recommended Environment
Hardware	PC/AT-compatible machine operating under Windows 95/NT*	PC/AT-compatible machine operating under Windows 95/NT*
CPU	486DX2 66 MHz	Pentium 90MHz or higher
Memory	16 MB	32 MB or more

continues

	Minimum Required Environment	Recommended Environment
Free disk space	10 MB or more (required at the time of installation)	30 MB
Display resolution	640×480 pixels	800×600 pixels or higher
Display colors	256 colors	65,536 colors or more
Software	Netscape Navigator for Windows (ver 2.0 or later)**	
Sound	—	Sound card
Network	—	Network interface card and Internet access

* Community Place Browser supports all PC-compatible machines that meet the above requirements.

** With the helper version, the Community Place Browser can be used without Netscape Navigator, but only a limited set of functions are available. To use the Multiuser Functions, use this software in the recommended environment.

APPENDIX E

WHAT'S ON THE CD-ROM?

The CD-ROM for *Java for 3D and VRML Worlds* is a tremendous resource for users of the book. The CD contains the following:

➤ Sony's Community Place VRML 2 browser (including online manual)

➤ Sony's Community Bureau VRML 2 server (including online manual)

➤ Tutorials that teach you how to get the most out of Community Place

➤ A VRML 1-to-VRML 2 file converter

➤ The complete VRML 2.0 spec

➤ VRML files and examples from the book

➤ Sony's Virtual Society Web Home Page

➤ An extensive resource list for links to VRML-related Web sites

Most of the CD-ROM content is in HTML format, making it easy to click-and-go to the various CD contents.

More in-depth descriptions follow.

THE SONY COMMUNITY PLACE VRML 2.0 BROWSER

Our goal is the creation of a Virtual Society, an online, electronic, three-dimensional CyberSpace. CyberSpace will be full of interesting places to visit, fun things to do, and most importantly, other people to meet.

The Community Place Browser is the window into this online world. It enables you to enter 3D worlds, to navigate around them, to interact with objects in these scenes, and to meet and chat with other users.

To allow this, the Community Place browser is a full VRML 2.0 browser with Java language support that enables you and others to build and experience interactive, multimedia 3D worlds.

However, Community Place is more than a stand-alone VRML 2.0 browser; it's part of a sophisticated multiuser shared 3D CyberSpace. Each browser, when connected to a multiuser server—the Community Place Bureau—will enable you to choose your 3D representation in that world, your avatar, and will use that avatar to represent you in the shared worlds.

Once connected to the Community Place Bureau, you enter the shared world. Within it, you can see other people, wave to them, chat in groups, or even have private conversations. The browser and server support it all.

In this software package you will find all you need to enable you to enter this world. The Community Place browser works well as a stand-alone VRML 2.0 browser, and we've provided some demo files for you to load and enjoy. We've also provided a shared VRML world, Circus Park, that automatically connects to a public server when loaded.

Enjoy!!

—The Sony Community Place development team

COMMUNITY PLACE BUREAU (MULTIUSER SERVER)

Shared Community Place PC server—Alpha Test Release

You should be familiar with the basic operation of the Community Place browser, and you should have connected to one of the Sony shared worlds to get a feeling for what it's all about.

You don't need to worry about this server if you just want to use the shared worlds that Sony, or another third-party, has created. These shared worlds will connect to publicly accessible servers that we at Sony run or that third parties have run.

THE WIN95 SERVER: WHAT'S IT ABOUT?

This server enables you to share VRML 1.0 and VRML 2.0 worlds by using the Community Place VRML 2.0 browser. Sharing a world is simple: you need to add one line to an existing VRML 1.0 or VRML 2.0 world file, which will tell the Community Place browser where the world server is.

You then run the server on a PC of your choice, and anybody loading the VRML 1.0 or VRML 2.0 file into a Community Place browser will be automatically connected to the shared world.

When connected, users can see other users, use a simple chat facility to talk to each other, and, if you set it up, express a little emotion with our avatar action panels.

So why are we telling you this here? Because the use of a Community Place bureau server running on your PC not only enables you to share scenes, but it enables you to share behaviors as well! Sounds fun? It is—shared animation, games, collaborative tools, and a host of other 3D ideas are trivial to build if you want.

ONLINE COMMUNITY PLACE TUTORIALS

These are the Community Place Development Tutorials. Within them you'll find tutorials and exercises to help you learn how to develop 3D VRML 2.0 worlds with Sony's browser, Community Place.

The tutorials were written by the VRML Crew at Sony Pictures Imageworks: John D. DeCuir, Jai Natarajan, and Christopher Janney, under the faithful guidance of their fearless leader, Janet McAndless.

- ➤ Introduction: Welcome to CP Development!
- ➤ Preface: Setting Up Your System for CP Development
- ➤ Tutorial 1: A Simple Interactive World
- ➤ Tutorial 2: Exploring Simple Transformations
- ➤ Tutorial 3: Beginning Animation
- ➤ Tutorial 4: Intermediate Animation: Interpolators and Scripting
- ➤ Tutorial 5: Adding Sound to Your World
- ➤ Tutorial 6: Beginning Shared Behaviors
- ➤ Tutorial 7: Advanced Shared Behaviors
- ➤ Tutorial 8: Adding a User Interface (Via Java AWT)
- ➤ Tutorial 9: Adding Avatar Behaviors
- ➤ Tutorial 10: Advanced Animation (Simple Particle Systems)
- ➤ Tutorial 11: Creating Intelligent Agents
- ➤ Appendix A: Modeling Tips/Tricks
- ➤ Appendix B: Troubleshooting
- ➤ Appendix C: Suggested Reading
- ➤ Index

CONVERTER (FROM VRML 1.0 TO VRML 2.0)

This program converts a VRML 1.0 file to a VRML 2.0 file.
Platforms:

➤ SUN(SunOS 5.5) (vrml1to2.sun)

➤ NEWS(NEWS-OS 6.0) (vrml1to2.news)

➤ SGI(IRIX 5.3) (vrml1to2.sgi)

➤ Windows 95/NT (vrml1to2.exe)

Extensive instructions are on the CD-ROM.

VRML 2.0 SPECIFICATION

The VRML Specification is the technical document that precisely
describes the VRML file format. It is primarily intended for
implementors writing VRML browsers and authoring systems. It
is also intended for readers interested in learning the details
about VRML. Note, however, that many people (especially
nonprogrammers) find the VRML specification inadequate as a
starting point or primer.

The Virtual Reality Modeling Language specification was originally developed by Silicon Graphics, Inc. in collaboration with
Sony and Mitra. Many people in the VRML community have been
involved in the review and evolution of the specification. Moving
Worlds VRML 2.0 is a tribute to the successful collaboration of all
of the members of the VRML community. Gavin Bell, Rikk Carey,
and Chris Marrin have headed the effort to produce the final
specification.

EXAMPLES FROM THIS BOOK

VRML- and Java-file examples from this book.

Please make sure to set up Netscape Navigator to use the Community Place Browser (refer to Appendix D, "Installing Community Place") before clicking the links to the VRML files.

CHAPTER 2

Chair

➤ chair.wrl

Bike

➤ bike.wrl

CHAPTER 3

Print line

➤ println.wrl (println.java)

Change sphere color

➤ ChangeColor.wrl (ChangeColor.java)

Mover

➤ mover.wrl (MoveIt.java)

Add route

➤ AddRoute.wrl (AddRoute.class)

CHAPTER 4

Light On/Off

➤ LightOnOff.wrl (LightOnOff.java)

Floating Agent

➤ FloatingAgent.wrl (FloatingAgent.java)

Rolling CD

➤ RollingCD.wrl (RollingCD.java)

Talkative Agent

➤ TalkativeAgent.wrl (TalkativeAgent.java)

Following Agent

➤ FollowingAgent.wrl (FollowingAgent.java)

Automatic Door

➤ AutomaticDoor.wrl (AutomaticDoor.java)

Switching Agent

➤ SwitchAgent.wrl (SwitchAgent.java)

Half-transparent Window

➤ Transparency.wrl

Man using LOD

➤ LodMan.wrl

Viewpoint

➤ Viewpoint.wrl (Viewpoint.java)

Car

➤ Car.wrl (Car.java)

Inlined Man

➤ InlinedLodMan.wrl

Man using PROTO

➤ ProtoMan.wrl (ProtoMan.java)

CHAPTER 5

Motd (Before executing this, please copy it to your local disk.)

➤ Motd.wrl (Motd.java)

Directory Browser

➤ DirBrowser.wrl (DirBrowser.java)

Open Sesame!

➤ OpenSesame.wrl (OpenSesame.java, OpenDialog.java)

Color Tester

➤ ColorTester.wrl (ColorTester.java, ColorPanel.java)

Road Mirage

Example Client

➤ ExampleClient.wrl (ExampleClient.java)

Example Server

➤ ExampleServer.java

Multiuser System

MuClient

➤ MuClient.wrl (MuClient.java, MuReceiver.java, MuProtocol.java))

MuServer

➤ MuServer.java, MuServer.java

CHAPTER 6

Double Face

➤ DoubleFace.wrl

Light On/Off Directly

➤ LightDirectOnOff.wrl

TV

➤ TV.wrl

Dynamic Shape Generation

➤ DynamicGen.wrl (DynamicGen.java)

Lion

➤ Lion.wrl

Lion Movie

➤ LionMovie.wrl (LionMovie.java)

Keep Value in Java

➤ ValueInJava.wrl (ValueInJava.java)

Keep Value in Wrl

➤ ValueInWrl.wrl (ValueInWrl.java)

Changing Sound Pitch

➤ SoundPitch.wrl

OTHER EXAMPLE WORLDS

The following is a list of other VRML and Java examples not found
in the book. Please make sure to set up Netscape Navigator for
the Community Place Browser (refer to Appendix D) before
clicking the links to the VRML files.

➤ jumanji
➤ shadow1

➤ blur
➤ depth

➤ blur1
➤ soft line effect

➤ blur2
➤ Waving effect (1)

➤ motion
➤ Waving effect (2)

➤ motion
➤ Waving effect (3)

➤ shadow
➤ Waving effect (4)

VIRTUAL SOCIETY HOME PAGE

Surfin' the Web like Zappin' the TV

Chat On-line like talkin' by phone

Shopping in a virtual city...

The Virtual Society project is designed to realize this dreamlike vision through the latest digital and networking technology. The goal is a seamless community between real society and electronic society—another kind of community, a virtual society that's fun, fast, and free.

RESOURCE LIST

Web URLs are ever-changing, so we regret that we can't guarantee how long each of these addresses will be active. Most will likely be around for quite a long time.

VRML-RELATED WEB SITES

Sony Virtual Society Home Page:

➤ http://sonypic.com/vs

➤ http://vs.sony.co.jp

Sony Pictures. Imageworks. VRML 2.0 tutorial:

➤ http://sonypic.com/vs/tutorials

The official VAG Web site:

➤ http://vag.vrml.org VRML
  Architecture Group's home page

The VRML FAQ:

➤ http://vag.vrml.org/VRML_FAQ.html

VRML mailing list archive:

➤ http://vag.vrml.org/VRML_FAQ.html
A complete Hypermail archive of the VRML mailing list

The VRML repository:

➤ http://www.sdsc.edu/vrml
Links to many useful pages

VRML 2.0 worlds:

➤ http://vrml.sgi.com/worlds/vrml2.html
Links to other VRML worlds

HotMix on SGI:

➤ http://www.sgi.com/Products/HotMix/
VRML info page by SGI

VRMLSite Magazine:

➤ http://www.vrmlsite.com
Monthly magazine full of tips for VRML authors

The VRML Forum:

➤ http://vag.vrml.org/www-vrml
How to join www-vrml ML

VRML 2.0 proposals:

Active VRML—Microsoft

➤ http://www.microsoft.com/intdev/avr

Dynamic Worlds—GMD and others:

➤ http://wintermute.gmd.de:8000/vrml/dynamicWorlds.html

HoloWeb—Sun:

➤ http://www.sunlabs.com/research/tcm/holoweb/holoweb.html

Moving Worlds—SGI and others:

➤ http://webspace.sgi.com/moving-worlds

Out of this World—Apple:

➤ http://product.info.apple.com/qd3d/VRML20/Out_Of_This_World.HTML

Reactive Virtual Environment—IBM Japan:

➤ http://www.ibm.co.jp/trl/projects/rve/vrml2top.html

JAVA-RELATED WEB SITES

Sun's Java Site:

➤ http://java.sun.com/
The latest version of JDK is available on this site.

Java Programming FAQ:

➤ http://sunsite.unc.edu/javafaq/javafaq.html

Java Tutorial:

➤ http://sunsite.unc.edu/javafaq/javatutorial.html

Java Mailing List:

➤ http://www.javasoft.com/Mail/external_lists.html

Visual J++:

➤ http://www.microsoft.com/visualj/
Microsoft's Visual J++ developers information

CONVERTER (FROM VRML 1.0 TO VRML 2.0)

This program converts a VRML 1.0 file to a VRML 2.0 file.
Platforms:

➤ SUN(SunOS 5.5) (vrml1to2.sun)

➤ NEWS(NEWS-OS 6.0) (vrml1to2.news)

➤ SGI(IRIX 5.3) (vrml1to2.sgi)

➤ Windows 95/NT (vrml1to2.exe)

Extensive instructions are on the CD-ROM.

INDEX

M

REGISTRATION CARD

Java for 3D and VRML Worlds

Name _____ Title _____

Type of
Company _____ business _____

Address _____

City/State/ZIP _____

E-mail/Internet _____ Phone _____

Would you like to be placed on our preferred mailing list?   ❏ yes   ❏ no

Have you used/purchased New Riders books before?   ❏ yes   ❏ no

Where did you purchase this book? Check one.
   ❏ Bookstore chain   ❏ Independent bookstore   ❏ Computer store
   ❏ Wholesale club   ❏ College bookstore   ❏ Other _____

What influenced your decision to purchase this title? _____
_____

Which of the following operating systems do you use? Check all that apply.
   ❏ Windows 3.x   ❏ Windows 95   ❏ Windows NT
   ❏ Macintosh   ❏ SGI   ❏ Other _____

What are the names of the software programs you use currently? _____
_____
_____

Which of the following best describes your work environment? Check one.
   ❏ Self-employed   ❏ Small business   ❏ Large business

Which of the following do you create/develop for? Check all that apply.
   ❏ Games   ❏ Motion pictures   ❏ Web sites
   ❏ Print   ❏ Other

What online services and Web sites do you visit on a regular basis? _____
_____
_____

What trade shows do you attend? _____

What computer book titles do you consider your most valuable sources of information?
_____

What applications/technologies would you like to see us publish on in the future?
_____